THE STORY OF
BATH

THE STORY OF
BATH
CATHRYN SPENCE

The History Press

First published 2016
Reprinted 2023

The History Press
97 St George's Place,
Cheltenham, Gloucestershire, GL50 3QB
www.thehistorypress.co.uk

British Library Cataloguing in Publication Data.
A catalogue record for this book is available from the British Library.

ISBN 978 0 7509 6402 9

Typesetting and origination by The History Press
Printed by TJ Books Limited, Padstow, Cornwall

CONTENTS

ACKNOWLEDGEMENTS

I would like to thank the many historians, archaeologists, journalists, commentators, authors, photographers and artists who have contributed to our understanding of Bath over the millennia. I have unashamedly drawn on their work, devoured their theses, poured over their images and been inspired by their passion and perception. Equally, I have had the very great pleasure of collaborating with some exceptional people over the last fifteen years in order to build my knowledge of this wonderful city. This book is dedicated to them all, as well as the dog walkers of Odd and Combe Down – for their love of Bath, for their friendship and for their unremitting encouragement during the writing of this book.

This edition is dedicated to Kath Jewitt (1967–2023).

ABOUT THE AUTHOR

D r Cathryn Spence is a museum professional, lecturer and historic buildings and gardens consultant. She is currently the Marquis of Lansdowne's consultant archivist and curator at Bowood House in Wiltshire and the Manager of the Lutyens Trust. She was previously the Curator of Archives at the American Museum in Britain and Director of the Building of Bath Museum (now the Museum of Bath Architecture). She has also worked at the National Portrait Gallery and the V&A Museum. In addition to her work as a consultant, Cathryn is an independent researcher, her specialism being the architectural, cultural and social history of Georgian Britain. She has recently published a substantial monograph on the eighteenth-century artist Thomas Robins, entitled *Nature's Favourite Child – Thomas Robins and the Art of the Georgian Garden* (published by Stephen Morris, 2021), which was long-listed for the William M.B. Berger Prize for British Art History. Cathryn wrote a regular monthly column for *The Bath Magazine*; much of the research undertaken for those articles served as the basis for the four books she has published with The History Press. She is a trustee of the Friends of the Victoria Art Gallery, Bath.

INTRODUCTION

The story of Bath revolves almost entirely around its unique thermal waters, but its position within a wide meander of the River Avon, surrounded by seven hills in a hot and swampy valley, is not a natural place to make a settlement.

Evidence indicates that it was not until the first century that the area we now consider to be the centre of Bath was occupied. It is an extremely compact city, however, and through a combination of rising and falling fortunes, the surrounding topography and the River Avon, Bath was kept mostly confined within the line of the Roman ramparts and wall for around 1,500 years. However, Bath's story – both true and imagined – is far richer and more varied than this would suggest.

According to legend Bath was founded as a symbol of Prince Bladud's gratitude for the curative powers of the waters. Having contracted leprosy, Bladud was expelled from his father's court and forced to roam the country as a swineherd. His pigs, which had also contracted leprosy, wallowed in the hot mud they happened across whilst foraging for acorns and were cured of the sores and blemishes that had obscured their hides. Noticing this miracle, Bladud too immersed himself and was healed. Fit and well, the young Prince was welcomed back to his father's court and, once he became King, returned and founded the city of Bath.

Over the centuries, Bath has been 'occupied' by the Romans, Saxons, Benedictine monks, Normans, Royalists, Parliamentarians, Tories, Whigs, Liberals and Conservatives – only the Vikings seem to have been kept from entering the gates. All have made their mark on our town. National, and international, events have affected Bath like any other city. Royal patronage has had a profound influence on its fortunes and validity. A list of Bath's highlights could include such an array of diverse events as the invention of Plasticine, to the discovery of the planet Uranus; from sanctuary for a key suffragette cell, to home to the exiled Emperor Haile Selassie; from healer of royal infertility, to the victim of a devastating bombing raid by the Luftwaffe in April 1942.

Bath's heydays were, unquestionably, during the Roman occupation of Britain and the Georgian era. I have, however, attempted to give equal weight to other time periods and have relied heavily on the important information provided by archaeologists, and, for later periods, contemporary newspapers. At its height in the second half of the eighteenth century, Bath welcomed 8,000 visitors a week during the season, making it one of the largest pre-industrial cities in the country.

Elements of Bath's history have been cleansed, in order to fit the image it created for itself. This is not a new thing; in September 1728, the mayor and aldermen sent a notice to all the national newspapers to assure everyone that Bath was not suffering from a raging distemper and the city was safe to visit. It has often been said that Bath had no industry, and the poor – since Elizabethan times – have been conveniently excluded or hidden in hospitals, workhouses or the ghettoes of Avon Street and Holloway, far from the residences of the wealthy or high-ranking visitor.

Readers will probably be taken aback to discover that Bath's greatest expansion was actually during the nineteenth century, when the town doubled in size with the construction of working-class homes for families employed by engineers Stothert & Pitt, woollen cloth factories Charles Wilkins & Co. and Carr Mills,

The origin of Bath

Bladud, the son of a British King, was a leper and for that reason was expelled from his father's palace. Becoming a swineherd, his pigs were infected with the leprosy, but by rolling themselves in the warm mud through which they had to pass in their wanderings, they were soon cured. Bladud was eventually discovered taking his morning dip by two of the king's courtiers, who promptly took him home to his father. When he afterwards became king, he built the city of Bath B. C. 863 upon the muddy swamps which had proved so salutary to him.

The Origin of Bath, Prince Bladud and the Pigs, humorous postcard published by R. Wilkinson, Trowbridge, 1950s. (Private Collection/Bath in Time)

iron and brass foundries, tin works, the railway, gasworks, the pin factory and the many breweries. In addition, there were the service industries – shopkeepers, servants, cabinetmakers, seamstresses, solicitors, bank managers and city officials to maintain the 'genteel'. But when we consider that the public message in 1839 was that Bath was 'best fitted for the retirement of individuals with independent incomes … [because] for those past the meridian of life, its quietness, beautiful neighbourhood, and warmth of climate, particularly recommend it', it is hardly surprising that we have failed to comprehend the full story.

This misconception was (and still is) engineered as part of Bath's tenacious survival instinct. Unlike other cities, Bath knows that its fortunes rest on its waters and the tangible, and intangible, elements that surround them. Industries can come and go, but as long as people are driven to visit, so Bathonians will find employment to service those visitors. Be it the leather-skinned attendants in the baths who would cut your corns for you, the servants and laundresses, the sedan chairmen, the innkeepers, the milliners and dressmakers, artists, tour guides, museum curators, street cleaners – or writers of history books – our economy is more resilient than that of a coal mining or fishing village, for example.

Over the centuries layers of history and culture have added to the attraction of the waters. People come to Bath as much for the architecture that grew up around the waters as they do to enjoy a luxury weekend in the spa. Fans of Jane Austen, Thomas Gainsborough, Charles Dickens, Walter Richard Sickert and Mary Berry are as equally drawn to this city as those who love Bath Rugby, the literature and music festivals, or the plethora of great shops and good restaurants.

The effect on Bath's economy when, in 1978, contamination in the outdated pipework forced the closure of the baths and drinking fountains for almost thirty years, was palpable. This was probably not helped by the 'sack' of some of Bath's oldest buildings during the 1960s and 1970s. For a moment in time, Bath did not value its waters or its cultural heritage – a lesson that the city does not need to be taught again.

Bath's story is one of constant reinvention: from muddy swamp to Roman spa, from Saxon wool town to fashionable resort, from bombed shell to heritage city. In 1987, UNESCO (United Nations Educational, Scientific and Cultural Organisation) recognised Bath as a place of Outstanding Universal Value for its:

Roman remains, eighteenth-century architecture, eighteenth-century town planning and its role as a setting for social history, inspired by its hot springs and natural landscape setting. The story of the city settlement extends over six millennia, from its earliest days when the hot springs were a place of worship for the Britons, to the contemporary city, which is an international icon of heritage and a thriving community.

Bath is far more than a World Heritage Site or tourist destination; Bath is a living, breathing city with 89,000 residents (swelled by a further 16,000 university students during term time) and a local economy worth £40,000 (GVA) per head – admittedly a large proportion of that is associated with the 3.8 million tourists who visit each year.

This book is an attempt to tell the story of Bath within the context of Britain's wider history. Inevitably it is a summary, but I have tried to show the depth of Bath's history, 'warts and all'. So many commentators have left us their thoughts, reactions and opinions on Bath over the millennia, and I have drawn heavily on their words, as well as including details about one or two of Bath's particularly colourful characters. Together, I hope that you will find this both an informative and entertaining story of Bath.

One

'GREAT BLADUD BORN A SOV'REIGN PRINCE'

A place as unique as Bath rightly has a rather remarkable founding myth. This myth – like all good folktales – has flourished with each generation, and more and more elaborate versions have been recorded. King Bladud's greatest advocate was the architect John Wood (1704–54), who famously proclaimed himself the restorer of Bath, because – in his mind – he was merely reinstating the glorious city that Bladud had built in the first millennium BC. The story continues to resonate today, and as recently as 2008 was the inspiration for a hugely successful fundraising venture called 'Bladud's Pigs'.

The first known version of the legend of Bladud was written by Geoffrey of Monmouth and dates from the twelfth century. In his *Historia Regum Britanniae* (*c.* 1138), Monmouth traced the royal line from the (imaginary) founder of Britain, King Brutus of Troy. Much attention was lavished on King Arthur, but we also learn that Bladud, the son of Rud Hud Hudibras, was the ninth ruler of Britain after Brutus, that he founded the city of Kaer Badum (Bath) in 863 BC, created the baths by making the hot waters boil up out of the earth, built temples dedicating them to Minerva with eternal flames, and was able to fly. He was smashed into many pieces when he fell onto the Temple of Apollo in Trinovantum (London). In his later poem, *The Life of Merlin*, we learn from Monmouth that Bladud's Queen was called Alaron and that the waters were particularly beneficial for healing female ailments. Monmouth, however, makes no mention of Bladud's leprosy or his pigs, the two fundamental elements of the story retold today.

In his article, *Bladud of Bath: The Archaeology of a Legend*, John Clark traces the subsequent accounts of Bladud and gives possible theories as to how the widely accepted legend came to be. In the 1440s, for instance, John Hardyng places Bladud in Athens studying philosophy, and it seems that his occupation as a swineherd was first written down by Robert Peirce, a doctor in Bath at the end of the seventeenth century. Peirce ascribes the tale to local tradition and establishes the associations with the local place names of Swainswick, Swineford and Hogs Norton.

It seems likely that Peirce was aware of the Reverend Robert Gay's account from around 1666. Gay's manuscript mainly dealt with the building of Stonehenge, but within his thesis he refers to Bladud's leprosy leading to him being ostracised from court, finding work as a swineherd and his health being restored by the thermal waters at Bath. Twenty-five years prior to Peirce's account, Henry Chapman included an amusing poem in his *Thermae Redicicae: The City of Bath Described* ... , suggesting that the story of Bladud founding Bath was the subject of general mockery at this time as well as of these more serious dissertations.

A tablet commemorating Bladud was first placed at the King's Bath in 1672 alongside a small, seated statue of Bladud himself. That inscription notes that he was a great philosopher and mathematician with links to Athens. At the opening of the new Pump Room in 1705, a thoughtful poem (or song) was performed and later recorded by John Wood:

> Great Bladud born a Sov'reign Prince,
> But from the Court was Banish'd thence,
> His dire Disease to shun,
> The Muses do his Fame record,
> That when the Bath his Health restor'd,
> Great Bladud did return.

Mary Chandler referred to 'Brute's great descendant' in her epic poem of 1734, whilst city guides and maps at this time also make mention of Bath's royal founder. And so, by the middle of the eighteenth century, Bladud's leprosy and his herd of pigs was a well-established component of the story, having been passed down through generations as a traditional tale – the origins of which are now lost. The concentration on Bladud's miraculous cure from leprosy must surely be connected with Bath's growing promotion as a health resort.

Bladud's story would probably hold very little interest to present-day Bathonians, and the city's many visitors if it were not for the vital effect it had on Bath's supreme architect, John Wood. Wood's additions to the story are perhaps the most substantial and, of course, give credence to his elaborate architectural accomplishments. He indeed places much emphasis on the pigs and also Bladud's position as an educated, enlightened man with extraordinary powers.

During the initial decades of the eighteenth century, it was common practice for architects to publish their beliefs about the pedigree of architecture. In 1741 Wood published *The Origin of Building, or the Plagiarism of the Heathens Detected*, an idiosyncratic hypothesis in which he manipulates evidence to prove his own ideals. Wood needed to prove that the origin of architecture was, in fact, God-given and that Britain's ancient builders, the Greeks and the Romans, were mere

(After) William Hoare: Prince Bladud from the frontispiece to John Wood's *A Description of Bath*, Vol.1, 1749. (Bath Central Library/Bath in Time)

W. Hoare delin.   *B. Baron Sculp.*

BLADUD,
To whom the GRECIANS gave the Name of
A B A R I S.

plagiarists. By the time *The Origin of Building* had been published, Wood was already working on *An Essay Towards a Description of Bath*, which comprised three volumes (although the third is very rare) over two editions. In *Origin*, Wood assigned himself a theoretical standpoint for which he quickly felt little sympathy (his conflict and contradictions are clearly shown in the heavily annotated manuscript version held by Bath Central Library).

In *Essay*, Wood constructs a history that saw Bladud being witness to the building of the Temple of Solomon in Jerusalem. According to Wood, Bladud brought those principles back to Britain, where he conveyed them to the majestic buildings he created when he founded the city of Bath. Wood states that this occurred in 483 BC, at least 400 years earlier than previous chroniclers had identified. Wood recounts the Monmouth version of Bladud's biography as also written by William Camden (1551–1623) in his *Britannia* (1586). He also refers to an account by Joseph Glanville, a former Rector of Bath, and Dr Peirce's *Memoirs*.

Wood, however, states that New Troy (where Bladud was buried) and Trinovantum (London) were the same place, but those former scholars had corrupted the word, misunderstood the progression of Brutus and his descendants and 'loaded [the history of Britain] with improbabilities'. The seven cities and two towns the Trojans founded, according to Wood, were all located between the south-west borders of Wiltshire and Gloucestershire and the River Tamar. And therefore the original capital of Britain, declared Wood, was irrefutably Bath – a new Troy, built by Bladud with temples to the sun and the moon.

In the second edition (1749) of *Essay*, Wood gave even more prominence to Bladud by including an engraving of the King dressed as a Druid with classical style buildings in the background.

Camden had written about the Druids, as had Michael Drayton in 1613. The Druids were established as being the true heirs of biblical Jewry and Classical Greece. They were more learned and ancient than the Romans. John Aubrey (1626–97) and William Stukeley (1687–1765) were at the forefront of a revival of interest in Druidism in the early eighteenth century, claiming that these Iron Age philosophers, priests, doctors and lawmakers were the builders of Stonehenge and Avebury. In 1702 John Toland published his *Critical History of the Celtic Religion and Learning*, in which he introduced Abaris, the Hyperborean Priest of the Sun. And then in 1726 Toland published his *History of the Druids*.

These many publications and sources were devoured, transformed, manipulated and retold by Wood with such brazen self-assurance that we can only admire his ability to sidestep any inconsistencies and conflicts with his reasoning to impose a dogged source for all his architectural creations. When classical mythology tells us that Pythagoras and Abaris visited Jerusalem and witnessed the building of Solomon's Temple, Wood was not deterred because Abaris was just another name for Bladud, who was – of course – Apollo, the sun god.

Bath's waters were governed by Apollo, who was worshipped by the Druids as Bel (Belenus). When a golden head was discovered during the construction of a drain along Stall Street in 1727, Wood claimed it to be Apollo. We now know it to be Minerva, although this was still being debated in 1888. It was therefore Bladud who taught Pythagoras astronomy and geometry and built the round temple Tholos at Delphi, before returning to build Bath.

Significantly, Wood makes many references to the Druids being 'the priests of the hollow oak'. Wood found architectural evidence to support these theories in the ancient stone circles of Stanton Drew, Avebury and Stonehenge – all within easy reach of Bath – and all-encompassing correlated measurements with the First and Second Temples in Jerusalem. These factors reinforced Wood's assertion that the origins of architecture were British.

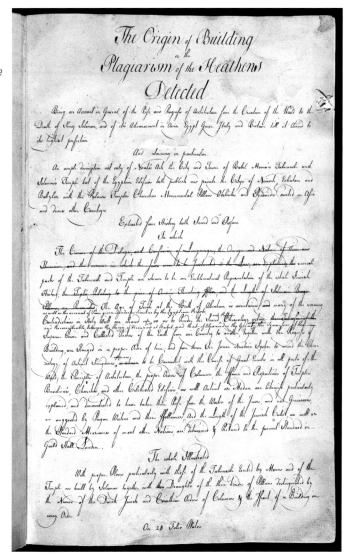

John Wood: Manuscript version with crossings out of *The Origin of Building or the Plagiarism of the Heathens Detected*, c. 1741. (Bath Central Library/Bath in Time)

It is fascinating to try and consider what exactly Wood's contemporaries thought of his strident decrees; even in the eighteenth century, before the benefit of archaeological evidence, Wood's proclamations would have been considered at best eccentric, but more likely the dogged falsehoods of a contumacious obsessive. The results, however, were widely and publicly admired – 'Queen Square,' reported the *Gloucester Journal* in 1732, 'will far exceed any public building … in England, and outdo everything in Bath'.

The folk tale retold today is a combination of these various narratives. Prince Bladud, the son of King Hudibras, contracted leprosy whilst studying in Athens. The fear of a leprosy endemic saw Bladud ostracised from his father's kingdom. Before he left, Bladud's mother gave him a ring, a token by which she would know him again should he ever find a cure. Forced to wander the country, Bladud came upon a poor shepherd with whom he exchanged his clothes to afford him greater anonymity. When he reached Cainsham (now Keynsham) Bladud found work with a swineherd droving pigs. Despite, frankly, the medical impossibility – his pigs also caught leprosy. To keep this disaster from his employer, he proposed to drive his pigs to the other side of the River Avon, to fatten them with acorns. Bladud discovered a shallow part of the Avon where he was able to cross, naming the place Swineford. His pigs, 'as if seized with a frenzy', ran away; Bladud pursued them up the valley and found the pigs wallowing in the hot marshy mud surrounding the springs. Eventually he persuaded the pigs to leave the mire by shaking his satchel of acorns; they spent the night resting in an area he named Swainswick.

When he washed the mud and debris from his pigs he was astonished to see that they were healed of the disease. Bladud took it upon himself to follow the example his pigs had set and wallowed in the water every morning and evening. Within a few days he too was cured of leprosy and returned to his father's kingdom. He put his mother's ring into her glass of wine and when she saw it she proclaimed that her son had returned.

Welcomed back into the family fold, Bladud was again able to enhance his education, returning to Greece for eleven years to study philosophy, necromancy and mathematics. When his father died, Bladud was crowned King. Forever grateful for the curative powers of the thermal waters, Bladud founded the city of Bath. He used his magical powers to make the waters boil up in three different places, building cisterns to retain the waters. He established his palace and court at Bath and reigned happily for twenty years, fathering the future King Lear.

Bath was then known as Caerbren and stretched from Wookey Hole in the west to Stonehenge in the east. At Odd Down, Bladud established a temple to Camolos, the British god of war. Also here, then called Camalodunum, was 'the great court of justice of the ancient Britons' and a 'stupendous mausoleum' to house Bladud's remains. Bladud's palace was on the Ham (where Wood envisioned his unrealised Royal Forum). He conferred a lordship and estate to his swineherd employer and together they created a north and south town. The north town, according to Wood, was still known as Hogs-Norton, or Norton-Small-Reward in the 1700s.

Having practised necromancy, Bladud had learnt how to fly from the dead, but ironically he died of a broken neck when he fell from a flight onto Solsbury Hill (to the east of Bath), which was identified by Wood as the site of a temple to

Apollo. And this is, of course, why Wood chose that his final resting place should be St Mary's Church, Swainswick – the nearest church to Solsbury Hill.

According to Wood, this important foundation story began to be ridiculed during the reign of Charles II by personalities such as John, Earl of Rochester. As a consequence, Bathonians became 'extremely cautious of repeating … what had been so solemnly handed to them: so that the tradition is now in a manner lost at Bath'. Referring to Peirce's Bath *Memoirs*, Wood recounts other momentous occasions when pigs have led historic heroes to their destinies, such as when Aeneas founded the city of Lavinium. In so doing, Wood was determined to prove that the tradition relating to Bladud was probable. As we will see in chapters 7 and 8, the founding story of Bath directed the placement and realisation of Wood's architectural set pieces.

The city fathers adorned Northgate with a statue of Bladud but it was so badly neglected that a poem, *King Bladud's Ghost*, was widely published recounting how unhappy Bladud was at how ungrateful the citizens had become. The Corporation was embarrassed into replacing the statue. Wood described the new statue as looking like a dressed puppet seated in a ducking stool – this seems a very good description of the statue that now resides at the King's Bath. Nevertheless, Wood's son, John Wood the Younger, upheld his father's admiration for Bladud and included an inscription about the King over the pump of his Hot Bath (1775–77).

Otherwise, commemorations of Bladud after Wood the Elder are limited. Bladud Buildings, built during the decade after Wood's death (1755–62) at the junction with Broad and George Streets, The Paragon and Lansdown Road became home to Bladud Bank (taking its name from the address) in 1790 and the Cross Bath featured a figure in relief of Bladud (after William Hoare). Despite this, it seems the story was still known because president of the Royal Academy and historical painter to King George III, Benjamin West (1738–1820), depicted the moment when Bladud and his drove of pigs happen upon the thermal waters in a large chalk and wash drawing undertaken during an extended stay in the city for his wife's health in 1807.

Bladud's story was included in the Bath Pageant, an extravaganza of 1909 comprising a cast, choir and orchestra of 3,576 locals (see chapter 11), but having originally been mooted as the narrator for the entire pageant, he was thought 'too mythical a person to seriously employ'. For some, however, this downgrade of Bladud was considered a slight – the mayor publicly declared his displeasure with the promoters of the pageant, claiming they were 'over scrupulous' in their discarding of the foundation myth of Bath.

It is fair to say that towards the end of the eighteenth century, more rational commentators and historians distanced themselves from the fabulous fable of

Bladud; instead they increasingly dedicated the pages of their theses to Bath being founded by the Romans.

Although a wonderful and compelling story, the truth – as far as archaeological evidence provides – is far less exciting. A complete archaeological understanding, however, is barred to us because of the important later buildings that now occupy those key central areas. A specialist in Roman archaeology would probably jump at the opportunity to discover what lies beneath the Abbey, likewise an expert in the Neolithic period would relish the prospect of digging under the Roman baths and temples. When opportunities are afforded because of major developments, our understanding of pre-Roman Bath is greatly enhanced. For example, extensive archaeological investigations were undertaken in 1998–99 prior to the development of the Thermae Bath Spa.

The team found evidence of the river gravels being exploited for chert and flint during the late Mesolithic era, and possible ritual activity associated with the Hot Spring prior to this. Prehistoric man left little impression on central Bath, however. Evidence shows that the land was persistently wet and wooded so would have been unattractive for a domestic settlement, but perhaps a good source of game. Archaeologists have derived that Mesolithic man took advantage of the plentiful flint as the raw material for his tools and the available hunting, but lived on the hills above Bath. These were the hunter-gatherers who first domesticated the dog to assist with hunting.

The temperature had increased, Britain was becoming an island as the melted glaciers raised sea levels and land bridges were submerged. This was a plentiful time; the Mendips (20 miles south-west of Bath) is a key British Mesolithic site.

An ornate gold-covered bronze sun disc, combined with the concentration of round barrows on the hills around Bath, has led academics to establish that the hot springs encouraged settlement in the surrounding area during the Bronze Age. Even during the Iron Age, Bath was only occupied imperceptibly. More substantial finds at Sion Hill and Bathampton Meadows, over 1 and 2 miles respectively from the spring quarter, show that the main areas of settlement were still outside what we would now consider to be Bath.

Earthworks of former field systems have been identified on Charmy Down and Bathampton Down. Their pattern has been recognised as being similar to the late Bronze Age reave systems on Dartmoor. Archaeologists agree that there is evidence of settlement at Little Down, Solsbury and Bathampton in the form of hillforts, but dating material is inconclusive. It is generally accepted that each hillfort would have had access to the uplands of Lansdown and Odd Down, probably as sheep pasture, valley pasture and meadowland, the more gentle slopes for arable, and the steeper being left as woodland.

It is not until the Celts created a causeway of gravel and boulders over the mud to enable their offerings to the goddess Sulis that there is any evidence of modifications being made to the springs. Coins from the first to fourth centuries have been discovered in the Hot Spring, suggesting that as soon as coins were available in this area they were being offered to the tutelary god(s), probably the goddess Sulis. This in turn supports the principle that the hot springs were subject to spiritual reverence long before the Roman invasion.

It is irrefutable that early man would have found the natural hot waters spiritually significant and would have made offerings here; however, until the Romans built cisterns to contain the water, central Bath would have been unsuitable for settlement. As we shall see, even during the Roman period the main areas of residential occupation were away from the spring quarters.

Two

AQUAE SULIS

A ccording to the historian Publius Cornelius Tacitus (*c*. AD 56–120), the Roman way of life of 'the lounge, the banquet, [and] the bath' was 'a form of vice brought by the conquering Romans to Britain, which seduced the hardy native inhabitants of the island'.

The Romans landed in Kent in AD 43 and between then and AD 47 they occupied much of southern England. Prior to the invasion, England had already come under the influence of Rome, mainly through trade links. Roman wine, glassware and jewellery were already popular. Roman culture, governance and military strength were already comprehended.

Initially Emperor Claudius' (11 BC–AD 54) strategic objective was to control the fertile and prosperous lands of the south-east of England. Most scholars have advocated that a wide military zone, controlled by a fortified road called the Fosse Way and stretching across the country from Exeter to Lincoln, was a deliberate measure to protect this more 'civilised' area. More recent research, however, has shown that the Romans took advantage of Britain's mineral deposits beyond this boundary early on in their administration. We also know that if the Fosse was ever a military road that function was quickly superseded by its role as the main transportation, trade and communication link connecting the south-west with the north-east.

It is arguable, then, that the Fosse Way – one of this area's most iconic Roman vestiges – was always intended as an efficient link between the important legionary fortresses at Exeter and Lincoln, providing access to established tracks and pathways, rather than as an armoured boundary. Nevertheless, Bath lay to the east of this delineation and importantly accommodated the convergence of three key roads: besides the Fosse Way, there was the road to the harbour at Poole in Dorset and the road from London to the port at Sea Mills in Bristol.

Due to the number of archaeological finds, and the presence of a ford near to the present-day site of Cleveland Bridge, this seems the most likely junction of these major roads, and thus the crossing point of the Avon. It would have therefore been strategically desirable to have a fort near here although, sadly, no tangible evidence has yet been found. Conjecture favours the area around Bathwick Street and Henrietta Park. Other propositions are Walcot, where early Samian pottery, high-quality imported glassware, *Terra Nigra* pottery, a small piece of armour and a first-century metalled road have been unearthed, and Victoria Park, where military equipment was discovered in the nineteenth century.

Throughout the AD 50s, the Romans proceeded gradually across Britain, taking control of lands to the north and west of the Fosse Way and progressing towards the border with Wales. The conquest of Wales was, however, dramatically interrupted by a rebellion led by Boudicca, the Queen of the Iceni (modern-day Norfolk) in AD 60–61. We have no evidence of how this bloody uprising affected Bath, but throughout Britain it appears that the aftermath saw a period of measured consolidation with no significant appropriations. Rome itself was in turmoil by the end of the decade: Nero, Claudius' successor, committed suicide in AD 68 sparking civil war, which was followed by the quick succession of four emperors. Stability eventually arrived with Vespasian (AD 69–79) and the start of the Flavian dynasty. And it is from this period that the majority of the archaeological finds in central Bath, but outside of the actual baths area, date.

As we have seen, the hot springs were already venerated before the Roman invasion. There is evidence that soon after their arrival the Romans drove a road through the centre of the shrine. One can only assume this was a deliberate act of desecration, despite there being evidence that the Roman invaders made use of the hot springs from the onset of their colonisation. Nonetheless, it was not until the reigns of Nero, and later, Vespasian, that the spa was properly developed.

Prior to the Roman invasion, the Dobunni, an indigenous Iron Age tribe who believed that the hot springs were sacred and had dedicated them to the goddess Sulis, ruled the baths. Post Boudicca's rebellion, the Romans respected the importance of these local deities, appreciating the collateral they afforded. Equally, bathing, and the social endeavours associated with public bathhouses was an important element of Roman cultural life. Bathhouses were built in towns and cities throughout the Roman Empire, but the complex at Bath was the most prestigious in northern Europe, mainly because the waters were believed to be curative.

Interventions commenced by Nero and halted by Boudicca's revolt and Rome's own upheavals were given priority during Vespasian's reign. By transforming this native shrine into a magnificent curative and religious centre, the Romans were perhaps promoting reconciliation and co-operation between the indigenous population and themselves as interlopers. Although determined to rid the land of aggressive opponents to their occupation, the Romans were respectful of established gods and goddesses. They adopted Sulis, seeing her to be similar to their own deity, Minerva. The Romans gave Bath its first recorded name of Aquae Sulis – the 'Waters of Sulis'.

John Poole: The newly excavated Roman Great Bath, *c.* 1890. (Bath Central Library/Bath in Time)

In around AD 70, work began on a massive reservoir with walls 2m high, lined with sheets of lead to enclose the Sacred Spring. Driving oak piles into the surrounding mud consolidated the unstable ground. Once the spring was tamed, work began on the temple and a suite of three luxurious swimming baths, including the Great Bath.

Unlike today, the Great Bath would have been roofed, initially with timber but later with a brick and tile vaulted roof, part of which can be seen at the Roman Baths Museum. The bath is flat-bottomed and still lined with forty-five sheets of lead mined from the nearby Mendip Hills. The natural hot water continues to flow into the Great Bath through a lead culvert in the north-west corner. Some water was drained off to supply the baths to the east, but the majority flowed out through a sluice-controlled drain that (still) discharges into the River Avon, ensuring that the consolidated ground does not become waterlogged and unusable again. The bath was therefore constantly being refreshed with warm water.

Because the water did not need heating it allowed for a far larger swimming pool than in any other bathing establishment in the whole of the Roman Empire. Pilgrims came from across the realm – inscriptions survive from Chartres, Metz and Trier – to make sacrifices or dedicate gifts to the deity Sulis Minerva. They thanked her for providing the health-giving waters and prayed for a successful cure, often by inscribing a message on a sheet of lead or pewter before throwing it into the Sacred Spring. From these messages we get a glimpse of their concerns: one man left a curse for whoever stole his cloak, whilst another laments the loss of his napkin. Excavation has also shown that gifts included coins, jewellery, pewter and silver items. The pilgrims would then immerse themselves in the waters.

Bathing was an important facet of Roman society – spiritually, curatively and pleasurably. It provided an atmosphere conducive for social interaction, intellectual discussion and business deals. At its height, the baths comprised an undressing room (*apoddyterium*), a cold plunge bath (*frigidarium*), a sauna (*laconicum*) and warm and hot steam rooms (*tepidarium* and *caldarium*). The complex was kept warm with underfloor heating provided by the hypocausts.

The ritual of bathing included being oiled and taking part in gentle exercise (to work up a sweat) before bathing. The quality of the oil and the number of attendants massaging you was an indication of your social status. The oil was scraped off with a *strigil*, taking with it sweat, dead skin, dirt and hair. If this detritus came from a gladiator it would have been made into an unction and sold on as a cure or beauty treatment. Many of the attendants, entertainers, beauticians and workers at the baths would have been slaves.

The architectural design of the baths allowed for spectators – it was important to be seen. Licentious acts were common, but reduced in the second century when Emperor Hadrian forbade mixed public bathing. Whilst Bath built additional facilities, other establishments across the Roman Empire introduced separate opening times for men and women to bathe.

Archaeology has shown that at its most extensive (in the fourth century) the bathing complex incorporated five baths, two swimming pools, sweat rooms (heated with hypocausts) and cooling rooms – all built around the Sacred Spring that had been enclosed within a large vaulted chamber in the second century. The magnetism of the curative waters continued to rise over a period of 300 years, and the complex of buildings was extended to accommodate the increasing visitor numbers. Subsequently Bath became one of the most significant religious spa centres in the entire Roman Empire.

The Temple of Sulis Minerva was situated to the north-west of the Great Bath, on the opposite side of the Sacred Spring. Only fragments of the temple have been discovered, but expert reconstruction and analysis has provided us with a clear indication of what the temple would have looked like. Built on top of a high podium, a set of sweeping steps led up to an impressive portico supported by four vast fluted Corinthian columns. The highly ornate pediment, fragments of which have been found, was rich with symbolism. The striking central feature of a Gorgon's head has become an iconic representation of the Roman Baths Museum. It is on display alongside representations of the four seasons and a

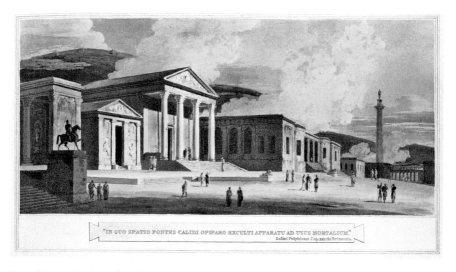

"IN QVO SPATIO FONTES CALIDI OPIPARO EXCULTI APPARATU AD USUS MORTALIUM."
Solini Polyhistor Cap.xxii de Britannia.

Samuel Lysons: Imaginary view of the Roman Temple of Minerva, 1802. (Bath Central Library/Bath in Time)

moon goddess. There are also depictions of helmets and an owl, which represent Minerva's attributes of military prowess and wisdom. Behind the portico lay a room where only the priests had access; they would tend the eternal flames that burnt around the statue of Sulis Minerva.

Solinus, writing in the early third century, described Bath as being 'furnished luxuriously for human use', with Minerva presiding over her temple and a perpetual flame (this is now agreed to have been achieved by the burning of Somerset coal). In 1727, whilst workmen dug a new sewer on nearby Stall Street, the gilded bronze head of this idol was discovered. It is now on display at the museum and is still considered to be one of the most significant finds from the Roman period in Britain.

The temple precinct would have contained a sacrificial altar, sited so that it was on the east–west axis through the temple and the north–south axis across the spring. It was here that animals were forfeited and their organs 'read' by an *haruspex* priest (which literally means 'gut-gazer'), to foretell the future of the person who had commissioned the sacrifice. It is established that the temple precinct must have been a very busy place full of pilgrims, scribes writing curses, slaves clearing up, merchants, priests, soldiers, souvenir vendors and suppliers of sacrifices – all set against the hum of the very many different languages from across the empire.

The Romans enclosed the bath and temple complex area within a series of walls with three main entrance gates to the north, south and west. The enclosed area

A. Gordon: Engraving of Minerva's bronze head, 1730. (Bath Central Library/ Bath in Time)

CAPUT hoc, ex ære inauratum, antiquo opere summoque artificio conflatum, Urbis inter rudera multis jam seculis excisæ sepultum, AQVIS SOLIS in agro Somersetensi XVI tandem sub solo ped. effossum A.D. CIƆ DCC XXVII. Æternitati consecravit Soc. Antiquar. Londinensis.

was no more than 24 acres, or 10 hectares, which is considered rather small for a Roman town. No public buildings – an indication of official civic activities – such as a forum, basilica or a market hall, have been found. Whilst a few high-class mosaic floors have been discovered within the walls, it is believed that these were probably priests' residences and not the properties of the mainstream inhabitants of Bath. Instead, archaeologists and historians concur that the evidence points to the 'town' of Bath lying to the north of the sacred precinct, stretching along Walcot Street, to the junction of those significant roads at Cleveland Bridge and then continuing along the London Road.

The area's name, Walcot, which doubtless derives from the Saxon word *wealqs*, meaning a foreigner, and therefore a native Briton, perhaps supports this (the Saxons called a Roman settlement '*ceaster*' and some documents from this period distinguish the area of the baths as Bathancester). It seems highly probable that

Walcot archaeological dig of Roman remains, 2 April 1991. (Bath Central Library/Bath in Time)

local entrepreneurs, traders and pedlars would have found a plentiful supply of customers at the site of a major road interchange, with an adjacent busy river way, at the main approach to a major religious spa, and at least 45km from the nearest town of any size. One can assume, therefore, that living standards for Bathonians during this period were relatively high.

A very small number of finds from the Claudian (AD 43–54) and Neronian (AD 54–68) periods have been linked to the builders of the baths and temples. Most finds within the walls post-date AD 69. Finds along Walcot Street, London Street, at Nelson Place and between the river and Walcot Street, however, show that a settlement had been established here around AD 50. It was substantial and abiding.

Archaeologists have found evidence of blacksmiths, potters and leatherworkers here, including the discovery of a rubbish pit near Walcot Street, which was found to contain leather shoe fragments, offcuts and a set of tools. Coins, pottery, metalwork and a tessellated floor have also been unearthed, indicating that this was a residential, as well as an industrial, area. Narrow stone and timber houses, probably of two storeys with shopfronts, would have lined the main road.

Behind, and closer to the river, would have been the higher status houses. The Roman road ran behind the site of Hudson's Bar and Grill (formerly the Hat and Feather public house).

A tombstone to *Vibia Secunda*, discovered before 1658 on the site of the Bell Inn, was the first documented Roman find. In 1815, during redevelopment of Hedgemead Park and the area around Walcot Methodist Church, large quantities of artefacts were uncovered (although unfortunately the exact positions were not recorded). More recent excavations, mainly in the late 1980s, support the theory that this was the site of Bath 'town'.

During the redevelopment of the Tramsheds in 2000–02, a few finds showed that commercial properties progressively spread down Walcot Street towards Aquae Sulis. Sadly, no archaeological work was undertaken during the construction of the underground Northgate Car Park in the 1970s – almost certainly this site would have provided evidence of how commercial and spiritual Bath were linked, if indeed they were.

Elsewhere in Bath, mosaics of some distinction have been discovered at Daniel Street in Bathwick (on the south side of the river) and behind Norfolk Crescent (on the west side of the city), which indicate that these were quality dwellings, although their relationship to the town is unclear. At least thirty villas are known within 15 miles of Bath, including at Box, Newton St Loe, Wellow, Monkton Combe, Brislington and Keynsham.

Lower Common Villa (north of the Upper Bristol Road) was discovered in 1983 and excavated between 1986–88. It was a substantial building with a stone gatehouse, stone walled enclosure and private bathhouse. The Wells Road Villa, on Prospect Place, was discovered in 1997. It was over 120ft wide (36.5m), and probably consisted of three ranges around a courtyard, with perhaps a fourth or a covered way. It had been damaged by ploughing in the Middle Ages, but it had at least one large tessellated floor. It too had its own bathhouse, and enviable views across the city.

In 1822 during road widening, a Roman coffin was found at Combe Down (1½ miles south of Bath). Over the next three decades a further five coffins were found in the area. And during the 1850s the Reverend Prebendary Henty Mengden Scarth, rector of Wrington, spent time cataloguing a large number of artefacts, coins and building materials found on the site of a villa. He published his findings in 1864. Sadly the exact location of that villa has not been satisfied and it was probably lost during surface quarrying in the late nineteenth century. Dating of the coins suggests that the villa probably dated from the fourth century and was vacated before the fall of the Roman Empire in the fifth century. The owners of this villa were probably overseers of the stone extraction which we know occurred at Combe Down during the Roman period.

Archaeology continues to add to our understanding of Bath during the Roman period. In 2007, workmen on the development site of the Gainsborough Hotel spotted some coins in what was probably the corner of a room in a Roman building within the walls. Comprising silver and base metal Roman coins and dating from 32–31 BC to AD 274, there were 17,577 coins in total, in eight bags. Why the coins were collected, by whom and why they were buried is only speculative. However, from the excavations undertaken by James Irvine in the 1860s we know that there were a number of high-status Roman buildings here, possibly part of another bathing complex – the site is close to the Hot Bath spring. A Roman altar discovered in the Cross Bath in 1809 further supports the idea that this area of Bath also had an important religious function.

Despite these finds and excavations, much of what we understand about Bath during the Roman occupation is educated supposition. For example, the lack of domestic finds within the walled area has led to the belief that the central site around the springs was sacred – and whilst I do not dispute that, some could argue that the amount of rebuilding on top of Roman Bath, and the reuse of Roman building materials perhaps means that these domestic indicators were cleared away centuries ago.

The fourth century was a time of unrest. Citizens were subjected to raids by barbarian tribes from northern Europe and Ireland. Villas around Bath were attacked and burnt. Rome itself was sacked in AD 410, with further raids throughout the century. Rome's downfall (after 500 years of dominance) was due to a number of factors: overexpansion and reliance on slave labour made administration and communication hard; defending such a large empire was costly, resulting in oppressive taxation, which left the citizens resentful and poor; and the legalisation of Christianity in AD 313 undermined the emperor's divine status. Once weakened, Germanic tribes such as the Saxons were able to invade and occupy far-flung territories like Britain.

The instability made it unsafe to travel, and therefore fewer visitors attended places such as the baths. Maintenance work undertaken on the Temple of Sulis Minerva from this period was not of such good quality when compared with what had been done before. After the middle of the century, secular masonry buildings started to encroach upon the temple precinct and there was a serious decline in the temple's condition and status. Equally, however, there are signs of continued use of the baths, suggesting that the leisure side of Bath continued, even if its religious status had been lost.

During the third and fourth centuries, the sea level started to rise, causing a succession of floods. To counteract this the floors were initially raised, but as time went on the floodwaters continued to swell, whilst the usability – and thus prosperity – of the baths dwindled. The baths became choked up with mud left behind by the receding floodwaters.

By the fifth century, the number of visitors to Bath had seriously declined, even at the very heart of the shrine, and rubbish was allowed to accumulate. Attempts were made to try and consolidate the layers of mud with layers of rubble. Eventually the floodwaters and thick, black mud won out. The vaulted roof collapsed over the spring and reservoir and the classical columns and pedestals were left in ruins. Bath's great complex started to be swallowed up by a cycle of floodwater, mud, rubble and rising sea levels; the structures falling in on themselves. The baths and temple precinct disappeared under the encroaching marshes. As you walk the streets today, remember that Roman Bath is now a subterranean world, deep below you, the levels having also risen with the building and rebuilding of properties over older foundations.

All the archaeological evidence indicates that after the fall of the Roman Empire, the once bustling suburbs of Bath, such as Walcot, had all but disappeared. But Bath did not collapse with the withdrawal of the Romans. Whilst the central area crumbled, the slightly higher surrounding parts continued to be inhabited. The bathhouse at Lower Common Villa was converted to a glass workshop; stone structures were replaced, albeit with timber buildings; pottery kilns were established in previously high-status villas; and burials from this date, whilst plain, do indicate that some citizens continued to prosper.

Three

AQUAEMANN TO CATHEDRAL CITY: SAXON AND NORMAN BATH

Although the Roman Empire in western Europe ceased to exist after AD 476, the influence of Rome on the general way of life did not disappear overnight. Probably throughout the fifth century, and perhaps into the early years of the sixth century, sub-Roman culture and ideologies coexisted with that of the Britons.

Sometimes referred to as the 'Dark Ages' and acknowledged as a period of widespread violence and warfare, the era between the collapse of the Roman Empire and the arrival of William the Conqueror actually saw considerable change and development, much of which is still apparent today. England established itself as a Christian country; the county shires were first established; modern English was developed; literacy became widespread; an impressive monetary system was adopted; the population expanded; there was increased urbanisation with the growth of centres such as York and London; and there was an architectural revolution with stone-built castles, churches and monasteries. To distance itself from its pagan past, Bath adopted the name 'Aquaemann'.

As we have seen, England had been subjected to a series of raids from northern Europe and Ireland during the fourth century. Villas around Bath were burnt down and the majority were not reoccupied. Instead, people sought shelter within the safety of the city walls. Naturally these people started to establish homes and businesses, encroaching on the temple precinct and salvaging any building materials they found there. A fall in the number of visitors to Bath, due to the unsettling nature of the countrywide conflicts and a series of floods from the Avon, meant that the baths became too difficult to uphold. Evidence also indicates that there was a major act of demolition around this time, when building stone and lead were robbed and recycled. This is confirmed by John Leland's description of Bath from 1542, when he refers to a statue – probably of Hercules – and Latin inscriptions that he saw embedded in the sides of more modern buildings or amongst the stones that made up the city's walls and gates. Leland understood that these antiquities had been reused for repairs and were not in their original, ancient positions.

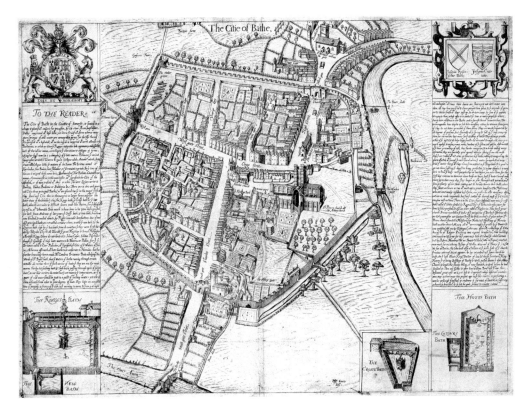

The Savile Map of Bath, 1588–1603. (Bath Central Library/Bath in Time)

In addition, framing Savile's map of 1588–1603 is a lengthy description of Bath and its foundation. Savile writes that the inside of the walls were ramped with earth almost to the top and embedded in this earth bank were Roman antiquities.

※ ※ ※ ※ ※

The barbarians from northern Europe, who originally came to plunder these shores, were invited by local leaders to settle along the coast and protect the country from all other raiders. These Saxon mercenaries, however, rebelled and spread out across the south and east. They made a number of attempts against the west, but were unsuccessful; their greatest defeat being at Mount Badon in around AD 520 (John Wood traced Mount Badon or Mons Badonica to Lansdown, but Bathampton Down also lays claim, as does Badbury Hillfort in Dorset and Bowden Hill in Linlithgow). The Saxons did not give up, and –

according to the *Anglo-Saxon Chronicle* – won a decisive victory in AD 577 at the Battle of Dyrham, capturing Cirencester, Gloucester and Bath.

This prolonged period of battles and raids saw a number of towns deserted. Gildas, a British monk, wrote in *The Ruin of Britain and Other Works*, 'the cities of our land are not populated even now as they once were; right to the present they are deserted, in ruins and unkempt'.

There are great tracts of time when we have little or no evidence of what Bath was like, but a poem, thought to have been written in the eighth century, is believed to be about Bath and supports Gildas' account:

In Ruin
Wondrous is this masonry, shattered by the Fates.
The fortifications have given way,
The buildings raised by giants are crumbling.
The roofs have collapsed; the towers are in ruins …
There is rime on the mortar.
The walls are rent and broken away
And have fallen undermined by age.
The owners and builders are perished and gone
And have been held fast in the Earth's embrace,
The ruthless clutch of the grave,
While a hundred generations of mankind have passed away …
Red of hue and hoary with lichen
This wall has outlasted kingdom after kingdom,
Standing unmoved by storms.
The lofty arch has fallen …
Resolute in spirit he marvellously clamped the foundations
Of the walls with ties
There were splendid palaces and many halls with water
Flowing through them
A wealth of gables towered aloft …
And so these courts lie desolate
And the framework of the dome with its red arches shed its tiles …
Where of old many a warrior,
Joyous hearted and radiant with gold,
Shone resplendent in the harness of battle,
Proud and flushed with wine.
He gazed upon the treasure, the silver, the precious stones,
Upon wealth, riches and pearls,
Upon this splendid citadel of a broad domain.

There stood courts of stone,

And a stream gushed forth in rippling floods of hot water.

The wall enfolded within its bright bosom

The whole place which contained the hot flood of the baths ...

Very little tangible evidence remains from this period either, but the West Wansdyke, or Woden's Dyke, named after a Saxon deity, is an earthwork that ran along high ground between Bath and Maes Knoll, and perhaps onto Dundry Hill, near Bristol. In 2007, archaeologists dug a number of test pits, which frustratingly offered no precise dating material, but it is thought to have been created around AD 600. They were, however, able to show that the earthwork was constructed under a consistent design and therefore purposefully and at one time. A section can be seen at Odd Down, behind Sainsbury's, although in a worrying condition.

It seems the West Wansdyke has little connection with the more famous Wansdyke in Wiltshire; Bath's was perhaps the border between the Romano-British Celts and the Saxons of West Saxon and Mercia. During the Saxon period there was a fluidity of smaller kingdoms across England, until the ninth century when they were consolidated to form four main realms – Northumbria, Mercia, East Anglia and Wessex. Bath was initially in Wessex, then Mercia, then back again to Wessex, before Wessex and Mercia were united at the beginning of the tenth century. Bath was strategically important, and once the kings of Wessex had taken total control of the area they invested in Bath's defensive walls.

The next significant mention of Bath in the records is not until AD 675, when an Anglo-Saxon charter tells us that King Osric granted 100 hides of land to found a monastery for women. We do not know for certain what these lands consisted of, but it probably relates quite closely to the estate identified in the Domesday Book of 1086. Abbess Berta (or Bertana) was granted land for the foundation of a nunnery, or perhaps a 'double house', where a male and a female community lived under the same roof and leader but practised separately. This would have then metamorphosed into a monastery as the nuns died, perhaps explaining why no record of the foundation of St Peter's is known to exist.

The first reference to monastic brethren dates from AD 757 with the foundation of the abbey church of St Peter. It is possible the foundation records of the monastery may have been lost, meaning that Bath would have had two significant religious houses established in the seventh and eighth centuries. The location of both the nunnery and monastery (or double house) has not been determined, but it was not unusual for Roman precincts to be reused by early ecclesiastical establishments. Two other medieval churches in Bath appear to have been positioned on sacred Roman sites; both St Winifred's Chapel and well on Sion Hill and Bathwick old church (demolished in 1818) were sited on Roman cemeteries.

Since the end of the eighth century, the north of Britain particularly was subjected to a series of raids by the 'Great Heathen Army' from Scandinavia. The first Viking raid, recorded by the *Anglo-Saxon Chronicle, was around* AD 787. The Danes were pagans and many Christian monasteries in Britain were raided and looted. A number of contemporary accounts illustrate the anguish felt as monasteries were burnt and monks killed by the Viking raiders, such as at Lindisfarne in AD 793 and Iona in AD 802. A large army of Vikings set sail in AD 865 with the intention of conquering the whole of Britain. By AD 874 all of the Anglo-Saxon kingdoms had fallen, except Wessex.

Wessex was ruled by Alfred the Great (AD 849–899), who famously hid from the marauding Danes in the marshes near Athelney (approximately 35 miles to the south-west of Bath) where he regrouped and later defeated the Vikings at Edington (approximately 15 miles south-east of Bath) in Wiltshire. The Vikings retreated to their stronghold at Chippenham (also in Wiltshire), but Alfred

besieged them and after a fortnight of no supplies the Vikings sent an emissary to Alfred. In 1982, a Viking sword was discovered at the corner of New Bond Street and Northgate Street – just outside the city walls. This artefact, however, may date from King Swein's assault on Britain in 1013, which saw the noblemen of Bath submit to his Viking army.

Alfred was unable to drive the Vikings out of Britain and so the Peace of Wedmore saw the Viking leader Guthrum baptised, and the country effectively cut in two. Bath – in the west – remained under Anglo-Saxon rule. Alfred improved the defences in the areas he controlled by building fortresses and building up a navy. Bath was redefended with over 4,100ft (approximately 1,250m) of

Lesley Green-Armytage: Bust of King Alfred, 14 Alfred Street, Bath, *c.*1973.
(Bath Preservation Trust/Bath in Time)

wall placed in front of the Roman foundations. The walls, 10ft (over 3m) wide and at least 20ft (over 6m) high, were on the one hand a great defence, but on the other a huge liability. When Bath was under threat so the city's walls were maintained, but when, for instance, the threat of French invasion subsided in the late fourteenth century so the walls were used as an open quarry for repairing and extending structures.

King Stephen (1135–54) came to inspect the walls in 1139–40, because Henry I's daughter, Matilda, had taken control of the west of England with the intention of claiming the throne. In 1369, when relations with the French were particularly bad, Edward III (1327–77) ordered a survey of all fortifications across Britain – Bath's were in a very sorry state and described as destroyed and broken and close to ruin. Edward made it the responsibility of everyone who benefitted from the city to contribute to the upkeep of its walls.

King Alfred was an impressive self-promoter, and we should perhaps take his battlefield successes with 'a pinch of salt'. Despite this, the *Anglo-Saxon Chronicle*, which he commissioned, is vital, being one of very few sources of information about medieval Britain. During the reign of Alfred's son, Edward the Elder (AD 899–924), Wessex and Mercia were united and a mint was established in Bath, ranking the city the thirtieth place of importance in England (Bristol was thirty-third).

During the reign of King Edgar (AD 959–75) Britain enjoyed a period of peace with the multi-ethnic character of England embraced by its leaders. It was at this time that the Church was reorganised and rekindled. Edward recalled Bishop Dunstan from the exile which had been imposed by his brother Eadwig, and made him Archbishop of Canterbury. Bath abbey was re-founded in around AD 963 as a Benedictine house, but its lands were now scattered.

Edgar's reformation was centred on the strict reform of the monasteries, sealed by the *Regularis Concordia of* AD 973, the same year in which Edgar was crowned King of the English at Bath abbey (Dunstan carefully orchestrated his coronation). This prestigious occasion must have been an impressive event, which continues to resonate today. The current coronation service is still based on the one compiled by Dunstan for Edgar. In 1973 Queen Elizabeth II visited Bath Abbey for a service to mark 1,000 years since the coronation of King Edgar. There is a stone commemorating this visit in the floor of the Abbey.

A series of short-lived rulers, both from the house of Wessex and their rivals, the kings of the Danes, mark the next century. Bath does not feature in the *Chronicle* and we have very limited knowledge of events, activities and developments during the eleventh century in Bath.

The Norman Conquest seems to have had little effect on Bath. William the Conqueror's (1066–87) survey, the Domesday Book, commenced in 1085, put

Queen Elizabeth and Prince Philip during their visit to Bath for Monarchy 1000, 9 August 1973. (Bath Central Library/Bath in Time)

Bath's population at just less than 1,000. The abbey had lands in Somerset and Gloucester, it held twenty-four burgesses (boroughs) paying 20 shillings a year, a mill and 12 acres of meadow. The mill was probably Monk's Mill, which stood where Parade Gardens is now; the meadow was probably the Hams. This independence and wealth was to be short-lived. Two years later, Bath was plundered during the national rebellion against the accession of William Rufus (1087–1100), William the Conqueror's second son.

Once King, William Rufus made his own physician, John de Villula of Tours, Bishop of Wells, and gave him the city of Bath and its priory. Rufus had decreed that bishops' sees should be based in towns, and preferably defended towns such as Bath. John of Tours took the opportunity to restore Bath after the devastating sack of 1088 and made it his home. He transferred the bishop's see from Wells to Bath (thus transforming the abbey into a cathedral) and called himself the 'Bishop of Bath'. Since he was not a Benedictine monk, Tours left the actual running of the monastery to the prior – this is why it became known as the Bath Priory. It is easy to understand Tours' preference for Bath – the abbey was well known and respected, the town was wealthy with high-status residents, and Bath enjoyed the benefits of both visitors to the town and those just passing through on the four major roads. Wells in comparison was quite provincial.

Although Tours thought little of the resident monks, he instigated the building of a major cathedral priory with a complex of church buildings, gardens and orchards enclosed by walls – a city within the city. Tours' grand Romanesque church was 90ft wide (27.5m) and more than 350ft long (106.7m), making it one of the largest Norman cathedrals in the country. It has been estimated that the abbey church we know now would have fitted into its nave. Leland noted that Tours 'pullid down the old Church of St Peter at Bath, and erectid a new, much fairer' one, 'with [a] great and elaborate circuit of walls,' added William of Malmesbury.

Tours' new church was certainly under way by 1106 and possibly begun in the 1090s. In addition, almost the entire south-east quarter of the old Saxon city was taken up with the auxiliary precinct. Tours established the bishop's palace and chapel, a private bath (or baths, known later as the Abbot's Bath and the Prior's Bath) fed with the overflow from the King's Bath, provision for the monks, and a cathedral school. The bath was refurbished and fitted with masonry arches for the comfort of bathers. From here on it became known as the King's Bath, probably named after Henry I (Rufus' younger brother, who seized the throne in 1100 after Rufus was killed in a hunting accident in the New Forest). *Gesta Stephani* (1138) includes a description of the bath:

Model to illustrate possible appearance of the Norman cathedral of John de Villula, 1951. (Bath Central Library/Bath in Time)

Through hidden pipes, springs supply waters, heated not by human skill or art, from deep in bowels of the earth to a reservoir in the midst of arched chambers, splendidly arranged, providing in the centre of the town baths which are pleasantly warm, healthy and a pleasure to the eye ... Sick persons from all England resort thither to bathe in these healing waters, and the strong also, to see this wonderful bubbling up of the hot springs and to bathe in them.

This description shows that the baths – and Bath – was attracting those seeking relaxation at a popular resort, as well as the sick praying for a cure. Bath was once again beginning to be recognised for its curative powers.

Outside of the precinct, Tours built Stall Street and reconfigured the South Gate by re-siting it 60m to the west of its Saxon predecessor. This helped establish a clear north–south route through the city, and increased the rentable space along these streets, which in turn provided greater income for the bishop to help pay for all these improvements. The original South Gate was later recut to form the Ham Gate in the thirteenth century.

Tours established hunting areas at Claverton and Prior Park. A critical portrayal of Tours, written by William of Malmesbury, says that he:

... completed many things nobly in ornaments and books, and filled the Abbey with monks eminent for literature and discharge of their duties. According to reports, his medical knowledge was founded more upon practice than science. He enjoyed literary society but indulged in sarcasm more than was fitted to his rank. He was a wealthy man and of liberal habits, but could not be induced, even on his death-bed, wholly to restore their lands to the monks.

Tours died in 1122 and his successors, Bishop Godfrey (1123–35) and Bishop Robert of Lewes (1136–66), continued to add to the building works, including the replacement of the church that was partially destroyed by fire in 1137. Bishop Robert added an infirmary, probably in answer to demand as Bath continued to establish itself as a place of healing rather than just recreation. The monastic library held four medical treatises.

The cathedral was completed by 1156. It has been said that what John of Tours created was a Christian version of the Romans' Aquae Sulis, and this is a very good comparison to aid our understanding of the magnitude of Bath's Norman renaissance.

When Rufus granted Tours the town of Bath it was so that he could establish his pontifical seat there. Moving the see from Wells, however, was not met with universal approval. In 1176, Pope Alexander III decreed that both Bath and Wells should be of equal status; Pope Innocent IV then substantiated this in

1245, by endorsing the title of Bishop of Bath and Wells. At about this time a wooden bridge was built at the end of Southgate Street. St Lawrence's, or Old Bridge, linked the two religious centres by making the journey between Bath and Wells easier. By 1304 the bridge had been rebuilt in stone.

In addition to the great cathedral, Bath had four parish churches. St James near the South Gate was established on this site in 1279 (it had been within the area now occupied by the Abbey precinct), St Mary de Stall, St Michael (within) and St Mary Northgate were all of late Saxon origin, yet none survive today.

The royal lodgings were situated within the priory precinct. We know King John kept a house in Bath from at least 1201, but by the time Edward I was on the throne he believed it was frivolous to expend on a house he so rarely visited. After 1276 no reference to a royal residence is known. This may be due to Bishop Robert Burnell taking Bath back from King Edward I in 1278. (Although Rufus had given Bath to Tours, Bishop Savarac returned the city to King Richard I in 1192, in exchange for Glastonbury Abbey.)

The bishop enjoyed a good income from the rents he received from the land owned and rented by the priory, which extended beyond the city walls to the Bath Hundred and the Foreign Hundred. These were administrative areas comprising not only parts such as the Ham and Walcot that are now part of the city, but also what would become Bath's surrounding parishes of Kelston, Freshford and Bathford. The Church effectively owned a third of the city and seventeen neighbouring villages. The priory dominated daily life, with citizens renting land, supplying services and having to seek the bishop's approval for any major changes to the town.

Although the monastic establishment at Bath was impressive it was never overtly crowded, there were not ever more than forty monks. Its most successful time was at the beginning of the fourteenth century, but the Black Death of 1348–49 curtailed this. The Black Death, which started in the Dorset port of Melcombe Regis, spread rapidly through the West Country. For example, 40 per cent of the population from the Bristol region fell victim. Bath was equally devastated and the number of monks fell to twenty. Consequently the buildings were not maintained and the monks became undisciplined and debauched. Instead, Wells, with its monumental cathedral commenced in 1175, became the focus of religious life in the region. Bishop Reginald had already discharged the bishop's palace to the priory for an annual rent of 20s in 1328.

❋ ❋ ❋ ❋ ❋

The residential and commercial properties of Bath were mainly timber framed with thatched roofs. Some very wealthy properties were in stone; the materials more often than not pillaged from the ruined Roman structures and the walls. In the spacious gardens behind were rubbish pits. Sewage was thrown over the city wall or, worse, into the streets. It was not until the sixteenth century that a town scavenger was appointed, whose job it was to collect the waste and cart it out beyond the city walls. Much of the urban rubbish was thrown on the Hams, which flooded regularly. The approach to the city must have been disgusting, and of course Bath, with its own airless quality, must have been eye-watering. The narrator in Richard of Devizes' *The Chronicon de rebus gestis Ricardi Primi* (1192) is a French Jewish cobbler, who gives advice to young French Christians intending to visit England. Whilst describing all the English cities he knew, the cobbler advised, 'Bath, situated, or rather buried, in deep valleys in the middle of a thick atmosphere and a sulphurous fog, is at the gates of Hell'.

The wool trade was vital to Bath's economy at this time. Geoffrey Chaucer's *Wife of Bath* is an example of those who were prospering from the cloth industry. It was these merchants who were becoming increasingly frustrated by the oppressive powers of the priory and the bishop. Bath was not purely a place of religion and thermal waters; its commercial and civic identity was gaining strength. A group of merchants decided to take advantage of Richard I's (1157–99) desperate need to finance his battles with France and his religious Crusades to Palestine. They met with him just before he set sail from Dover in 1189 (he was crowned King on 3 September 1189) and secured a charter, which stated that 'the citizens of Bath, who are its Merchant Guild' have the right to trade freely, wherever they travel, without payment of taxes. This charter, confirmed in 1246 by Henry III, was effectively the foundation of the Corporation of Bath, which ran the city's civic and commercial activities for the next 600 years.

Bath had a mayor by 1230 and was represented in Parliament from 1268. The first evidence of a guildhall is in a document from 1355, and investigative work undertaken by Elizabeth Holland has pinpointed the location of the first guildhall to be in the car park behind the current Guildhall on the High Street – adjacent to East Gate. Over the next century, secular powers increased to control tax collection, beggars, crime, fraud, trade, employment and wages.

The 1379 poll tax, imposed by Richard II on his accession, provides fascinating evidence of Bath's population, their wealth, their trades and where they lived. It records 328 male individuals, equating to about 1,100 residents, most of whom were labourers or servants. The dominant wool trade employed three weavers, six fullers, eleven spinners and eight tailors. There were only two hostelries mentioned and no one appears to have been employed by the baths.

The northern suburb, where Broad Street and Walcot Street converge, was far more greatly populated than the area below South Gate. St Michael's Church, near North Gate, was probably founded in the late eleventh or early twelfth century to service the community that was establishing itself just outside the walls. The plots of land are well organised and equal, suggesting a systematic development here. Richard II's poll tax demanded that the wealthiest in the country pay 10 marks (1 mark was the equivalent to about 14s); Bath's richest four men paid an average of 5s each.

Although the power of the priory was diminishing, it kept its own flock of sheep from which a large quantity of raw wool was produced; the monks also bought in bales of wool from other merchants. The priory employed a team of spinners and weavers to produce the cloth, finished in the Monks' Mill (both a grist mill for corn and a fulling mill for cloth). There is evidence of other fulling mills in Bath, at Twerton for example, showing that the monks did not completely monopolise the profession. In 1260, the local townspeople secured the rights from the priory to make use of the pasture at Kingsmead for grazing.

As John Wroughton has shown, Bath's increasing affluence can be understood by the growing number of more luxury trades that start to appear in the fourteenth and fifteenth centuries, such as a goldsmith, tailors, shoemakers and a tannery in Southgate Street supplying leather. Bath was an important and busy town, holding a twice-weekly market on Wednesdays and Saturdays when outsiders were allowed within the city walls to both sell and buy goods. The market was accommodated by the widening of the late Saxon street that led south from North Gate. The hot waters were still important, and since the thirteenth century, fresh spring water from the hills around Bath was piped down improving the conditions and health of the citizens.

Bath held four annual fairs, and the fees paid to the organiser or landowner by the stallholders made fairs very lucrative, whilst the influx and concentration of customers provided a healthy financial boost to the traders. Research has shown that Bishop John of Tours was first granted the right to hold a fair by Henry I in 1204. This fair was located on the High Street and held on the Feast of Saints Peter and Paul, 29 June. Due to the abbey's dedication to these two saints, this was a holy day all Bathonians would have observed, ensuring prodigious attendance. By the nineteenth century this was known as the Cherry Fair and ran for ten days.

At the end of the thirteenth century, Bishop Robert Burnell returned the see to Bath and the priory began to regain ownership of its lands. Edward I (1272–1307) approved two further annual fairs, one at Lansdown, held in August and known as St Lawrence's Fair because of the proximity to St Lawrence's Chapel (now part of Chapel Farm). It was established in 1304 and specialised in sheep. The other fair was based at Bear Flat, and was known as the Holloway Fair; it specialised in horses, with some of the proceeds going to support the leper hospital on Holloway. After the Dissolution of the Monasteries, the Corporation applied to Henry VIII for the right to hold another fair on the High Street, but in February and on Lady's Day. By the eighteenth century, this was primarily a cattle fair.

※ ※ ※ ※ ※

Bath has a long tradition of offering charitable assistance, possibly because the hot waters have long been considered curative. The area around the Cross Bath and new Thermae Spa is historically known as Bimbery. The Hospital of St John the Baptist was founded here in 1174 by Bishop Reginald Fitzjocelyn de Bohun (1141–91), 4th Bishop of Bath. The charity, for the poor and infirm of Bath, continues to serve the local community over 800 years later. It was not a hospital in the way we understand that term today, but a place of refuge for the disadvantaged. More like a small monastery, it was established to provide food and shelter for the needy, who in turn were expected to pray for the soul of their benefactor.

In 1435, William Philips, a former mayor and wealthy clothier, provided accommodation for poor visitors seeking a cure. After his death in 1444, his four almshouses were passed to the people of Bath and became known as St Catherine's Hospital. St Catherine was the patron saint of Bath and associated with spinning and cloth-making and hence Bath's Merchant Guild. Since 1249, members of the guild had owned the Chapel of St Catherine's in the Church of St Mary in Stall Street. Philips also had this chapel rebuilt and refurbished. In 1984, St John's Hospital took ownership of St Catherine's Hospital, which continues to offer almshouse flats to this day.

St Mary Magdalen Chapel on Holloway, 1950s. (Bath Central Library/Bath in Time)

On Holloway, Walter Hoast gave his house and the adjoining private chapel of St Mary Magdalene to the poor in around 1096, under the jurisdiction of the abbey.

The dedication to Mary Magdalene links the chapel with the nearby leper hospital, because tradition assumes (although biblical texts do not specifically identify) that it was Mary who anointed Jesus prior to his crucifixion whilst he was at the house of Simon, the leper. Committal to a leper, or lazar, house was a sentence of living death. Lepers underwent a symbolic funeral on admission, in which they were declared dead to the world and born again to God. It was part prison, part hospice.

Henry Edmund Goodridge (1797–1864), now more famously associated with his work at Beckford's Tower, was a prolific Bath architect and added the chancel and small three-stage tower in 1830–34, although the tower was not connected through until 1889. The east end of the chapel had to be rebuilt after suffering bomb damage in 1942.

Magdalene Cottage, adjacent to the chapel, was originally the leper hospital and in existence prior to 1212 when a legacy was left to the 'house of lepers in the suburbs of Bath'. This hospital was not owned by the Corporation, but instead came under the jurisdiction of the Crown. In 1263, Brother Nicholas, master of St Mary Magdalene, promised prayers to a couple who had granted property to the hospital. Another thirteenth-century grant mentions the brothers and sisters serving God there. There would have been money coming in from rents to help fund the hospital, and as we have seen, proceeds from the annual Holloway Fair and alms would have been collected on the lepers' behalf, but it was always a fairly poor foundation.

Prior John Cantlow petitioned the Pope in 1486 to unite the hospital to Bath Priory, because it was 'ruinous, impoverished and in debt'. There were no longer brothers living there and only two or three poor people were recorded as inmates. Prior Cantlow repaired the buildings and added the Tudor porch in 1495:

> This chapel flourished with foremost spectacle
> In the honour of Mary Magdalen Prior Cantlow hath edified
> Desiring you to pray for him with your prayers delectable
> That such will inhabit him in heaven there ever to abide.

Bath Priory was dissolved in 1539 and, as a consequence, the hospital fell into decline. The new master, Simon Shepherd, took the proceeds and provided no support. He was just one of many who, over the next 300 years, abused the charity they were supposed to help manage. Although a further bequest in 1560 appears to have put the hospital on a better footing once more.

By the end of the fourteenth century leprosy was on the decrease and leper hospitals across the country gradually closed or became hospitals for the sick and infirm. In Bath, however, the spa waters continued to attract sufferers of contagious skin diseases well into the sixteenth century.

The hospital was eventually converted into an 'asylum for idiots' sometime before 1660. Neglect followed, until 1761 when the Reverend Dual Taylor repaired the chapel and rebuilt the hospital. John Wood described it as a small poor house for the reception of 'idiots', but very few were maintained there and for a long period it only had one occupant. The last inmate to be cared for at the hospital was a Mary Phillips, who died in 1855. A year later the charity was wound up and eventually merged with the Bath Idiot and Imbecile School, begun as the Bath Institution for Idiot Children and those of Weak Intellect by Charlotte White. In 1894, under the Bath Municipal Charities Act, both charities came under the remit of St John's Hospital.

✳ ✳ ✳ ✳ ✳

By the end of the fifteenth century Bath was still a small, walled city, but accounts show that the healing properties of the water were well known. Its qualities as a place of resort were also recognised and Thomas Chaundler wrote in 1452:

> Nothing is more elegant and magnificent. Amongst its charms are shady groves, flowery meadows, pleasant streams, transparent fountains, and above all, the very nature of the place is formed for delight; for the very hills themselves with which beholders cannot satisfy themselves, or be weary of surveying; so that the whole region round about may rightly be esteemed and named a sort of paradise, to which nothing in the whole world is equal in respect of beauty and delight.

Four

CHURCH AND CHARITY:
TUDOR BATH

By the time Henry VII had crushed Richard III at the Battle of Bosworth and claimed the English throne in 1485, the large Norman church of Bath had fallen into decay and the monks had become undisciplined. Furthermore, Wells (20 miles south of Bath) was taking over as the focus of religious life for the region, after the bishops preferred to reside there throughout the fourteenth century.

When Bishop Oliver King (*c.* 1432–1503) visited Bath in 1499, he lamented the state of the abbey. He found that a succession of wanton and egotistical priors had led to not only the immorality of the monks, who had 'frittered themselves away in pleasures', but also substantial debts and the sustained neglect of the priory buildings and the abbey. King reluctantly concluded that any restoration would be far too costly.

Whilst still in Bath, King had a vision that comprised the Holy Trinity and a ladder with ascending and descending angels. At the foot of the ladder was an olive tree supporting a crown. King heard a voice that instructed him, 'Let an Olive establish the Crown, and let a King restore the Church'. King interpreted his vision, which is commemorated on the church's west front, as a direct challenge from God. Rather than abandon Bath abbey to its fate, King appointed William Bird as Prior Cantlow's successor and together they reformed the institution, bringing into force a strict budget and a more pious regime for the monks. The priory's surplus income was then diverted to the building of a new church – rather than rich living.

King's church was to be considerably smaller than the Norman church it replaced, making it less expensive to build and maintain, but this was also more appropriate for the now far smaller community of monks. King, however, insisted the church still be elegant and so he employed Robert and William Vertue, whose stonework for Henry VII in London had so impressed him. The Vertue brothers created a beautiful fan-vaulted roof to rival any that they were installing at Westminster Abbey. Unfortunately, both King and Bird died before 'one of the last great medieval cathedrals to be built in England' was completed.

※ ※ ※ ※ ※

Henry VIII's (1491–1547) defiance of Pope Clement VII's authority and subsequent divorce of Catherine of Aragon and marriage to Anne Boleyn came at a time when there was a groundswell of public opinion against the power, wealth and corruption of the Catholic Church. Henry's early reign was characterised by his youth and vigour, scholarship and musical talents, and was a period of great national pride, financial stability, increased wealth, investment in the navy and extensive building projects. Henry was a popular monarch. Many Members of Parliament resisted foreign interference in England's affairs, in much the same way as the 2016 European Union referendum showed that over 50 per cent of voters felt that the laws passed in Brussels were imposed on us against our will.

Henry's break with Rome was not purely driven by his own desires; there was support throughout England for the rebellion, including from the Archbishop of Canterbury, Thomas Cranmer. Ironically, in 1502 both the Spanish and English royal families had been concerned to receive the Pope's permission to sanction the marriage of Henry to his widowed sister-in-law. In addition, Henry penned an important attack on the instigator of the Protestant Reformation, Martin Luther, in 1521, which won him the title 'Defender of the Faith' from the Pope.

Shortly after Henry ascended the Crown in 1509 he married Catherine. Their union was a happy one and lasted almost twenty-four years, but it only produced one surviving heir – Mary, born in 1516. Henry was desperate for a son. His own accession had been the first peaceful succession for many years, he desired a male heir to ensure the House of Tudor continued unchecked. Catherine was in her forties and started to withdraw from court life, Henry – six years her junior – still enjoyed socialising and had fallen in love with Anne Boleyn. Henry believed his lack of a legitimate male heir was a punishment from God for his marrying his brother's widow. He believed his union with Catherine was unlawful and he wanted an annulment. This would put things right in the eyes of the law and the Church, and a new marriage would then be rewarded with a healthy boy.

In either late 1532 or early 1533, Henry married Anne; the Pope responded by excommunicating both Henry and Cranmer. The Act of Submission of the Clergy, the Act of Succession and the Act of Supremacy, passed by Parliament in 1534, made Henry 'Supreme Head on earth of the Church of England', and taxes that had once gone to the Vatican now passed to the English Crown.

Henry obviously enjoyed the increase in his wealth and the power he now held. His decision to go after the monasteries and find them guilty of moral laxity, veneration of relics and living a non-religious life was clearly in order for him to take advantage of their wealth and lands. Again, this decision was not made in a vacuum. Previous monarchs had suppressed religious houses and

Henry himself had previously sold off monastic estates to fund the universities in Oxford and Cambridge and foreign wars. Other European and Scandinavian monarchs also seized monastic income; the writings and philosophies of church reformers Martin Luther and Desiderius Erasmus had had a significant influence throughout the Continental kingdoms.

In the summer of 1535 Henry's commissioner, Dr Richard Layton, visited Bath. Layton reported that Prior William Holloway (Bird's successor) was a virtuous man, but the monks were 'worse than I have any found yet, both in buggery and adultery – some of them having ten women'. He sent evidence of the use of relics and, although the buildings were in good repair, related that the priory was £400 in debt. Most historians agree that the reports made by all the commissioners at this time were exaggerated, or at least paid special attention to any of the notorious aspects that would provide Henry and Thomas Cromwell with the evidence they needed to dissolve a monastic house.

Prior Holloway had predicted the end and did what he could, through bribes to Henry and Cromwell and friendships with local dignitaries, to secure as favourable a dissolution as possible for himself and his fellow monks. The voluntary surrender of the priory was signed on 29 June 1539. The Merchant Guild was offered the abbey and its lands for a bargain price of £500, but they feared that they would later be accused of – and punished for– defrauding the King and so turned the deal down.

All assets were stripped and sold off, including 80 tons of lead from the church roof, leaving it open to the elements and to assuredly deteriorate. The precinct and some surrounding plots of land were sold to Humphrey Colles on 16 March 1543, who, two days later, sold the lot on to Matthew Colthurst from Hinton Charterhouse (approximately 6 miles south of Bath). Colthurst converted the prior's lodging house in Abbey Green into his family home (now called Abbey House) and successfully won his campaign to become the Member of Parliament for Bath in 1545. On Matthew's death in July 1559, his estate passed to his son, Edmund. Edmund, in turn, gave the church, churchyard and adjacent land to the Corporation of Bath in 1569. This was probably a mixed blessing, seeing as the roofless and glassless shell of the abbey church would have been far more of a liability at this time.

The priory occupied a quarter of the land inside the city walls and had dominated city life for hundreds of years. Many of the citizens' livelihoods depended on the monastery, either directly through services provided to the monks, employment in their mills, or via the renting of land for grazing and farming. Even though church attendance was compulsory, faith was a welcome component in people's lives. The Church instructed when people could marry, it dictated days for fasting and days for feasting; the many holy days – between

W. Day: West front of the Abbey Church, Bath, *c.* 1830. (Bath Central Library/Bath in Time)

FRONT OF THE ABBEY CHURCH.
BATH.

forty and fifty – had to be respected by attendance at three church services during the day, meaning these were non-working days. In turn, the monks provided education, assisted the poor and attended the sick.

The Dissolution caused the closure of many schools that had been run by the monks, including the cathedral school founded by John of Tours. Amongst its alumni was Adelard, one of Europe's greatest scientists and philosophers. Adelard (*c.* 1080–*c.* 1152) was born in Bath, but travelled extensively before returning to his hometown where he probably taught. He translated a number of key Arabic texts on mathematics, geometry, astrology and astronomy into Latin and wrote several influential texts that drove the twelfth-century enlightenment and included a number of noteworthy medical advances. The disadvantage to the country of this loss of scholarship, especially at a time of a renaissance in art, science and literature was recognised by Henry VIII, but it was during the reign of Edward VI that endowments and funds from property previously owned by the monasteries were granted to establish – or re-establish – thirty-three grammar schools, including King Edward's School in Bath.

King Edward's was founded in 1552, and financed through the income generated from 102 properties in the city that King Edward gave for this purpose. Originally situated on the now demolished Frog Lane, it moved in 1583 to the disused St Mary's by Northgate.

Eventually, in 1754 the school moved to a purpose-built building, designed by Thomas Jelly and situated on Broad Street. The building still stands, although King Edward's moved to its current site on North Road in 1959.

John Leland (c. 1506–52), Henry's antiquary, was employed 'to make a search after England's Antiquities, and peruse the Libraries of all Cathedrals, Abbies, Priories, Colleges, etc. as also all places wherein Records, Writings and secrets of Antiquity were reposed'. In other words, Leland's task was to liberate the priceless contents of every monastic library. He undertook a tour of the country recording his travels in his *Itinerary*. He is thought to have made two visits to Bath, firstly in 1533 and again in 1542. He approached the city via Holloway, crossing the bridge with its 'great gate with stone arch ...[and] five fair stone arches', and then travelled up Southgate Street remarking on:

> ... fair meadows on each hand. The city of Bath is set both in a fruitful and pleasant bottom, the which is environed on every side with great hills; out of which come many springs of pure water that be conveyed by diverse ways to serve the city. Insomuch that lead, being made near at hand, many houses in the town have pipes of lead to convey water from place to place.

THE NORTH GATE OF BATH. ABOUT 1650.

W. Lewis: The North Gate of Bath in about 1650, 1879. (Bath Central Library/Bath in Time)

JOHN LELAND,
FROM A PICTURE BY HOLBEIN.

Thomas Charles
Wageman (after) Hans
Holbein, portrait of
John Leland, 1546.
(Bath Central Library/
Bath in Time)

Leland noted the four gates and the wall 'of no great height to the eyes', but from the foundations (visible on the outside of the walls) it was more impressive – illustrating just how the internal ground levels had risen since the Romans first built the city walls. He recorded that there were two springs dispensing hot water; and described the Cross Bath which was 'much frequented of people diseased with leprosy, pox, scabs and great aches; and is temperate and pleasant, having 11 or 12 arches of stone in the sides for men to stand under in time of rain'; the Hot Bath, which had only seven arches, and where bathers initially thought the water would scald them, but once acclimatised they found it pleasant; and the larger King's Bath which had a high stone wall and thirty-two arches for men and women to stand separately in. 'To this bath do gentlemen resort … the colour of the water … is … a deep blue sea water, and reeketh like a seething pot continually, having a somewhat sulphurous and somewhat unpleasant savour.'

In 1554, the baths came under the control of the city for the first time. Although still considered as an amenity for the poor and sick, a greater appreciation of their potential value started to grow. And the reputation of the waters and their benefits started to reach a wider clientele. Distinguished physicians were beginning to promote the medicinal benefits of the waters. William Turner, the 'master of English physicke', included a section on the baths in his 1538 herbal remedy book. Later, in 1572 John Jones, another revered doctor, recommended the waters both for bathing in and drinking. Soon after his book appeared a drinking fountain was installed at the King's Bath.

These texts and concepts were only available to the wealthier classes who were literate, able to employ the services of a physician and could afford to travel. As a consequence, Bath started to enjoy the patronage of wealthy invalids and a steady increase in resident physicians. Many of these doctors set up lodging houses, providing a 'package tour' of health and spa to Bath for their patients from across Britain. The dozen or so inns available in Bath at this time were fine for the usual clientele, but the more sophisticated visitor considered them dirty, overcrowded and uncomfortable.

At about this time the city fathers decided to professionalise the running and maintenance of the baths. A sergeant was appointed, who supervised the whole set-up with a small staff. The sergeant effectively leased the baths, paying the city 40s for the privilege. He made his money from the users, whilst the staff received a small wage from the city and tips from the bathers. The Cross and Hot Baths were emptied and cleaned daily, the King's Bath twice a week.

As the crowds increased the city decided to build another bath adjoining the King's. Exclusively for women, it was in use by 1576 but had no recorded name until the following century when it was called 'Queen's' after Queen Anne of Denmark, who visited in 1613 and 1615. To mark these visits the Corporation erected a central tower, topped with a globe and a crown and the inscription *Anna Regina Sacrum*. Entrance to the King's Bath, after the Dissolution, was through the churchyard of St Mary de Stalls, and facilities here were also improved. In 1578 a seat and drinking fountain was added over the spring. It became known as 'the kitchen' and is clearly seen in engravings of the bath at this time. Lodging houses and inns started to flourish in the area, with some establishments procuring their own private entrances – or slips – to the waters.

Establishing itself again as a health resort was a significant development. Bath's cloth trade was in decline by the 1540s due to a combination of entrepreneurs taking production outside the city walls, to areas such as Freshford and Twerton and slightly further afield to Beckington, leaving many locals unemployed, and the increased competition from East Anglia. By the 1580s there were reports of great distress, decayed buildings, poverty and hunger due to soaring inflation, failed harvests and unemployment. The authorities were justly concerned about public disorder; clothiers who retained raw materials were ordered to re-employ their former workers and those who refused were reported to Queen Elizabeth. But this was merely a short-term answer and actually saw those clothiers fall into even deeper debt. Bath's future fortunes lay with its waters and its attractiveness as a resort.

In 1572, the Corporation had petitioned Elizabeth I for the right to restore the priory church. For thirty years it had been plundered, exposed to the elements and now used as a quarry for building stone and road repairs. The Corporation identified that a ruinous church was not a positive advertisement for the town. The Church was still at the centre of people's lives, and residents and visitors alike needed somewhere appropriate to come and hear sermons and pray. Bath was also keen to firmly establish itself as a Protestant town. The five city-centre

Bellott's Hospital, photograph before 1858. (Bath Central Library/Bath in Time)

churches, which were in poor repair and unable to support individual livings, were united and consolidated at this time into one rectory, managed by the Rector of Bath.

The aim was to divert all religious activity and income to the priory church – it would become Bath's only parish church and thus the old parish boundaries could be removed. Consequently, the Parish of Saints Peter and Paul was established in 1583.

The restoration of the church was so large an undertaking that Queen Elizabeth decreed that donations could be collected throughout the country for a period of seven years. By the time she visited Bath in August 1574, the chancel had been re-roofed and an inaugural service was held there. The restoration continued in fits and starts, as these major projects tend to do even today with the ebb and flow of funds, but it is agreed that the church was completed in 1617.

Elizabeth I's visit must have been such an engaging event for all Bathonians. She travelled with an impressive entourage, which contemporaries described as consisting of 300 carts laden with household furniture, curtains, tableware and soft furnishings to ensure the Queen's comfort. It was estimated that five or six horses were required to pull each cart, and those horses would need to be refreshed at every overnight stop. Her Privy Council, ladies-in-waiting, barons, earls, Knights of the Garter and around fifty Gentlemen Pensioners, who guarded the Queen, all travelled with her.

Bath was suitably spruced up in anticipation of the royal visit with streets cleaned, buildings repaired, roads mended and a new public privy built. Despite her visits reputedly being so expensive to the host as to ruin them, John Wroughton has shown that Elizabeth's accounts reveal that she paid nearly £400 for her two-day visit, covering the cost of food and drink, the stabling and feeding of her horses and making donations to the poor.

The Queen saw the church and her courtiers marvelled at the hot waters, and for Bath this visit had been a resounding success, promoting the city to fashionable tourists. Sir Walter Raleigh (*c.* 1554–1618) visited Bath three times in 1587, 1589 and 1599 to take the waters and encouraged other noblemen to do the same. The Royal Charter granted by Elizabeth in 1590 acknowledged – and thus invigorated – Bath's system of governance by a mayor and corporation (populated by local men) and paved the way for the city's transformation from apathetic ecclesiastical municipality to an empowered centre of health and well-being.

Bath's waters had come to be recognised as an important national asset, mainly due to the many different ailments including gout, dropsy, joint pain, leprosy and infertility it was claimed to cure. This gave Bath a much-needed boost; new lodgings and facilities sprung up to accommodate the increasing number of visitors. Further physicians set up practices in Bath, some even had their own supply of the thermal water piped to their consulting rooms via subsidiary plumbing. The Elizabethan nobility and gentry, including many of Elizabeth's own courtiers, flocked to the increasingly popular spa and St John's Hospital took unique advantage of the situation by providing lodgings for the wealthy paying visitor alongside its role as an almshouse.

The proximity of the spa waters encouraged the foundation of further charities, including Bellott's Hospital (1608/9) by Lord Burghley's steward, Thomas Bellott. It provided somewhere for approximately twelve poor strangers to stay whilst they visited Bath for the cure. In 1652, Lady Scudamore added to the facilities by providing an endowment to secure the services of a physician. Rebuilt in 1859, the coat of arms above the doorway is Lord Burghley's and from the original building. This period also saw the Cross and Hot Baths, traditionally frequented by the poorer classes, being patronised by higher society. As a consequence, in 1576 Dr John de Feckenham established the Lazars, or Lepers, Bath, which was fed from the overflow of the adjacent Hot Bath.

An act of charity saw parishes sending their sick poor to spas such as Bath or Buxton at the expense of the parish. The problem was that in Bath they tended to stay on after the 'cure', establishing residency and the right to poor relief from their new home. Many towns seized on this opportunity to offload their paupers. The new poor begged from the wealthy visitors, but were similarly in competition and confrontation with the resident beggars who had set up a ghetto on Holloway. Across the country a population explosion, unemployment and inflation had led to large numbers of people relying on begging and vagrancy. The nursery rhyme, 'Hark! Hark! The dogs do bark. The beggars are coming to town', is thought to refer to these bands of beggars – the dogs barking to alert their owners there were strangers in the vicinity.

The problem became so great that two sixteenth-century Acts of Parliament, dealing with beggars and poor relief, mention Bath. The genuine poor and sick were permitted to beg, but any able-bodied beggar could be stripped naked, tied to the back of a cart and whipped until his body was covered in blood, before being expelled from the city. Persistent offenders could be branded with a 'V' and enslaved to a local farmer for two years. These punishments were harsh, but ineffective. Increasingly vagrants also turned to petty crime.

In the meantime an unnecessary burden was put on the poor relief, collected in the local parish for Bath's own poor and sick parishioners. The Beggars of Bath became a recognised social category and 'go to Bath' a common phrase used to dismiss importunate beggars anywhere in England. Ultimately beggars and petty thieves threatened Bath's renaissance as a health resort for the wealthy.

The Poor Relief Act of 1572 was an attempt to control the ever-increasing numbers of unsightly sick and poor. Each individual 'diseased or impotent' visitor to Bath had to have a licence issued by two justices from their own county showing they were in genuine need of the waters, that their parish would continue to support them financially and that they were obliged to return home, whatever the outcome of taking the waters. Without this licence people were turned away at the city gates and immediately punished (branded and bound) for being a vagrant. Those genuinely in need who arrived with the correct papers were, however, welcomed to the city and shown compassion. As, of course, were the affluent visitors attracted to the city by the new leisure facilities.

It was sustained royal patronage, commenced by Elizabeth I, that brought the opulence of the court to Bath, raising the town's status and fortunes and turning what was a small, poor market town into a grand and wealthy city.

Five

THE BATHS

The reason Bath exists, and central to its entire social, economic and spiritual history, is the 275,000 gallons (1.25 million litres) of natural thermal waters that are forced up along the Pennyquick fault every day. It seems only right, then, that Bath's baths should have a dedicated chapter.

These are Britain's only natural, hot mineral waters (other thermal springs exist in the UK, but these are tepid and the flow not plentiful enough to support public baths). The waters have inspired great human creative genius, with the many buildings built across the millennia dedicated to containing and utilising this extraordinary resource. It is these factors that are central to Bath's award from the UNESCO as a place of Outstanding Universal Value.

Rainwater which fell approximately 10,000 years ago is heated by the earth's mantle to an estimated 69°C (156°F), cooling to an average 45°C (113°F) as it reaches the surface through faults in the limestone below Bath. There are three main springs, all with slightly different temperatures: the hottest is the Hot or Hetling Spring which, at 48°C (120°F), is hot enough to scald human skin. The Cross Spring, at 42.8°C (109°F), is the coolest and the King's Spring rises at an average of 45.6°C (114°F).

Scientific analysis has shown that the thermal waters contain high concentrations of sodium, calcium chloride and sulphate, as well as other trace elements. In around 1607, William Camden (1551–1623) recorded that the spa waters were of a blue or sea colour, and sent up thin vapours with a strong smell because they rose through veins of Brimstone and 'a clamy kind of earth called Bitumen'. He stated that the temperature changed during the day, causing the baths to be shut between 8 a.m. and 3 p.m., when their great heat stirred up the filthy sediment. This is concurred by Celia Fiennes (1662–1741), who visited towards the end of the seventeenth century and noted that the baths were allowed to refill themselves twice a day, and the scum was cleaned off the top.

After the Romans left Britain it is not clear who took responsibility for the baths until they came under the jurisdiction of the Bath Priory. After the

Dissolution, there was an interval of about fifteen years before the Corporation managed to seize control. From Leland's descriptions from this period, however, we know the baths remained busy with 'people diseased with leprosy, pox, scabs and great aches'.

On taking charge, the Corporation appointed a sergeant, or keeper of the baths, which was basically a franchise agreement, the keeper being motivated to manage the facility well to ensure his profit share was substantial. The Corporation – made up of men who owned businesses in the city – realised that the baths were key to everyone's prosperity. A programme of improvements, at the baths and across the city, were implemented at this time. The investment was noted by William Harrison in 1577, 'What cost of late hath been bestowed on these baths ... they are not only very much repaired and garnished ... but also better ordered, cleanlier kept'.

At the end of Bath Street is the Cross Bath, situated in the south-west quarter of 'old' Bath, in an area once known as Bimbery. The neighbourhood is central

John Fayram: The Cross Bath and Melfort Cross, 1738. (Bath Central Library/Bath in Time)

to Bath's mineral water and charitable history that, for centuries, went hand-in-hand. The Cross Bath dates back to the early 1100s, with the site having first been utilised by the Romans; there are remains of a Roman stone-built cistern beneath the current structure and a Roman altar was discovered here in 1809.

Cross Spring, which is now recognised as a sacred site, feeds the Cross Bath, and their names probably derive from this site being a place of pilgrimage. St Aldhelm, who introduced the more moderate Benedictine rule, 'peace, pray and work', died in ad 709 and his body rested in Bath on its way from Doulting (where he had died) to his burial at Malmesbury. At each of the stopping places his friend, the Bishop of Worcester, commissioned crosses. In the nineteenth century, fragments of a stone cross were discovered here, which could have marked the spot of St Aldhelm's resting place, close to the Cross Bath. The bath may therefore have been named after its association with St Aldhelm.

The cross was greatly enhanced by the Earl of Melfort after the birth of James II's son. James II and his wife, Mary of Modena, were struggling with infertility until the successful conception and birth of a male heir after Mary visited the Cross Bath in 1687. Dismantled because of its popery connotations, the only known remnant from this cross is a small child statue in a niche in Old Bond Street.

The Cross Bath, the most private and with the most comfortable temperature, became the most fashionable. A visitor's guide from the 1700s encouraged those 'easily affected by heating substances' to initially use the Cross Bath because it was safer. Persons complaining of kidney and liver disease were particularly recommended to use this bath. Dr Edward Jordon, author of *The Nature and Uses of our Baths in Somersetshire* (1631), advised his patients to spend an hour in the hotter baths, followed by two hours in a more temperate one. He described the Cross Bath as:

> … almost triangular, twenty-five feet long and of equal breddth at the widest part. It has arched seats on all sides, three dressing rooms and as many flights of steps. It is surrounded by a wall. The springs here are smaller than in the Kings and Hot and it is there not so hot.

The Cross Bath has had many forms over the centuries, including a major refurbishment in 1593–94 that introduced a sluice to allow for daily cleaning and three dressing rooms. Lord Brooke financed a gallery for spectators and a pump for drinking the water in 1674 in gratitude for his cure. A second gallery was added in 1687, but by the following century the musicians, employed to entertain the bathers, were stationed here. Bathers were supplied with fashionable chocolate drinks, and soon the Cross Bath earned the best

reputation for decency and order – gentlemen kept strictly to one side of the bath, and the ladies to the other.

The structure we see now, however, is principally by John Palmer, who effectively rotated the building in 1797–98 so it faced east and could act as the terminus to Baldwin's new Bath Street. In the nineteenth century, the Cross Bath was neglected and became known as the Tuppenny Hot – a cheap swimming pool for locals. It is now fully restored (1987–2006) using the original plans by Palmer.

As its name suggests, the Hot Bath is fed by the hottest of the three springs. It was known as Alsi's, possibly after Aelfsige, Bath's first abbot, who was later Bishop of Winchester and Archbishop of Canterbury. Originally sited in the middle of Hot Bath Street, it was rebuilt in its new position by the Corporation to a design by John Wood the Younger in 1775–77.

It was subsequently redesigned by A.J. Taylor between 1925–27, and from 1948 until 1976 treatment using Bath's mineral waters was available for all on the National Health Service. Prior to the foundation of the NHS and since 1739, patients at the Mineral Water Hospital had the right to bathe there.

The Hot Bath is now integrated within the new Thermae Bath Spa. Working with Donald Insall Associates, architects Nicholas Grimshaw and Partners created an iconic new suite of baths and spa facilities, including the restoration of five historic buildings. They sympathetically restored Wood's symmetrical,

Carlo Chinca: The Refurbished Hot Bath, 2003. (Private Collection/Bath in Time)

square-within-a-square design, dispensing with the changes Taylor had made and adding a glazed roof.

Over the centuries, it has been claimed that Bath's waters can cure over ninety different ailments. Dr William Turner included eighty-six in his book *The Baths of Bath in England* (1568), including gout, dropsy, diseases of the nostrils, deafness, bladder stones, forgetfulness, the premature birth of babies, depression, joint pain, leprosy, and significantly, infertility.

It was during Tudor times that the waters came to be recognised as an important national asset. This gave the small West Country town a much-needed boost; new lodgings and facilities sprang up to accommodate the increasing visitors. Physicians also set up practices in Bath, and visitors were advised to consult a doctor before visiting the baths. Dr Jordon warned that those who 'self-medicated' were the ones who left the city 'without benefit'. Originally the Cross and Hot Baths were frequented by the poorer classes, but by the late sixteenth century they were increasingly popular with higher society. This led to the establishment of the Lepers Bath in 1576. Its founder, Dr Feckenham, also provided a hospital for seven visitors requiring accommodation whilst they sought a cure from the serious skin disease.

The Horse Bath was constructed on the advice of Dr Turner in 1598. He felt that a facility to cleanse horses from the mire they had collected on their journey to Bath would support the effort to keep the streets clean. He also thought it would improve the health of the animals. A culvert for the overflow from the King's Bath passed under the city wall here and fed the Horse Bath, before flowing into Bum Ditch and then on to the River Avon.

The site of the new Thermae Spa (2006) was originally the Tepid Bath, built in 1829 by George P. Manners specifically for swimming. The water came from the King's Spring and was cooled in a large reservoir in York Street before being pumped into the bath. Renewed interest in the spa led to the Corporation building the New Royal Baths, by Wilson & Willcox (1867), behind Bath Street. In 1920, the Tepid Bath was demolished to make way for A.J. Taylor's Beau Street Swimming Bath which helped alleviate the suffering of many wounded veterans from the First World War. This bath was demolished in 1998 for the Thermae Bath Spa project.

For over 10,000 years the natural thermal waters that rise in Bath have been a source of fascination, spirituality, pilgrimage and cure. Although the popularity of Bath's spa has wavered over the millennia, the water has flowed constantly. In 1978, after harmful amoebas were discovered in the outdated pipework, Bath became a spa in name only. For almost thirty years, litres upon litres of hot mineral water washed directly into the River Avon. Throughout this period there were regular attempts to restore the spa, but all were defeated by the huge

Carlo Chinca: A view of the rooftop pool, Thermae Bath Spa, 2003. (Private Collection/Bath in Time)

capital cost. In 1997, the Millennium Commission announced that it would support the Bath Spa Project with a grant worth £7.78 million.

The crowning glory of the Thermae Spa, or New Royal Bath, is the open-air rooftop pool. Submerged under the hot mineral water, bathers can enjoy a unique view across Bath's skyline – an experience especially enchanting after dark. Grimshaw's contemporary design comprises a stone cube, resting on four great mushroom pillars, enveloped by glass. Within the strict rigidity of the building, the internal design plays on curves and circles and free-flowing sinuous lines. These forms are enhanced by the use of fibre optics to produce atmospheric lighting.

On the ground floor is the Minerva Bath, above the four circular steam room pods, with portholes pierced through the stone cube to the outside. Within the Hot Bath area there are twelve treatment rooms, which offer many different spa treatments. This is a modern facility that shows respect for the historic buildings already on the site and the associated millennia of use. Cynics were skeptical about the site, design, quality of the build and the popularity of the waters, etc., whilst others showed their support by making donations to the project in the form of subscriptions. Their optimism was rewarded with a number of free visits or subsidised spa treatments for the first three years of operation. Even the most disparaging disbeliever would have to admit now that the Thermae Spa has been a momentous success, both in terms of visitors to the baths and the subsequent benefit to the local economy.

The King's Bath, named for Henry I, was originally the largest of Bath's baths. It had thirty-two arches and access was via the slips at each of the four corners. In the centre the tower, added in 1578, was known as the 'kitchen' because this was the hottest part of the bath. The structure provided recessed seats for bathers and a drinking fountain. Metal rings attached to the walls which bathers could hold on to or be tied to, were added towards the end of the sixteenth century.

The balustrading around the bath, as seen in Thomas Johnson's illustration of 1675, was probably donated by Sir Francis Stonor, who paid for the work in around 1624 as a thank you for the benefit he received from the waters for his gout. The King's Bath was effectively cut in half by the Pump Room expansion in 1751, rebuilt by Thomas Baldwin in the 1780s, and reduced again further in 1790–95.

The Queen's Bath was added to the south side of the King's Bath in 1576, and fed from the overflow through an opening in the wall between the two baths. It was originally intended for the poor who travelled to Bath for the cure, but was utilised when attempts were made to segregate the sexes. The bath was named Queen's after Queen Anne of Denmark. The temperature in the Queen's was cooler, and a smaller, separate cistern – known as the parlour – was more temperate still. There were eight arches in the walls for shelter. It measured about 25ft (7.6m) square. People entered via one private and two common slips on the west side. The bath was demolished in 1885, and beneath it – to the south – the Roman circular bath was discovered.

As Bath's popularity grew so the facilities became crowded. A wider demographic was now visiting and the finer visitor was tiring of the clientele at the King's and Queen's Baths. And so, during the peak of Bath's Georgian heyday, the Duke of Kingston built a private bath on the south side of the Abbey in order to provide a facility for these nobler and wealthier visitors – admission was costly at 5 shillings. During these works in 1755 remains of the Roman 'Lucas' Bath were discovered, but not excavated. Instead, the duke went ahead with his plan to provide a roofed suite of five baths and small pump room, fed with water supplied by a Roman culvert.

Because they were expensive, they were exclusive. Wealthy visitors found them much more elegant and convenient to use. Philip Thicknesse reported that the Kingston Baths were 'now the only place where persons of condition or delicacy can bathe decently'. Stimulated by this competition, the Corporation gave Wood the Younger his only civic commission, to reconstruct the Hot Bath, in 1775. The Kingston Baths were enlarged by Dr Wilkinson during the first half

Emerging from below the Queen's Bath, 1878. (Bath Central Library/ Bath in Time)

of the nineteenth century, and then acquired by the Corporation in 1870. The Kingston Baths were demolished in 1923 in order to facilitate the excavation of the Roman East Baths.

Bath's cold mineral waters were also highly prized for their medicinal virtues; it was said that because the springs broke through the ground to the east, they were the purest possible and particularly beneficial for eye disorders. In 1707, Dr Oliver recommended in his *Practical Dissertation on the Bath Waters* that a public cold bath be made. Whereupon, wrote John Wood, 'Mr Thomas Greenway, one of the Free-stone Masons of the City, directly engaged in the Work; and made a handsome Bath, in one of the rooms of a house built by him up on the Beach, at the Foot of Beaching-Cliff' (on Claverton Street, Widcombe).

The bath measured 15ft by 8ft (4.5m x 2.4m), was lined with stone and had an elaborate stone moulding running around almost three of its four sides. It was fed by a spring, said to have risen on the spot, and in the north-east end of the bath was a gully that led directly out to the towpath. Originally this gully was enclosed and there were probably steps over this end. Halfway along the south side of the bath was a lion's mask, 8in wide by 10in high. It had nearly freestanding ears and apparently only one eye, and served as a conduit through which the water flowed into the stone-lined plunge pool.

The Cold Bath House was highly considered and patronised by many people of quality whilst they were staying in Bath. It was featured on Strachey's map in 1732, and given an appreciative write-up in Cruttwell's *Bath Guide* of 1777. The Cold Bath remained popular until the early nineteenth century when it fell into decline and the building was subsequently used as a tenement, carpenter's workshop and café; the bath itself being concealed below a concrete floor. The building was demolished for the relief road in 1966.

❋ ❋ ❋ ❋ ❋

Of the original, post-Roman baths, three survive, and visitors can bathe in both the Hot and Cross Baths and admire the portion of the King's Bath that remains during a tour of the Roman Baths Museum. And, whilst in the museum, possibly feel a little jealous of all those who, until 1978, were able to experience swimming in the Roman Great Bath during the 'Roman Rendezvous', which became a popular part of the Bath Festival from 1962.

'Roman Rendezvous', the Great Bath, *c.* 1965. (Bath Central Library/ Bath in Time)

Six

'SCORBUTIC CARCASSES AND LACKERED HIDES': THE SEVENTEENTH CENTURY

Elizabeth I died in 1603 leaving no heir, and the Crown hitherto passed to her cousin James Stuart. He became James VI of Scotland and James I of England and Ireland, resulting in the three nations being united under one ruler for the first time. Scotland did, however, retain its own parliament and legal system. The smooth succession was deeply welcomed in England, whilst James, for his part, eagerly admired the unexpected wealth he saw as he made his progression from Edinburgh to London in the spring of 1603.

Within two years, however, a group of thirteen disgruntled Catholics had hatched the Gunpowder Plot. They had hoped that James I would be more lenient towards their beliefs, but when this optimism proved groundless they planned to blow up the King and the House of Lords. Sir John Harington (1560–1612) of Kelston (the inventor of the flushing lavatory) reported that at least three of the traitors, Robert Catesby, Thomas Percy and Thomas Wintour, had had a number of meetings in Bath. At one meeting, in August 1605, they conceded that more conspirators were required. It was agreed that Sir Everard Digby and Catesby's cousin, Frank Tresham, be recruited. Some believe that it was Tresham who wrote anonymously to his brother-in-law, Lord Monteagle, to warn him to stay away from the opening of Parliament. Rapidly, the letter was passed to the King via Robert Cecil, 1st Earl of Salisbury, and the plot was uncovered.

The Jacobean period was rich in poetry and literature, with the works of John Donne (1572–1631), William Shakespeare (1564–1616) and Ben Jonson (1572–1637). Through the new methodologies championed by Francis Bacon (1561–1626), the foundations of how we approach scientific analysis today were also laid. Inigo Jones (1573–1652), Britain's important Classical Renaissance architect, made his first trip to Italy to study the antiquities of Rome.

Dutch and Flemish painters, such as Marcus Gheeraerts (c. 1561–1636) and Paul van Somer (c. 1577–1621), dominated the arts. Whilst gardeners also showed favour to the Dutch style by introducing canals, topiary, knot gardens and herb gardens. The empire also continued to grow, with the foundation of the first British colonies in North America at Jamestown (1607) and Plymouth (1620).

Yet, despite John Wood insisting that Inigo Jones designed Bath's new market and guildhall (1625), Bath remained parochial during the seventeenth century, although I'm sure many residents took advantage of the crops of Virginian tobacco that had begun to be imported to Britain at this time. Marek Lewcun has shown that in 1623 there were six grocers, four apothecaries and six other tradesmen selling tobacco in Bath.

By 1600, Bath's resident population was around 2,000 (compared to London with 200,000), and John Speed's map of 1610 provides a wealth of information about Bath at the turn of the seventeenth century. It was probably based on Henry Savile's more intricate and refined map of around 1603.

Both maps show that Bath was still mostly contained within the walled area, with expansion to the north around St Michael's Church and to the south, on the main route to Wells. At North Gate (A), the tower of St Mary's Church is shown

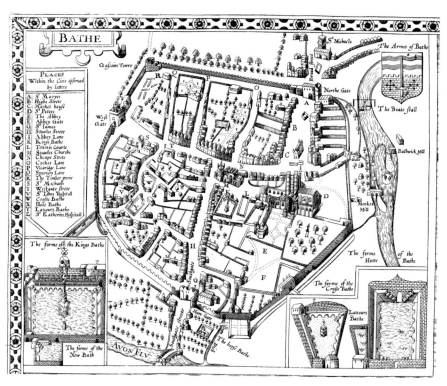

John Speed: City of Bath, Somersetshire Map (detail), 1610. (Private Collection/Bath in Time)

(this was the town's prison), and next door in the nave was King Edward's School. Just to the south, the diamond shape indicates St Mary's Conduit, a fountain where people could retrieve fresh water. To the east the rope ferry, accessed via Boatstall Lane, took passengers across to the Bathwick Meadows and mill.

In the centre of the High Street (B) is the Market House (C), built around 1552. This building was replaced in 1625 with a two-storey structure that could house the market and the council chamber. The ground floor was open to the elements, being constructed with sixteen stone arches, which made it ideal for the fishmongers' stalls.

To the south, the city stocks and pillory (erected in 1412), used for the punishment of particularly abhorrent crimes such as sexual offences, can be seen. The nave of the abbey is shown open to the elements, the roof not being finished until after 1608 when James Montague, Bishop of Bath and Wells, donated over £1,000 for the building's completion. In Abbey Orchard is what Speed seems to denote as a statue, but on closer inspection of Savile's map it appears to be a man on stilts knocking the fruit off the trees. Curious, when the only other person represented by Savile and Speed in the body of their maps is the ferryman from Boatstall Lane.

The three main gates of north, west and south are shown, as well as the East Gate and Ham Gate. The fourteenth-century East Gate was originally constructed for the monks to use in order to reach their mill. It was much smaller than the three main gates and, unlike those, still exists. It was also possible to reach the Boatstall Lane rope ferry from here, the ferryman pulling passengers to and from Bathwick. Unlike the other gates it remained open at night (other than at times of war).

By the Ham Gate is the Horse Bath and Bum Ditch. The latter was an open drain; it was fed by the stream that took the excess water from the King's Bath to the river via the Isabel Mill. The Ham Gate was closed up for safety during the Civil War (1642–46) and never reopened. In 1623, a public toilet was built near here, over the stream that then ran into Bum Ditch and thus into the river. Vignettes on both maps illustrate the five baths: King's Bath, New Bath, Cross Bath, Lazours (Lazars, or Lepers) Bath and Hot Bath.

In the north-west corner is Gascoyne's Tower, a repair to the city wall reputedly built by a local resident in the late fifteenth or early sixteenth century as a punishment for an incident of civil unrest. John Wood wrote that the tower became an ammunitions store during the Civil War. Below is Timber Green, or Sawclose, an open area for logging and where cockfighting was staged. Bear and bull baiting were also popular and sponsored by the Corporation (these sports were banned in England in 1849).

The south-west quarter is dominated by the baths and hospitals and, despite featuring in the key, St Catherine's is not marked on the Speed map (its position was just north of the city wall to the west of the South Gate). Despite Bath's compact size there are plenty of open spaces and the majority of properties appear to have large gardens behind. When Samuel Pepys visited in 1668, he recorded that there were 250 houses and a population of less than 1,200. Residents and businesses were still largely confined within the city walls, only the weavers had settled outside the city limits, on what is now Broad Street, using the area above present-day George Street to hang and dry their wool.

Speed's map was printed in *Theatre of the Empire of Great Britaine*, which included a number of town and county maps. Savile's map, on the other hand, includes a review of Bath's history and its commendations, which suggests it was a product of Bath's growing emphasis on increasing its visitor numbers. The town could no longer depend on the wool and cloth trade for its welfare, and so the city's leaders made a concerted effort to establish Bath as a centre for tourism.

After Elizabeth I's visit, Bath was seen by outsiders to have improved itself greatly, offering better lodgings and provisions. Royal visitors tended to stay at Westgate House or Abbey House. Other visitors could choose to stay in one of the numerous lodging houses run by local physicians, or in one of the new inns such as the White Hart, Three Tuns, Raven or the Bear. By 1641, eighteen inns were recorded.

'Bath is a little well-compacted Cittie and beautified with very faire and goodly buildings for receipt of strangers,' wrote Dr Tobias Venner in 1628. Venner (1557–1660) also recommended Bath's proximity to the river, its good air and the fertility of its soil. Venner was a well-respected doctor and a memorial was erected in his memory in the Abbey. He advocated the introduction of 'dry-pumping', whereby the hot water was pumped, or bucketed, just onto the afflicted body part.

For amusement Bath offered a bowling green near the Abbey, and by the end of the century another was positioned just outside the walls above North Gate (recalled by the current Green Street). There was a fives court, again just outside the walls but this time by West Gate. A tennis court, shown on Speed's map near the King's Bath, is not shown on Joseph Gilmore's later map, suggesting it was swept away during the seventeenth century. It was certainly sacrificed when the Pump Room was built (opened 1705). There were pleasant places to walk, particularly in the Abbey grounds, and probably theatrical performances, and the Abbey itself was still used as a place for social assemblies (not just religious ones). Sir Edmund Verney wrote, 'We pass our time awaye as merrily as paine will give us leave.'

Getting to Bath, however, was difficult. Stagecoaches were expensive, slow and hazardous, with the threat of accidents as well as robbery. Lying at the bottom of a valley surrounded by seven hills made access treacherous. Highwaymen chose to attack coaches as they proceeded up a hill, and therefore at a slower pace. Celia Fiennes found that the wheels of her coach got firmly wedged in the rocks on its ascent and it took several men to free the vehicle. Another correspondent felt that the Alps would have been easier and less dangerous to cross than the rocky, narrow and uneven roads to Bath. Visitors tended to come, therefore, during the spring and summer months and on horseback. Having to change your horse regularly along the route made the venture expensive – and increasingly exclusive.

❅ ❅ ❅ ❅ ❅

In around 1625, Bath's increasing prosperity and the growing power of its governing Corporation was shown by the replacement of the market hall on the High Street with an elegant, new, double-gabled guildhall with arcaded market below. A large arched window was inserted into the northern façade and a smaller window on the south. The statues of King Osric (some commentators say it is King Coel) and King Edgar presided on the north front.

The Corporation took control of Bath, imposing new rules on property owners and leaseholders, all with a view to see the city's appearance – and thus its reputation – improve. The requirement to fix the roads and paths adjacent to your property, keep the area clean, and replace thatched roofs with tiles or slate were all part of the Corporation's careful management of their asset. The aim was to firmly establish the city as a leisure, and not just a health, resort, guaranteeing employment and financial security and perhaps even wealth for the citizens of Bath.

However, pollution increased in line with the town's prosperity. The growth in industry required coal-fired boilers in order to produce soap, pottery, beer and leather etc. Homeowners also added to what John Evelyn called 'the horrid smoke' that contaminated everything, with a greater number of hearths and chimneys being added to their houses. A city scavenger was appointed in 1613, and residents were expected to put their rubbish in his cart rather than litter the streets or dump their waste over the walls. Unfortunately not everyone complied: the open culverts that ran down the streets were often clogged with human and animal effluence, ashes and entrails from the activities of the many butchers and fishmongers, despite a 12d fine being imposed from 1633.

In 1631, Dr Edward Jorden recorded that 'the butchers dress their meat at their own doors, while pigs wallow in the mire … [the streets are no more than] dung hills, slaughter houses and pig stys'. Celia Fiennes abhorred the thick air, made worse by the steam from the baths, and the bowl-like topography. John Wood included an anonymous account, apparently dating from the 1600s, in his *Description of Bath*. '[Bath] is a place standing in a hole; in a quagmire; impenetrable to the very beams of the sun; and so confined by inaccessible hills, that people have scarce room to breath in the town, or come at it without danger to their lives'. John Evelyn, who visited in 1654, complained of the 'uneven, narrow and unpleasant' streets.

Systematic cleaning only seems to have occurred when the Corporation took decisive action, either motivated by a crisis or an impending royal visit. However, Bath did use its ability to create a stink to its advantage too. In 1685, the Corporation closed the city gates to the Duke of Monmouth and his 'pitchfork' army, and before they did so they ensured that the night soil men had spread their foul smelling 'wares' at the foot of the walls to ensure a repugnant reception.

※ ※ ※ ※ ※

Security was provided by two constables, elected annually from within the members of the Corporation. It was their responsibility to keep the peace by working with the magistrates to deal with illegal begging, public disturbances and general criminal activity. The constables supervised the bellman and watchmen, who patrolled the streets at night. The bellman rang out the time on the hour and alerted the populace should he come across a fire or see any wrongdoing. The gates were closed at night, and the streets were patrolled between 10 at night and 3 in the morning, or 9 and 5 in the winter.

The other long-running problem was the time-honoured practice of nude, mixed bathing. We know, for instance, that Bishop Beckington was shocked by the behaviour in the baths in 1449 when he wrote, 'the heavenly gift of warm and healing waters … is turned into an abuse by the shamelessness and uncleanness of the people of that city'. A letter to Lord Zouche in 1621 demanded that men and women be forced to bathe at different times.

Dr Jordon recorded that 'both sexes bathe promiscuously, whilst the passers-by pelt them with dead dogs, cats and pigs'. Whilst, in 1634, William Harrison remarked that the bathers appearing 'so nakedly and fearfully in their uncouth, naked postures would a little astonish and putt one in mind of the Resurrections'.

Thomas Johnson's well-known drawing of the King's Bath from 1675 (British Museum) confirms the practice, as does John Wood when he wrote of this period, 'the baths were … like so many bear-gardens, and modesty entirely shut out of them, people bathing by night and day stark naked'. Samuel Pepys wrote in his diary, 'methinks it cannot be clean to go so many bodies together in the same water'. An anonymous writer, who visited Bath towards the end of the century, graphically described the baths and the associated activities in a pamphlet published in London in 1700:

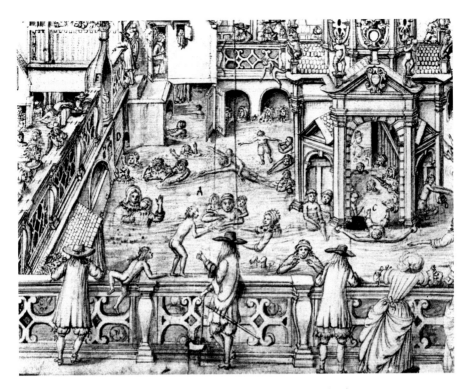

Thomas Johnson: The King's Bath (detail), 1675. (Bath Central Library/ Bath in Time)

The first we went to, is call'd the King's; and to it joyns the Queen's, both running in one; and the most famous for Cures. In this bath was at least fifty of both Sexes, with a Score or two of Guides, who by their Scorbutic Carcasses, and Lackered Hides, you would think they had lain Pickling a Century of Years in the Stygian Lake; Some had those Infernal Emissaries to support their Impotent Limbs: Others to Scrub their Putrify'd Carcasses, like a Race Horse ... At the Pump was several a Drenching their Gullets, and Gormandizing the Reaking Liquor by wholesale.

From thence we went to the Cross Bath, where most of the Quality resorts, more fam'd for Pleasure than Cures. Here is perform'd all the Wanton Dalliances imaginable. Celebrated Beauties, Panting Breasts, and Curious Shapes, almost Expos'd to Publick View: Languishing eyes, Darting Killing Glances, Tempting Amorous Postures, attended by soft Musick, enough to provoke a Vestal to forbidden Pleasure, Captivate a Saint, and charm a Jove: Here was also different Sexes, from Quality to the Honourable Knights, Country Put, and City Madam's ... The Ladies with their floating Japan Bowles, freighted with Confectionary, Kick-Knacks, Essences and Perfumes, Wade about, like Neptune's Courtiers, suppling their Industrious

Joynts. The Vigorous Sparks, presenting them with several Antick Postures, as Sailing on their Backs, then Embracing the Element, sink in Rapture ... The usual time being come to forsake that fickle Element, Half Tub Chairs, Lin'd with Blankets, Ply'd as thick as Coaches at the Play House, or Carts at the Custom House.

Thomas Johnson's illustration is significant for all the details it shows, including the sixteenth- and seventeenth-century buildings that overlooked the baths. Most were lodging houses (now all gone), one of which was owned by Dr Robert Peirce, who worked at Bellott's Hospital, but who also treated patients at his home. He advocated both drinking and bathing in the waters.

The baths were open to the skies, and provided entertainment for what John Wood described as 'idle spectators'. Johnson's illustration also shows the 'diving boys', who would dive for coins thrown in by onlookers. Not all the bathers are naked; some are dressed in the heavy canvas shifts that bellowed out with the water and concealed their body shapes. The arched recesses provided seats for the bathers. Many commentators spoke of the strength of the currents, and welcomed the opportunity to sit down, be supported by one of the guides or to hold on to one of the metal rings. Dressing and undressing was achieved in comparative privacy in the entrance passages or the cramped dressing rooms. On the left-hand side of the King's Bath, Johnson shows the niche that houses the statue of Bladud and in the centre the ornate 'kitchen', the hottest part of the bath and where the spring rose.

A number of accounts show us that people visited the baths at all hours. Samuel Pepys recorded that he was bathing in the Cross Bath at 4 a.m., whilst Willem Schellinks (1623–78), a spy from Amsterdam, bathed at 5 a.m. Schellinks visited Bath in July 1662, and stayed at the Bear. He not only produced an important drawing of the King's Bath (Austrian National Library), but he also left a vivid description of the rituals associated with taking the waters at this time, and the various treatments and services offered by the attendants:

It is the general custom to go [to the baths] very early in the morning and in the evening after the meal. One undresses to the underskirt in one's lodgings, the men put on underpants under their shirt, the girls and women an entire shift; so prepared, one is carried to the bath in a sedan ... chair; at the steps into the water, where men and women are waiting to help the strangers. All round and everywhere are seats in recesses, also rings to hold on to. If the seat is too low one asks for a cushion, so I was given a stone, soft and smoothed by the water. The water is fairly hot, so that one nearly breaks out in sweat. It is customary to drink some hot wine boiled up with sugar and herbs to prevent faintness. Some people stay in the water for two to three hours. We saw a lady who had pumped on her shoulder and on her head 800 pumpstrokes, and a gentleman 1000 strokes of very hot water straight from the pipes from the first spring. For weakness, headaches, etc. some people get on doctor's orders 1800 strokes pumped on for several days. There are also people in the bath who are ready with knives, scissors etc. to cut people's corns, warts and nails, to earn some money. So too are some people, who, when one steps out of the bath, spread out a woollen cloth to prevent one from having to stand on the stone floor. One then drops the underpants, has a linen sheet and a bathrobe thrown round one's body, enters a sedan chair and is carried back to one's lodgings. There one goes to lie in the linen sheet in a warmed bed, and sweats profusely for one or two hours, whilst somebody dries off the sweat with warm dry towels, and one drinks some mulled wine to regain one's strength. Meanwhile the musicians come, usually without being asked, to entertain the guests and to welcome them. There are always a lot of people there from all over the place, many staying for weeks and months, hence the prosperity of the place.

❁ ❁ ❁ ❁ ❁

King James I died in 1625, and having been predeceased by his son, Henry Frederick, the throne passed to his second son, Charles I. Charles passionately believed in the divine right of kings, insisting that he ruled under the direct will of God and answered to no earthly authority. This was a conviction shared by both James I and Louis XIV of France.

Bit by bit, Charles alienated himself from his subjects: he imposed taxes without gaining parliamentary consent; he married Henrietta Maria of France, a devout Roman Catholic (who described Bath as squalid!); and it was perceived that he had not supported the Protestant forces sufficiently during the Thirty Years War. His subjects disliked and mistrusted Charles; he was seen to have Catholic sympathies and a dangerous level of arrogance.

The continued breakdown of relations between the Crown and Parliament led to the Civil War (in 1642–46 and 1648–49). The Civil War saw families and communities divided over those who were loyal to King Charles I, the Royalists or Cavaliers, and those who would unseat him, the Parliamentarians or Roundheads.

Alexander Popham of Hunstrete House was one of Bath's two MPs. A staunch Puritan, he supported the Parliamentarian side. The other MP was William Basset of Claverton Manor, who was a Royalist. In the Bath Corporation the Royalists, led by Henry Chapman, were in the minority and the Parliamentarians, led by Matthew Clift, had the support of the local Puritans. Bath had an important Puritan community, extending their influence over the city and strengthening its Protestant and Parliamentary sympathies. Even so, Bath paid the taxes the King demanded.

Chapman was the innkeeper of the Sun and his brother-in-law was Clift, a mercer and draper. Despite their opposing views, the members of the Corporation rubbed along and there are no records of seriously fractious or strained relations. The only incident was when the order came to expel the Royalists from the council chamber in October 1647. Some members were reinstated within months, illustrating how equable the Corporation was at this time. Bath was not strategically important for either side, both commandeering and occupying the city at different stages during the war.

During the Royalist occupation (July 1643–July 1645) the citizens revived anti-Catholic traditions, such as celebrating the anniversary of the failure of the Gunpowder Plot. Equally, the tomb of Lady Jane Waller, Sir William Waller's first wife (a Parliamentarian) was vandalised during the Royalist occupation. Damage was done to property by both sides: in 1649 the landlady of the Catherine Wheel on Parsonage Lane, Mrs Power, was let off the annual rent to the Corporation in consideration of the damage done to her 'Katharine Wheele' by soldiers during the Civil War. (Tragically, the garrisoned soldiers also brought typhus within the city walls. The mortality rate, for 1643, more than tripled in Bath's three central parishes.)

There were two main skirmishes that affected Bath during the Civil War. The first at Warleigh and Claverton, and the second at Lansdown. In 1643, a cannon ball was notoriously shot across the River Avon from near to Warleigh Manor, passing through the outer wall of William Bassett's Claverton home and lodging in the chimney breast, apparently just missing his family as they sat down to eat. At least three Parliamentarians and one Royalist soldier were killed and their remains were buried in the grounds of St Mary's Church, Claverton.

This small skirmish was merely a taster of the far more devastating Battle of Lansdown that saw two lifelong friends come together

Portrait of Sir Bevil Granville, 1648.
(Bath Central Library/ Bath in Time)

on opposing sides. During a temporary truce, Sir William Waller wrote an extraordinary letter to his childhood friend, Sir Ralph Hopton (Royalist), 'the experience I have had of your worth and the happiness I have enjoyed in your friendship are wounding considerations when I look upon this present distance between us'.

The opposing sides met at Lansdown on 5 July 1643. The Parliamentarians numbered about 1,500 foot soldiers and 2,500 cavalry. The Royalist army comprised about 4,000 foot soldiers and 2,000 on horseback. Despite this imbalance the Royalists lost about 300 men and the Parliamentarians only twenty. The site where Royalist Sir Bevil Granville (1596–1643) fell from his horse, having received a lethal blow to his head with a pole-axe, is marked by the Bevil Monument. Granville was carried to the rectory at Cold Ashton, where he died the following day.

According to Mary Delany, his great-granddaughter, 'at the very moment he was slain, he had the patent for the Earldom of Bath in his pocket, with a letter from King Charles I acknowledging his services'. The monument was erected in 1720 by Granville's grandson, the griffin on the top being the family's heraldic symbol. The battle is considered to have ended indecisively. The Parliamentarians withdrew to the city with Popham in charge.

Shortly afterwards the Royalists won a decisive victory at Roundway Down, near Devizes in Wiltshire. As a consequence, Sir Thomas Bridges was appointed Royalist Governor of Bath and commanded a garrison there of 140 men. In turn, Parliament's recently formed New Model Army defeated the Royalists at Naseby in June 1645, and as the Parliamentarians took control, Royalist William Bassett lost his seat to James Ashe. Determined not to give up, however, Charles' supporters were still causing friction and skirmishes. The Long Parliament began negotiations with Charles, but radicals were resolved that Charles should be tried for treason. A military coup by the New Model Army saw the Long Parliament purged and replaced by the Rump Parliament (1649–53). Charles I was subsequently found guilty and beheaded in January 1649.

Oliver Cromwell (1599–1658), a commander in the New Model Army, waged a horrific campaign against Catholics in Scotland and Ireland, confiscating their land. He dismissed the Rump Parliament by force in April 1653 and became Lord Protector of the Commonwealth in December 1653. Attitudes changed and even staunch Parliamentarians, such as Popham, supported the Restoration of Charles II. Cromwell died in 1658 and was succeeded by his son, Richard. Richard was not a strong leader and was forced to abdicate only eight months later. The time was ripe for Charles II's supporters to see the monarchy restored.

Charles returned to London in May 1660. Hundreds of Bath's citizens formed a procession to St Mary's Conduit, which is said to have run with claret, to drink the King's health. Bath was the first city in the country to proclaim Charles II King, on 12 May 1660, followed by twenty-four hours of celebrations for 'the most glorious and joyful Coronation'. The Bath Corporation and its citizens were keen for a return to stability, where trade could improve and the economy be stimulated and visitors would again be able to travel to patronise the baths, lodging houses, shops and coffee houses that made up Bath's industry. The Civil War and subsequent period of the Commonwealth had halted Bath's transformation from weaving town to town of pleasure and leisure. Yet, thankfully, Cromwell had not felt the need to 'reform' Bath as he had Buxton, who saw their baths closed down by the Protector.

❋ ❋ ❋ ❋ ❋

By the 1680s and 1690s Bath was offering more entertainments and facilities to amuse the visitors, including balls held at the town hall and travelling bands of musicians and actors – called mummers – who would perform pantomimes at the guildhall. Now associated with Christmas, during the seventeenth century the theatrical harlequinade of Pantaloon, the old man, Columbine, his beautiful daughter, Harlequin, her lover who was at odds with Pantaloon, and his servant, Clown, was extremely popular throughout the year.

The wooden, shack-like structures that had run along the outside of the King's Bath were removed and replaced with stone buildings in the 1660s. Purpose-built shops, so rare outside of London at this date, started to spring up. Bath's first coffee house was opened around 1679, and a number of cake houses providing snacks flourished. The main shopping areas were around Northgate Street, Cheap Street and Stall Street.

The workshops of masons, smiths and leather workers based in Southgate Street also had areas to trade from. The number of mercers in the city indicates the high level of trade that was being struck with the wealthy visitors. Research has shown that up to 1625 there were sixteen shoemakers and twelve glovers, supported by two tanners and two curriers – another clear indication of the numbers of fashionable, wealthy visitors that Bath was welcoming, since Bath's residents alone could never have supported so large a leather industry. Other trades included silversmiths and goldsmiths. William Marsden was a noted silk weaver and there were at least four bookshop owners between the 1630s and 1690s.

The walls were repaired after the Civil War and by 1668, when Pepys visited, he found the city to be mostly built of stone, with clean streets, although they were still narrow.

The devastating plague that claimed 100,000 people in London in 1665 brought panic to Bath, as it did to all other places in Britain. Large numbers of people fled the capital, but in order to protect Bath the Corporation decided that anyone who welcomed someone from a plague-ridden area into their house would be fined £10. The night watchmen were also charged with making sure no one entered the city or they would be fined too.

One refugee who somehow managed to circumnavigate the ban was Dr Thomas Guidott, who established himself as an eminent physician in Bath and produced an important birds-eye view of the King's Bath in 1687. He advocated that an hour, or an hour and a half, was sufficient to cure any ill, and the patient could tell when to leave by the extent of the 'shivels' on his fingers.

❋ ❋ ❋ ❋ ❋

Despite having a large number of illegitimate children with his many mistresses, Charles II was desperate to conceive a legitimate heir, and so brought his wife, Catherine of Braganza, to Bath in 1663. They remained childless and so the succession passed to Charles' brother, James (1633–1701), in 1685. Unlike Charles, who downplayed his beliefs, James II did not hide his Catholicism nor his devotion to the concept of absolute monarchy.

James and his wife, Mary of Modena, also struggled to conceive a legitimate heir. Their visit to Bath, however, was more fruitful and Mary gave birth to a son in 1688. In celebration, the Secretary of State the Earl of Melfort greatly enhanced the cross in the centre of the Cross Bath.

Elsewhere, panicked by the birth of a royal Catholic heir, English Protestants begged William of Orange and his wife Mary, James II's daughter with his first wife, Anne Hyde, to take the throne in 1688. William, who had long been anticipating such a call, accordingly set sail with an army for England. James II fled to France a few weeks later, and William and Mary were crowned as joint monarchs the following year.

This was the Glorious Revolution, and Protestants in Bath – as across England – were restored to their positions of authority. The Crown and two political parties ruled the country equally. Throughout the country, signs or symbols of Catholic sympathies were removed, including the Melfort Cross in Bath. It was slowly dismantled and made more 'Protestant'. William and Mary's coronation was marked with a specially commissioned song that gave thanks that 'Rome's priests' with their 'hocus pocus' religion had been driven from England. In honour of the royal couple, the annual February Fair in Bath was renamed the Orange Fair.

James II still had many supporters in Ireland, and in March 1689 he landed there with a French army. William assembled his own troops to meet this challenge and in 1690 he decisively defeated James at the Battle of the Boyne. James promptly returned to France, leaving William free to consolidate his hold on power. The death of Mary in 1694 left William as sole ruler of the three kingdoms, and by 1700 all eyes were turning to the problem of the succession.

Because neither William, nor James II's surviving daughter, Anne, had any children, Protestants were terrified that the throne would eventually revert to James II, his son, or one of the many other Catholic claimants. To avert this danger, the Act of Settlement was passed in 1701, directing that after the deaths of William and Anne the throne would return to the descendants of James I's daughter, Elizabeth Stuart. Sophia, Electress of Hanover (Elizabeth's daughter) and her heirs accordingly became next in line to the English throne.

In 1702, William died and was succeeded by Anne. Five years after this, a formal union of the kingdoms of England and Scotland was engineered in order to ensure that there would be a Protestant succession in Scotland too. Henceforth England and Scotland officially became one country, and when Queen Anne, the last of the Stuart monarchs, died in 1714, it was to the throne of the United Kingdom of Great Britain that George I, the first of the Hanoverians, succeeded.

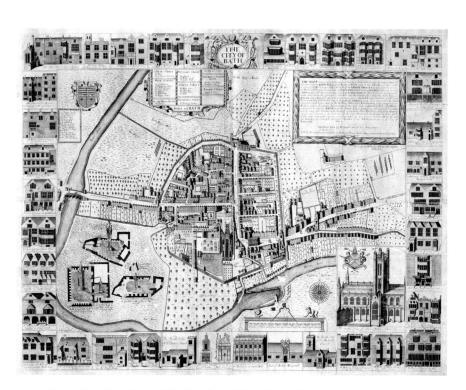

Joseph Gilmore: City of Bath Map, *c.* 1694. (Bath Central Library/Bath in Time)

By the end of the seventeenth century, Bath had started to expand; this is clearly revealed when a comparison is made between either Savile or Speed's maps and that drawn by Joseph Gilmore, a Bristol mathematician, in 1692–94 (the version most commonly known dates from 1731). Such a comparison is also vital to our understanding of just how dramatic Bath's transformation was going to be during the following century.

Between the beginning and end of the 1600s, the city walls remain largely unchanged but, within, the town is beginning to fill up and become crowded. The courtyards and gardens in the area behind the redundant St Mary's Within are now jam-packed with tenements. The rows of houses are longer and more uniform, for example on Southgate Street, where many of the properties are shown to have privies at the bottom of their gardens (on the east side these dropped directly into Bum Ditch). The houses, which would have started the century as two storey and thatched, were now more likely three or four storey with stone or slate roofs.

Sawclose is far less open, having been crammed full with lodging houses, although its purpose as a timber yard is still suggested by the lumbers. The open spaces around the Abbey have become more formal and buildings have started to encroach on the precinct. The greatest expansion, though, is to the north around St Michael's Church and Broad and Walcot Streets. A large, new bowling green has been added and the conduit, once a stone trough, is now represented as a fine stone edifice. Visitors still entered the city through one of the three main gates.

Gilmore included vignettes of the Hot, Lazars (or Lazours), King's, Queen's and Cross Baths and the Abbey encapsulated within a frame of individual key buildings. By doing so, Gilmore not only highlighted the guildhall and the many inns, conduits, churches, hospitals and lodgings (a significant number owned by aldermen) that were available, but also showed the sophistication of Bath's newer buildings. Only 'Mrs Savils Lodgings Nere the hott bath' endures in the same form. Once known as Hungerford House, it was built on the site of Dr Feckenham's leper hospital. A private property now called Abbey Church House, it was badly damaged during the Second World War but rebuilt.

Gilmore's vignettes provide a wonderful insight into the lost buildings of Bath. They show modern, three-storey lodging houses that must have towered over the medieval lanes and streets. The visitors, however, were pleased with the improved accommodation and amenities. This is Bath on the cusp of a magnificent transformation, helped along by the patronage of Princess Anne, who visited in 1692, although it was her visits as Queen in 1702 and 1703 that really made the difference.

❋ ❋ ❋ ❋ ❋

The period 1500–1700 was a time of massive social upheaval. The Dissolution of the Monasteries was followed by the Civil War. The medieval town plan of Bath, however, is hardly altered; there is no significant growth of this provincial town. Once, where the Church had dominated now the power lay with the city's corporate body. A mayor and the Corporation (comprising a maximum of ten alderman and twenty councillors) had replaced the bishop and the prior – a situation officially recognised by a Royal Charter in 1590.

Along with the change in Bath's fortunes due to the Dissolution, the weaving industry was also decreasing. It was fortunate, then, that the sixteenth century saw a revival in the popularity of the waters, mainly due to the increase in leprosy and smallpox and Bath's fame for 'curing' infertility. Local and national philanthropists provided facilities for the truly sick, which conveniently kept the 'unsightly' diseased and poor, mostly, away from the higher ranks of society.

Moneyed benefactors, grateful for the curative powers of the waters, improved the bathing experience for all. Doctors flocked to the town, many publishing important theses that further fuelled the rich man's desire to make the arduous expedition to take the waters of Bath. And, fortunately for the historian, many writers and artists also made the journey and left us with a rich legacy of invaluable first-hand accounts of this remarkable city.

Seven

A TRIO OF ENTREPRENEURS: EARLY GEORGIAN 1690–1760

I t is no exaggeration to say that Bath altered beyond recognition in the 1700s. Its dramatic change in fortunes from merely a health resort to a fashionable get-away is traditionally credited to Queen Anne's visits of 1702 and 1703. Increasing numbers did visit the city, but they tended to come in the summer months, when the roads were dry and passable.

Public amusements centred on bowling and walking, with visitors complaining about the lack of facilities to occupy their time. Bath was ripe for commercialisation and, although a number of entrepreneurs exploited its potential, it is Richard 'Beau' Nash (1674–1761) who is acclaimed for creating 'the most distinguished spot in the kingdom' for the affluent invalid who sought pleasure along with their medication.

Two other names, however, are also synonymous with Bath's transformation: the architect, John Wood the Elder (1704–54), and entrepreneur, Ralph Allen (1693–1764). It was lucky happenstance that found these three ambitious men in Bath at the same time, each reliant on the other to facilitate their individual aspirations. Bath's success was their success.

※ ※ ※ ※ ※

Queen Anne, the last Stuart monarch, began her reign in 1702. She had suffered ill-health for most of her life: she contracted smallpox aged 12 and may have suffered from the blood disease porphyria. She had numerous agonising miscarriages, and none of the five children she birthed reached adulthood. Her class and ill-health made her visits to Bath habitual, but her fame, authority and large entourage were of huge service to the West Country town as it teetered on the brink of unimaginable notoriety and prominence.

Anne's reign is characterised by the War of the Spanish Succession, which saw significant victories by John Churchill, Duke of Marlborough, against the French. Anne rewarded this national hero (who was married to her best friend, Sarah) with a large Oxfordshire estate on which they built Blenheim, courtesy of the public purse. The Duke of Marlborough regularly visited Bath for his health; the Duchess, however, tolerated these trips for his sake only.

The Treaty of Union, which came into force on 1 May 1707, was another noteworthy event during Anne's reign. Passed between England and Scotland, the treaty was a contentious solution to the instability created by the often opposing politics of the two nations. Anti-Unionists and Jacobites continued to oppose the union and the much hoped for stability, economic benefits and peaceful co-operation was not immediately forthcoming. Modern political agendas show that, for some, Scotland's independence is still craved.

Since the Act of Succession was passed, the Crown passed to George, Elector of Hanover, in 1714. There were at least fifty relatives with a stronger claim to the English throne, but George was the first Protestant in line. (Still to this day, no Roman Catholic has the right to the succession.)

George spoke very little English and spent as much time as he could in his beloved Hanover. It is not surprising, then, that those who supported the succession of James Francis Edward, Prince of Wales (the Old Pretender, 1688–1766), became increasingly agitated. There were Jacobite risings planned in Scotland, London, Cornwall and the West in 1715. Up and down the country supporters of the House of Stuart attacked property and people, burnt effigies and drank to the Pretender's health.

The Cornish plot unravelled when the postmaster at St Columb opened a letter from Jacobite James Paynter's servant. Some judge that there is evidence to suggest that the postmaster was none other than Ralph Allen.

One of the main headquarters for the rebellion in the West was based in Bath. Here Catholics and Jacobites could hide in plain sight because the town was full of strangers for most of the year. Conspirators could gather and plot under the pretence of 'taking the waters'. A letter to the *Flying Post* on 8 October 1715 stated, 'This place [Bath] has all summer been a nest of Tories and Papists, and the factious part of the inhabitants caress them as much for their hatred of the Protestant succession as for the money they pay for their lodgings.'

Major General Wade (1673–1748) was sent to Bath to establish a garrison and quash the rebels. An arsenal of weapons and at least 200 horses were quickly discovered. Leaders of Bath's 'Fifteen' were captured, including Sir William Wyndham and Lord Lansdowne. The Corporation was forced to apologise for allowing 'the concourse of Papists, Nonjurors, and other disaffected persons' in their town. It announced Bath's allegiance to King George through a zealous and public celebration of the failure of the Jacobite rising.

Loyalty to General Wade would prove very advantageous for the town. He financed the demolition of a number of old houses obstructing the natural routes around the Abbey and the fashionable grove – this became Wade's

Passage. He gave the Abbey a stone christening font and a marble altarpiece and commissioned Johan van Diest to paint the portraits of Bath's thirty-one councillors, the town clerk and the town recorder.

❋ ❋ ❋ ❋ ❋

Richard Nash was born in Swansea. He underperformed at school, at university, as a lawyer and as a soldier, but what he did excel at was socialising and gambling. Nash came to Bath in around 1704, reputedly for a respite from the hedonistic life he led in London. He was quickly on good terms with Bath's Master of Ceremonies, Captain Webster, and assisted in the smooth running of Bath's emerging social life. He was thus the natural successor when Webster was killed in a duel. With a vision for social enterprise and a head for business, Nash utilised his skills and his connections and – quite simply – revolutionised the fortunes of this modest West Country town. He invested in the roads into Bath, enforced a strict set of rules for social etiquette and was involved with the setting up of Bath's first Assembly Rooms with Thomas Harrison.

For Bath to become truly successful, Nash needed to retain control over every aspect of public socialisation, and so he banned all private parties and encouraged Harrison to provide somewhere for the wealthy visitors to meet. John Wood tells us that much energy had been spent in improving the private buildings of Bath, but the 'company' were forced to meet in a booth to drink their tea and chocolate and to play cards, whilst balls had to be held at the guildhall.

Harrison's, which opened in 1708, provided a handsome public arena for the company to enjoy the fashionable beverages of the day, socialise and gamble. The original building, set against the east side of the Borough Wall, part of the Abbey Wall on Terrace Walk, was quite modest. It overlooked Harrison's Walk, which Harrison laid out for his clientele with the gardens and paths bordering the River Avon. These gardens still exist as part of what is now Parade Gardens and remain a popular open space in central Bath.

In 1720 Harrison employed William Killigrew to add a large ballroom. This enticed non-gamblers to also frequent the rooms, guaranteeing that Harrison's was *the* place to be seen – and to see. Contemporary accounts often make mention of Harrison's, and the fine members of society who frequented the rooms. Bath's popularity was such that Lady Irwin complained in the autumn of 1729:

The Company increases daily, but everybody complains that they are people that nobody knows: for my own part I think it is of no great difference whether 'tis a crowd of quality or plebeians. Harrison's rooms are so full every night 'tis to me very disagreeable; if one had an inclination 'tis next to impossible to get a table to play, which I have only done once since I came. My sister Mary seems to relish the place as little as I do.

Harrison died on 14 January 1735 and the Rooms were taken over by Lord Hawley and his mistress, Elizabeth Hayes, and subsequently by his servant, Charles Simpson. Simpson further enlarged and remodelled the Rooms in 1749; some documents suggest it was practically rebuilt at this time.

Thomas Bodely, writing in *The Bath and Bristol Guide* of 1753, described Simpson's as 'lately built, [and being] 90 feet long and 36 feet broad; ... very lofty, the Ceiling, Stuko Work, enrich'd with Ornaments'. The structure was two storeys, and Simpson used the basement as a playhouse. The impressive façade comprised three equal bays with two tall, arched sash windows in each bay. The ground floor, on the same level as Parade Gardens, also had two windows in each bay but depictions differ as to their size and shape. This is quite possibly due to the continued remodelling of the building.

Images of the interior of Simpson's are rare, but a sketch by Thomas Robins (V&A Museum) confirms Bodely's account. The *New Bath Guide*'s 1792 description of the ballroom is similar, but it also elaborates on other details, the Rooms now under the tenancy of James Heaven:

> The view of the river, valley, and adjacent hills, [from the ballroom] makes it one of the pleasantest morning rooms in the kingdom. There is in it a portrait of the late Richard Nash Esq.; and it is elegantly furnished with chandeliers, girandoles, etc. The Card-room is 60 feet long and 30 feet wide, with a coved ceiling, and has in it another portrait of Mr. Nash. There are also two Tea-rooms, 40 feet by 24 each.

Bath's growing popularity meant that another assembly room was established in the same area. In 1728, the London apothecary, Humphrey Thayer, instructed John Wood to erect Lindsey's Assembly Rooms for retired singer, Dame Lindsey. The Rooms were opened on 6 April 1730. Catharine Lovelace held the lease fleetingly from 1736–37 before Walter Wiltshire, whose name is more readily associated with these rooms. Lindsey's was particularly distinctive due to the attic storey windows, which were circular with radiating sash bars.

After church, at about noon, the company would parade out on the walkways around the Assembly Rooms, Orange Grove, Harrison's Walks, etc. and this would last for about two hours. They would retreat about 4 or 5 o'clock for dinner, after which they would meet again at the Pump Room, followed by further walks, before withdrawing to the Assembly Rooms to drink tea before the main amusements of the night.

Visitors paid a subscription for the two balls held each week, one at Lindsey's on Tuesdays, the other at Harrison's on Fridays. The balls started at 6 p.m. when Nash, or the two most distinguished visitors, opened the ball with a minuet. There was an interval for tea at 9, and it was all over by 11 p.m. Additional fees were payable for walking in the private gardens, concerts, reading the papers and the use of a pen, ink, writing paper and blotting paper – all available at the coffee houses. Of course, additional money was needed for the gaming tables (the opportunity for 'deep play' or high-stake games was available at Bath). Lodging rooms cost 10 shillings a week and a servant's garret 5 shillings; these prices were halved out of season.

❊ ❊ ❊ ❊ ❊

Drinking the waters became popular after Dr Jones' recommendation in 1572 led to the erection of a drinking fountain in the King's Bath in 1578. By 1673, Bath's mineral water was being bottled and sold across the country. By the end of the seventeenth century all the baths had had pumps installed for both drinking and pumping or bucketing.

The taste of Bath's waters is probably best described by Charles Dickens' character, Sam Weller, who said it was reminiscent of 'warm flat irons', or Tobias Smollett's vividly repellent suggestion that the water drunk in the Pump Room had actually seeped through from the King's Bath, 'In that case, what a delicate beverage is every day quaffed by the drinkers; medicated with the sweat, and dirt, and dandruff; and the abominable discharges of various kinds, from twenty different diseased bodies, parboiling in the kettle below.'

In 1704, Dr William Oliver (1659–1716) published his essay on the waters (which would later form the basis of his *Practical Dissertation on Bath Waters* published in 1707), in which he encouraged the erection of a purpose-built room so that the season could be extended through the winter months. John Wood concurred:

> the Guardians of the hot fountains … soon came to a resolution to build a handsome room on the north side of the King's Bath, and to set up a new Pump in it, that people of rank and fashion might drink the waters, and walk about, at all seasons of the year, without the danger of catching cold, which the exposed situation of the old pumps made them liable to.

The building, designed by John Harvey and constructed of Bath stone, was opened in around 1706 to a revival of an old song honouring Bladud's discovery of the healing hot waters. The north front comprised five large, arched sash

(After) Thomas Robins: A View of the King's and Queen's Baths, including the Pump Room, 1764. (Bath Central Library/Bath in Time)

windows over 14ft (4m) in height. Each window had a door for access and ventilation. A small orchestra situated in a gallery projecting from the west wall would entertain the company.

An immediate success – in actual fact, *too* successful – Dr Oliver complained that it was too small to be convenient. Smollett's character Lydia described 'the noise of the music playing in the gallery, the heat and flavour of such a crowd, and the hum and buzz of their conversation, gave one the headache and vertigo the first day; but afterwards all these things became familiar and even agreeable'.

The Pump Room was remodelled between 1732–34 and then extended in 1751. Providing an 'all-weather' venue, alongside the improvement to the country's roads through the turnpike trusts, extended the fashionable season at Bath. After around 1730 Bath developed two seasons. The main one was between September and December, meaning that it was no longer in competition with some of the other resorts such as Tunbridge Wells. A more subdued season was held from late April to early June. By the end of the eighteenth century these two seasons had merged, leading to people 'wintering' in Bath, or retiring there permanently.

A further factor that helped Bath attain a second season was the agricultural revolution. In simple terms, the invention of the seed drill, the advancement of theories around crop rotation, Charles 'Turnip' Townshend (1674–38) and selective breeding all enabled Bath to sustain a winter season. Rather than leave a field fallow, as was usual in crop rotation, during the eighteenth century farmers started to grow root crops on the 'resting' field – root crops not only restored fertility to the soil, but also provided winter feed for cattle. Previously cattle were slaughtered at the beginning of the winter, but by feeding them turnips throughout the wintertime, fresh milk, butter, cream and meat became available all year round.

※ ※ ※ ※ ※

Daniel Defoe (1660–1731) noted that Bath had changed since his childhood:

> The whole time indeed is a round of the utmost diversion. In the morning you (supposing you to be a young lady) are fetch'd in a close chair, dress'd in your bathing cloths, that is, stript to the smock, to the Cross-Bath. There the musick plays you into the bath, and the women that tend you, present you with a little floating wooden dish, like a bason; in which the lady puts a handkerchief, and a nosegay, of late the snuff-box is added, and some patches; tho' the bath occasioning a little perspiration, the patches do not stick so kindly as they should.

The practice of taking a small bowl with you to the baths was certainly prevalent in the seventeenth century. Ned Ward admired 'the ladies with their floating Japan-Bowls, freighted with confectionary, knick-knacks, essences and perfumes'. Samuel Gale wrote that the bowls were 'tied to their arms with ribbons and wim upon the surface … to keep their handkerchiefs, nosegays, perfumes and spirits in case the exhalation of the water should be too prevalent'.

Defoe noted that at the Baths:

> … the ladies and the gentlemen pretend to keep some distance, and each to their proper side, but frequently mingle here too, as in the King and Queens Bath, tho' not so often; and the place being but narrow, they converse freely, and talk, rally, make vows, and sometimes love; and having thus amus'd themselves an hour, or two, they call their chairs and return to their lodgings.

※ ※ ※ ※ ※

The unpopular George I was succeeded by his son George II in 1727. George II had made far greater efforts to ingratiate himself with Britain's citizens since he had accompanied his father in 1714 and took the title of Prince of Wales.

After Bath's involvement with the Jacobite risings, the Corporation was keen to show its loyalty to the Hanoverians. General Wade was duly elected as

Bath's MP four times. Much pomp was made to celebrate royal birthdays and coronations. Allen raised a small army during the last battle fought on English soil, at Culloden in 1745, and, although George II never visited Bath, his children and grandchildren patronised the city regularly.

The Pump Room was the central focus of Bath's social life. It provided an expedient place for fashionable society to meet during the day, listen to music and consult the Subscription Book, which detailed who was in town and where they were staying. The local newspapers also recorded who was in town. Some of the earliest patrons of note included the Duke of Marlborough in 1716; the Archbishop of Armagh, who travelled from Dublin in 1718 to take the waters; and Princess Amelia, who was a regular visitor to Bath throughout the 1720s, often visiting twice a year.

In 1727 she accepted an official invitation to visit Bristol. She travelled from Bath in Tomkin's London Wherry, landing at Temple Slip. The church bells rang out, and a twenty-one cannon salute marked her arrival. The following year Bath celebrated her birthday. Mr Goulding 'had the honour of treating the populace in the day, and the Earl of Essex the quality with a ball at night'. A number of the fashionable engravings from this time feature Princess Amelia's fishing lodge, an ornate building on Harrison's Walk, adjacent to the river.

Thomas Loggan: Fan view of Harrison's Walk (detail), *c.* 1749. (Private Collection/Bath in Time)

Thomas Rowlandson: Spring Garden Breakfast, Plate 11, Comforts of Bath, 1798. (Bath Central Library/Bath in Time)

The poet, Alexander Pope (1688–1744), wrote to Martha Blount in 1714, 'I have slid, I can't tell how, into all the Amusements of the place; My whole Day is shar'd by the Pump-Assemblies, the Walks, the Chocolate houses, Raffling Shops, Plays, Medleys, etc.'.

The usual daily routine was to visit the Pump Room after morning bathing, between 7 a.m. and 10 p.m. and again at 4 p.m. In between time the company found other diversions, including proceeding to Spring Gardens (established before 1735) via the ferry for breakfast. These public breakfasts, according to the Reverend Penrose, were held in:

> ... a large handsome Building ... capacious enough to hold many Sets of Company, having six windows in the side,... and proportionally wide ... the Tables were spread with singular Neatness. Upon a Cloth white as Snow were ... every Thing belonging to the Equipage of the Tea Table,... interspersed with sweet Briar, which had a pretty Effect both on the Sight and Smell. At the Word of Command were set on the Table Chocolate, Coffee, Tea, Hot Rolls buttered, buttered hot cakes.

The gardens were open for breakfast twice a week, normally Mondays and Thursdays. Fetes, charitable benefits, illuminations, fireworks, public teas, music and celebrations of significant anniversaries such as the King's birthday were also hosted. Fireworks became a regular feature.

These displays were quickly dominated by Signor Giovanni Invetto, who provided spectacles at a number of locations around Bath, including Villa Gardens and later Sydney Gardens. He also made and sold fireworks from his lodgings at the Seven Stars on Borough Walls. You are right to think this a dangerous pastime – in 1789, Invetto lost his wife and child in an explosion at his home.

A letter from April 1753 describes the gardens as 'the fair Elysium … where sweet variety tempts every sense to rapture'. There were groves, parterres, gravel and grass paths (straight and serpentine), grass areas, a pond and a canal. The beds were planted with violets, pinks, roses, vegetables and shrubs. The gardens certainly had a reputation for pleasure; they were magical, and perhaps furtive enough to encourage even greater social freedom.

This sense of clandestine enchantment was invigorated by the need to take a ferry across the Avon to gain access to the pleasure grounds. Before Pulteney Bridge was commenced in 1769, guests either took a passenger boat from near East Gate or via the Whitehall Ferry from South Parade. The perilous nature of such transportation was lampooned by Christopher Anstey in his *New Bath Guide*, Letter XIII:

> In handing old Lady Bumfidget and daughter,
> This obsequious Lord tumbled into the water;
> But a nymph of the flood brought him safe to the boat,
> And I left all the ladies a'cleaning his coat.

Another area for fashionable parading was the Orange Grove, between Harrison's Walks and the Abbey. Originally part of the churchyard for the Bath Priory, after the Dissolution it was developed as a public space with areas for bowling. By the late seventeenth century, when it had become obvious that Bath needed to provide better facilities, this area was laid out with gravel walks and trees. The grove became a convenient and pleasant centre between the baths, Pump Room, Lower Assembly Rooms, Abbey and lodging houses.

In 1735, Nash erected an obelisk as a memento of William IV Prince of Orange's (1711–51) successful health-seeking visit of 1734. Orange Grove, as it then became known, was home to a number of prestigious architect-designed buildings, including Nassau House and Winchester House. Visitors were well catered for with an abundance of boutique shops: James Leake's bookshop,

George Speren's toyshop, the Fan and Crown (a place to buy trinkets and mementoes) and the earliest known coffee house, Sheyler's on Cheap Street.

Coffee houses sold alcoholic drinks as well as coffee, tea and drinking chocolate. They were more refined than the alehouses and so tended to be frequented by the company. Visitors could also catch up with the latest newspapers from London, which were only a day out of date. Men would normally take breakfast at a coffee house, but later in the century women-only coffee houses were also provided.

Before Bath's 'upper town' was developed, Orange Grove was one of the more sought after locations. John Wood wrote, 'People of fortune have lately preferred [Orange Grove] to any other Place, within the Walls of the City, to take up their Abode'. Lady Luxborough chose to lodge here, as did the Earl of Howith, who wrote that Nassau House was his favourite residence in Bath. 'I think Bath a more comfortable place to live in than London,' wrote Mrs Pendarves to Jonathan Swift in April 1736, 'all the entertainments of the place lye in a small compass and you are at your liberty to partake of them or let them alone just as it suits your humour.'

These fashionable areas were featured regularly on fans, engravings, trinket boxes and other souvenirs. George Speren (1711–96) appears to have been one of the first to publish fans with specific views of Bath's landmarks. On 9 July 1737, he advertised four copper engraved fan views in the *Country Journal*, comprising:

> An exact Prospect of the Summer-House, Walks and Gardens, with a fine View of the River Avon, and fields adjacent.

> Orange Grove, the Gentry on the Walks, the Shape, the East End of the Abbey Church, the Obelisque in Memory of the Recovery of his Royal Highness the Prince of Orange; and a View of a neighbouring Village.

> A perspective view of the Church-yard, the Quality assembling to the Pump-Room to drink the Water.

> A View of the Inside of Mrs. Lovelace's great Room, and the Ladies and Gentlemen taking their Diversion therein.

Jonathan Pinchbeck was a rival fan maker, but based in London where he ran his Fan Warehouse on the Strand. His 'Bath Medley' fan, 'being an accurate and curious Draught of the Pump Room at Bath' with a portrait of Princess Amelia, was sold at John Wickstead's, the toyshop next door to Speren's. Thomas Loggan

(1706–80), the self-styled 'Little Fan-maker' (he was only 4ft tall), occasionally included a self-portrait on his fans. He opened a shop in Abbey Churchyard, which he advertised as a 'Circulating Library', but its merchandise of fans, lacquer boxes and porcelain suggests it was actually another toyshop.

Speren collaborated with the artist Thomas Robins (1716–70) who provided designs for the fans and an important engraving, the *Prospect of the City of Bath*, published in October 1757. Robins, who was born in Charlton Kings near Cheltenham, made a living as an artist travelling around the country depicting the seats of gentlemen. He was also a regular visitor to Bath. Within his sketchbook, now in the V&A Museum's collection, there are at least forty-five sketches of Bath and its environs. These topographical sketches date from around 1754–65, and are hugely important as a record of Bath during this key transitional phase. His sketches included the old buildings and mills nestled amongst the new Palladian terraces.

Depictions of the Circus, which appear in the sketchbook and on the fans, illustrate just how notoriously slow was its development. Beset with complicated negotiations over the water supply, Robins captures the Circus when only the south-west segment had been built. Strewn around the foreground are blocks of ashlar stone and segments of column, but with no sign of any builders, just a group of fashionable visitors gathering around Beau Nash. Speren and Robins enjoyed a long-term collaboration, with Speren publishing a number of fans and engravings by Robins, and in October 1752 Robins advertised that he was based at Speren's shop, offering art classes to the gentry.

❋ ❋ ❋ ❋ ❋

Several of Nash's eleven rules tried to quash gossiping, an unfortunate yet very natural by-product of socialising and fashionable frivolity. A way around these rules was to pin anonymous limericks on the trees of the fashionable parading areas. A commentator noted, 'On several of the trees [of Orange Grove] was hung a lampoon on the marriage of one Mr. S ... a Drungmonger and the famous Madam S ... of London'.

Nash's code of conduct, which was published and posted up in various public places, ensured everyone understood what behaviour was acceptable, but also – importantly – guaranteed that if you followed the rules you could ensure not to make a social faux pas and be accused of being vulgar.

Nash pioneered the relaxation of Britain's strict social hierarchy, encouraging friendships across the classes that would never have been acceptable anywhere else, especially in London. He welcomed every individual visitor to Bath. He intervened when novice gamblers were being swindled and warned ladies off unsuitable suitors. He made himself instantly recognisable in a world without television or 'celebrity' magazines by dressing in an elegant, yet extravagant manner – earning him his nickname of 'Beau'. The company immediately knew who was in charge and sought out his company. Artists made sure that their images of Bath's walks and groves were fashionable by regularly including a likeness of Nash in his distinctive black wig and white, beaver-trimmed tri-corn hat. He assumed the title of 'King of Bath', and was trusted. He had made Bath both safe and enjoyable, and therefore popular.

Nash was undone by the very activity that had made him – gambling. A change in the law in 1739 saw the games faro, basset and ace of hearts banned. An indication of just how strongly Bath was associated with gambling is shown by the fact that this act actually included a clause peculiar to Bath – the £20 fine payable for playing or arranging illicit games in Bath was to be paid to the Mineral Water Hospital.

Parliament extended the ban in 1740 to include all dice games, and again in 1745 to include roulette. Nash's income fell dramatically, making it obvious to all that he had been taking a cut from the gaming tables. The company – who had happily benefitted from his organisation, investment and vision for Bath – were affronted by what they considered to have been a disingenuous way to make money. The next twenty years of his life were not so glamorous, but when he died at the age of 87, the city gave him a lavish funeral and a memorial in the Abbey inscribed 'Bathonie Elegantiae Arbiter'.

❋ ❋ ❋ ❋ ❋

In 1707, the city wall was purposefully breached with the intention of developing and expanding the city. George Tryme, a wealthy clothier and member of the Corporation, leased the land he owned around the walls and south of Barton Ground to speculative builders with the express desire to erect a number of higher-class dwelling houses. Tryme, like Nash, saw the opportunity to prosper from Bath's burgeoning popularity. He also built a small theatre at nearby Upper Borough Walls, funded by subscriptions from 'people of the highest quality'.

Eighteen houses were built on Trim Street, and although no architect's name appears on surviving deeds, it is likely that either Thomas Greenway or John Strahan – both of whom were active in Bath at this time – were responsible. As Bath continued to develop, so more of the walls came down until 1754, when the remaining parts were eradicated. The North and South Gates were demolished at about the same time, whilst the West Gate survived until 1776, when it too was removed.

We know that Strahan was the architect of Avon Street, another early development of fashionable lodging houses. John Hobbs, a Bristol deal merchant, employed the land surveyor and architect in around 1726 to lay out some streets on meadowland which formed part of the Great King's Mead, to which Hobbs had tenant's rights. The development also included Kingsmead Square and Beaufort Buildings (later Beauford Square). Avon Street, which originally ran uninterrupted directly down from Kingsmead Square to the river, dates from 1727. Strahan's fifty-one houses were built of Bath ashlar stone and formed an elegant row; although of two storeys, plus an attic and basement, they immediately seemed slight when compared to John Wood's contemporary buildings at Queen Square, commenced in 1728.

As Bath's urban spaces spread northwards driven by John Wood's vision, the earlier developments of Avon, Kingsmead and Trim Streets quickly fell out of favour. Trim Street was soon inhabited by tradespeople such as upholders, stay makers, coach builders, stationers and a private educational facility for young ladies. The Old Bath Fire Office kept their fire engines here, with instructions for clients to go to Trim Street first to alert the firemen, who were guaranteed to remove their furniture safely! Although Trim Street did not attract the high-class lodgers Tryme had hoped for, it did give legitimacy to the city's expansion outside the confines of the wall.

Without question, Bath's greatest architect and visionary was John Wood the Elder. Similarly, he was undoubtedly a very difficult and driven man. He had elaborate, majestic – even esoteric – plans for Bath, but needed landowners and moneymen to back his eccentric ideals in order to bring them to fruition. The Corporation either did not share his vision, or felt unable to put their trust in a 'jobbing builder'. Wood was forced to look further afield – in fact, to the fields of Barton Farm, just outside the city walls in the manor of Walcot. He approached Robert Gay, a barber surgeon from London and the owner of the estate since 1699. What Wood achieved here, through blind stubbornness and determination, is the acclaimed architectural splendour and town planning that is still heralded today, over 300 years later. On these fields outside the city limits, Wood established Bath's architectural style, the basic principles of which were copied by all the architects who came after him.

Wood was born in Bath and baptised in St James's Church (now demolished). He received a good but basic education at Bath's Bluecoat School. We know that his father, George, was a builder, and perhaps Wood was apprenticed to him. What is obvious is that the young Wood took advantage of the opportunities and connections he made during his early career in London and Yorkshire to satisfy his intellect. Through reading, site visits and practical experience he refined his beliefs, and combined his passion for Palladianism with his obsession with ancient

British history, and almost certainly Freemasonry. Through these seemingly conflicting preoccupations, Wood created an ambitious, yet commercially viable, harmonious and handsome blueprint for Bath's development.

In 1725, when he was only 21 years old, he developed an extremely ambitious strategy as he 'began to turn [his] thoughts towards the improvement of the city [of Bath] by building'. With the Palladian buildings at Queen Square, built between 1728 and 1736, Michael Forsyth expounds that Wood 'set fresh standards for urban development in scale, boldness and social consequence'. Wood undoubtedly took his inspiration from Inigo Jones's Covent Garden piazza (1631–37) in London and perhaps Dean Aldrick's Peckwater Quadrangle at Christ Church, Oxford (1706–10). The elegant and palatial north façade, comprising seven individual townhouses with architectural emphasis on the central house to suggest a grand entrance, is heralded as Wood's greatest triumph. The other three wings purposefully act as foils to this ostentatious palace front. The east and west sides of the square are the wings of the 'palace', enclosing a forecourt, with the intention of it all being viewed from the south – the side Wood chose to live until he died.

Although an existing property thwarted Wood's intended design for the west side, the two balancing villas he devised worked well. (The space was eventually filled by John Pinch the Younger in 1830.) Wood had cannily designed simple townhouses to appear far more majestic, like the grand country houses of the aristocracy, or the royal palaces of Europe's wealthiest monarchs. No self-respecting Georgian of rank could resist the elegance of these new lodgings and what they suggested about their standing in society. An indication of how profitable Bath was becoming is perhaps denoted by the number of local merchants, physicians and surgeons who took on leases at Queen Square.

'The intention of a square in a city,' wrote Wood, 'is for people to assemble together.' He understood that polite society enjoyed parading, and in order to do that Wood provided wide streets with raised pavements and a thoughtfully designed central garden. The formal garden was laid out with gravel pathways and low planting and was originally enclosed by an elegant stone balustrade. The obelisk, of which Wood was 'inordinately proud', was erected in 1738 in honour of Frederick, Prince of Wales. It formally rose from a circular pool to a point 70ft (21m) high, but a serve gale in 1815 truncated it.

Wood's Queen Square, named in honour of Queen Caroline, the wife of George II, is confident and strong and immediately proved popular with the more prominent members of Bath's own society. In all respects Wood was a phenomenal town planner, rather than an architect, in that he not only designed the buildings, but the spaces in between them.

All Wood's developments were built speculatively; this meant that whilst Wood leased the land from Robert Gay for £137 per annum, designed the frontages and divided the ground into separate building plots, he sublet those plots to individual builders or masons. They had two years' grace in which to get the walls up and the roof on, after which they had to pay a more substantial rent. As Bath was booming, most plots were reserved before the two years were up, providing the builder with the necessary income to complete the house. Ultimately, this meant less work and risk for Wood. In addition he received £305 per annum in rents, leaving him a healthy profit of £168 – the equivalent today (in terms of average earnings) of £306,000.

With the addition of St Mary's Chapel, Bath's first proprietary chapel, on the south-west corner of the square in 1732, Wood created the perfect 'town' within the city. St Mary's was demolished in around 1875 for road widening, but a plaque (provided by the Bath Preservation Trust) marks the spot. Also here, amongst the undergrowth, is a stone temple. This is almost certainly the original 'kitchen' from the centre of the Queen's Bath. It stood for many years in the garden of No. 14 Queen Square, but was thankfully recognised by Ruth Coard, restored by stonemasonry students and repositioned here in 1975.

Queen Square, explains Michael Forsyth, is the initial component of 'the most important architectural sequence in Bath'. In the north-east corner of Queen Square is a distinctive corner house, built by Wood in 1734–36 for Richard Marchant, a wealthy Quaker, and fellow governor of the Mineral Water Hospital. It marks the start of Gay Street (1735–40), which is the work of Wood the Elder as far as George Street, and continued by his son, Wood the Younger after 1755 to form the main link between Queen Square and the Circus. Gay Street is quite plain after the richness of Queen Square; it was designed purposefully to act as an interlude between these two spectacular architectural set pieces. Wood knew how to affect people's emotions through the urban spaces he created.

The exploitation of the topography means that there is little clue to the wonder that awaits you as you climb the steep hill of Gay Street. You quite literally step into the Circus (1754–67), built on a plateau sliced into the Lansdown hillside. According to Wood there had always been a temple to the sun and one to the moon here. The Circus – Wood's temple to the sun – is undoubtedly one of Bath's most famous landmarks. Its design, diameter and number of dwellings are derived from the ancient Druid monuments of Stonehenge and Stanton Drew. The 525 *metopes* on the Doric frieze are often seen as evidence of Wood's link with Freemasonry. However, although there are similar elements, few of the complete emblems are wholly Masonic. Tim Mowl has shown that a number were actually derived from George Withers' folio *Emblemes* (1635).

Perhaps the most striking and indisputable symbolism, however, is the equilateral triangle created by the points of the three roads that enter the Circus, representing the Holy Trinity, set within the circle of Wood's structure, a symbol of eternity. Equally, the stone acorns running along the parapet relate to the legend of Bladud's discovery of the medicinal qualities of the hot springs (his pigs had been foraging for acorns). Acorns are also a reference to the Druids, who were the Princes of the Hollow Oak. Originally the central area was a cobbled open space where the only spontaneous element was the sky – the Plane trees were added in the early nineteenth century.

Sadly, just three months after work began on the construction of the Circus in 1754, Wood the Elder died, leaving his son, also John Wood (1728–81), to complete his vision. The construction of the Circus was not without difficulties or delays, but Wood the Younger did himself and his father a great service here. More than anyone else, Wood the Elder believed wholeheartedly in Bath's potential. He was involved in a number of key economic developments in Bath, such as the founding of the Mineral Water Hospital and the navigation of the River Avon.

During the thirteenth century numerous mills and weirs had been constructed along the Avon between Bristol and Bath. Whilst making the most of the river's power (and creating fishing ponds) these obstructions stopped the river being navigable. Attempts had been made since at least the 1500s to navigate the Avon, but it took over 200 years for a scheme to get off the ground. Wood identified the need to improve the River Avon as 'a necessary prelude to the architectural developments' he visualised for Bath. In fact, Bath's continuing success relied very heavily on the commercial sector being able to bring in the supplies the fashionable visitors demanded.

Objections came from West Country businessmen, farmers and miners who feared the competition from cheaper goods from Wales and the north. Nonetheless, in May 1724, John Hobbs, the Bristol deal merchant behind the development of Avon Street, set up a stock company to make the river navigable. Work to deepen and widen the Avon between Bath and Bristol began in 1725. Wood was offered the contract for a 600-yard stretch at Twerton and it was during this contract, signed on 10 March 1727, that Wood claimed he introduced the real use of the spade to Bath and improved productivity by two-thirds.

The first barge travelled from Bristol to Bath in December 1727 carrying deal, pig-lead (iron) and meal. Broad Quay was built in 1729 in order to facilitate the landing of goods; it was '480ft in length by 97ft in breadth … [and] contained eleven houses'. Bath became like an inland port, exporting commodities such as stone, woollen cloth, furniture and, in turn, importing coal, copper, iron, slate and wine. Passenger ferries passed regularly between Bath and Bristol too. Yet the navigation was beset with fraud and sabotage: bargemen refused to declare their total cargo, often resorting to violence and criminal damage rather than pay the lockkeeper the full toll.

❀ ❀ ❀ ❀ ❀

The Act of 1572 that had regulated the numbers of the sickly poor coming to Bath lapsed in 1714. Growing numbers of desperate invalids started to descend on Bath. A charity to form a hospital that could provide the facilities needed by the visiting poor to receive mineral water treatments, was established in 1716. Of course, the immediate benefit of such an institution was to rid Bath's increasingly fashionable streets of these unsightly sick and infirm visitors, but despite the commercial benefits, it would be unjust to not recognise this undertaking as being equally humanitarian. Bath has a long history of charitable provision, and whilst the authorities wanted to ensure that those who were really in need could access help they also hoped to deter vagrants and beggars.

The foundation stone of the Bath General Hospital (now the Royal National Hospital for Rheumatic Diseases, but affectionately known as the 'Min' for Mineral Water Hospital) was laid in 1738, and several of Bath's best-known philanthropists and entrepreneurs were involved from its earliest days, raising funds, donating their services and serving as trustees – including Ralph Allen, Wade, Nash, John Wood, the surgeon Jeremiah Peirce and medic William Oliver. The artist William Hoare donated portraits to adorn the walls of the new hospital.

Wood's intention was to restore Bath, because he believed it had once been the most important settlement in ancient Britain. His master plan consisted of three major building projects: an Imperial Gymnasium, a Royal Forum and a Grand Circus. Central to his Imperial Gymnasium was a general hospital, and one of his original designs for this building was circular. Difficulties finding a site and differences of opinion over the hospital's design meant that Wood had to abandon his original scheme in favour of the uninspiring rectangular block on the corner of Union Street. His circular design would, of course, come into force at the Circus twelve years later. (The Min was acquired by the local Royal United Hospitals Trust in February 2015, and continues to specialise in rheumatology, chronic fatigue and pain management.)

❀ ❀ ❀ ❀ ❀

In the rare third volume of John Wood's *Essay* (*c*. 1743), he gives a full description of his intention for the flat land between where the railway station now stands and the edge of the Abbey grounds. The Royal Forum (1740–48) was to be an enormous rectangle, 1,040ft (317m) long by 624ft (190m) wide, dissected by a canalised River Avon and centred upon 'an octangular bason of water' where the river was to be widened to create 'the haven of Bath'. On each side would have been wide piazzas 'for people to celebrate their feasts and festivals, and carry on their commerce'.

The best place to appreciate the scale of Wood's phenomenal vision is from the existing South Parade (1743–49), which represents merely one corner of his momentous plan. North Parade, Pierrepont and Duke Streets are also part of the scheme.

The Corporation were wary, doubting any development earmarked for an area with such a propensity to flood. In December 1729 the river had swelled leaving Harrison's Walks under 4ft (1.2m) of water. With Nash's influence and the success of Queen Square, Wood eventually became absolute contractor in 1739. In a feat of incredible engineering and enormous expense, Wood raised the foundations by 18ft (5.4m) to form level and flood-free terraces. This new level affected the medieval buildings in Abbey Green, for example. The pavement had to be raised and the original entrance levels are now the basements.

Wood's design for the north and south ranges were similar to the palace front he had successfully accomplished at Queen Square. His vision, however, was frankly ruined by Ralph Allen. As a sub-leaseholder Allen strove to cut the costs he and his fellow lessees had to bear. Wood noted that the 'Scheme, contrived by one of the Tenants ... to lay aside the Ornaments; to alter the Proportion of the Walk; and to erect the Terrass Wall with Rubble Stone' had been 'in Violation of the Articles' and had led 'to the Destruction of a Design, which, on Paper, hath given Pleasure and Satisfaction to Multitudes, among all Ranks of People'. The absence of any reference to Allen in Wood's first edition of *Essay* has been read as evidence of a quarrel, but it can only be a matter for speculation.

The Parades are now a rather disappointing feature of Bath's cityscape. Few visitors admire this scheme as they do Wood's other achievements. In the eighteenth century, however, the development's proximity to attractions such as the Assembly Rooms, Harrison's Walks with Delia's Grotto, the Pump Room, the theatre on Orchard Street (via Wood's St James's Portico) and Whitehall Steps, and the ferry that took visitors across to Spring Gardens, ensured its popularity with Georgian society. Numerous contemporary fan and engraved views depict this area alive with people enjoying Bath's widest pavement; Duke Street is 50ft (15m) wide. Nevertheless it was, and still is, a damning shame that Wood's dream for this part of Bath went unrealised. 'The Parades ... rather disappointed me,' says Evelina in Fanny Burney's novel of the same name:

One of them is scarce preferable to some of the best paved streets in London, and the other, though it affords a beautiful prospect, a charming view of Prior Park and the Avon, yet wanted something in *itself* of more striking elegance than a mere broad pavement, to satisfy the ideas I had formed of it.

❋ ❋ ❋ ❋ ❋

Ralph Allen, alongside Wood and Nash, is key to Bath's success at this time. He too was involved in the development of the Mineral Water Hospital and he was one of the thirty-two shareholders and one of the three treasurers appointed to the Avon Navigation Scheme.

Born in 1693 in Cornwall, Allen came from the 'middling sort', in terms of class. His father was an innkeeper, the majority of whom had some education and business sense, but they would not have been a wealthy family. It is surmised that Allen helped his uncle and then his grandmother run the local post office in the then thriving St Columb, before perhaps moving to Exeter to work for Joseph Quash, and then to Bath.

By March 1712 he had been appointed Bath's postmaster, to add to his role as the local cross-post controller – he was only 19 years old. The cross-post was a government scheme served by six main routes all originating from London, which had the country's only sorting office and all letters had to go, therefore, via London. Quash operated the cross-post between Exeter and Oxford, via Bath. In 1719 Allen proposed a way of generating franchises in order to extend

Anthony Walker: Prior Park, the seat of Ralph Allen Esq.,1750. (Bath Preservation Trust/Bath in Time)

the cross and bye-posts and create a network of postal roads that did not pass through London. He also set out to rid the service of corruption. He signed the first of many contracts with the General Post Office in 1720. Although slow to start, the business was to make Allen his first fortune, revolutionise the country's postal service and, it is estimated, save the General Post Office £1.5 million.

If Allen's biography is accurate, he was not in St Columb during the 1715 Jacobite rising, but in Bath. Allen was friendly with General Wade (he owned a portrait of the military politician), and Wade was one of Allen's financial guarantors when he made his bid to extend the country's postal system. If Allen did tip Wade off, it was about intelligence he had received as *Bath's* postmaster, not St Columb's.

In 1725, the same year that Allen was made an Honorary Freeman of the City and elected a councilman, John Wood the Elder sent him his ambitious plan for Bath. The following year, despite not yet realising a profit with the cross-posts, Allen started to buy up the stone quarries at Combe Down which had been worked since at least Roman times. The two entrepreneurs shared a vision that would bring them profit and power. Wood was a fervent advocate of Bath stone; he even turned down a lucrative contract because the client, John Wicksted, intended to use cheap stone, plaster the surface and paint it to look like brickwork. 'Such an instance of whim and caprice!' exclaimed Wood.

In 1728 Wood went with Allen to pitch for the contract to supply stone for the Greenwich Hospital project in London. They were up against the popular and favoured Portland stone. Bath stone was thought to be too soft, and there was, according to Wood, great hostility to it, 'some of the opponents maliciously comparing it to Cheshire Cheese, liable to breed Maggots that would soon devour it'. Shortly after this disappointment he and Allen started to work on designs for a mansion that would show Bath stone 'to much greater advantage'.

Prior Park was conceived with ample ornamentation inside and out to show the value, beauty and versatility of Bath stone. It was built on one of John of Tours' deer parks, hence the name. The building that Wood designed responded perfectly to the site of the natural amphitheatre at the head of a steep valley, but – in retaliation – he also undertook to surpass Colen Campbell's unrealised plan for his masterpiece Wanstead House, in Essex. (Campbell was a member of the committee who had rejected Bath stone for Greenwich.)

When Allen took over the stone quarries his plan was to make the industry more economical. He introduced the renowned stone-carriages and tramway in 1731, which transported the stone from the quarries 500ft (152m) above the River Avon, down Ralph Allen's Drive, to the Dolemeads wharf below. Bristol engineer John Padmore designed the trucks, tramway and cranes. This cut the cost per ton of stone by a quarter and was such a success that their old rival,

Portland stone, had to reduce its price by a third in order to compete. The newly navigable river enabled Allen to ship his stone to Bristol, London and beyond.

Allen also turned his attention to the masons. He lowered their rate of pay, but in return promised them constant employment and regular, weekly wages. He settled at least some of his labour force into tied cottages, which Wood designed for him in 'two small towns'. The accommodation that Allen offered his artisans was modern, of a good standard and distinguished design. The two 'towns' survive today and are interesting for both their architectural and social concerns; they are probably the oldest surviving examples of industrial housing. Nonetheless, free enterprise depends on control. This was not merely a philanthropic gesture, it was driven by the purest kind of capitalism.

The 'towns' are made up of Wood's archetypal terraces. They consist of ten and eleven houses and are about 2 miles apart. One is at the foot of Prior Park Road, near the River Avon, and the other on the top, at Combe Down. They were obviously considered together as they are thematically related. The top houses were designed for the quarrymen, who were 'concerned in digging, raising, and transporting the unwrought stone down to a common yard by the waterside'. The men could gain access to the mine at the rear of these cottages from Davidge's Bottom. In the 1770s, Earl de Montalt, who married one of Allen's nieces, renovated and enlarged these top cottages and the terrace was subsequently renamed De Montalt Place.

The masons who worked the stone were supplied with houses at Withy Bed, near to their stone-dressing sheds at the Dolemeads and the wharf at Widcombe. These lower houses, now known as Ralph Allen's Row, were erected in 1736 and have distinctive end units, with the eight middle houses linked by shared porches and a pilaster strip.

Between 1739 and 1744, Allen's friend, the poet and garden theorist Alexander Pope, designed the surrounding estate to comply with the fashionable priorities of the day. He commanded us to 'consult the genius of the place', which required a more naturalistic approach to landscape gardening and to avoid straight lines and conformity. An ongoing programme of restoration by the National Trust, who have owned the gardens since 1993, has seen the reinstatement of a number of elements from Pope's original design, including Pope's Wilderness, the Serpentine Lake and the cascade down through the 'room' to the lake by the Palladian Bridge.

Allen commissioned the Palladian Bridge in 1755; it is one of only four in the world and responds to the bridges at Wilton House and Stowe by proclaiming Allen's political allegiance to the Patriot Whigs. Allen and his friends, Pope, Dr Oliver and Jerry Peirce, were Whigs, but they increasingly aligned themselves with those who were critical of Robert Walpole's administration and those that followed Walpole's resignation in 1742. The Patriot Whigs were formed by William Pulteney, 1st Earl of Bath, in 1725, and they held meetings at Stowe, where Richard Temple, 1st Viscount Cobham, acted as mentor to a number of the rising stars, known as 'Cobham's Cubs', including George Grenville (his nephew) and William Pitt the Elder, both of whom would be future prime ministers. Pitt married Grenville's sister Hester in 1754.

Allen welcomed his friend Pitt to Prior Park on a regular basis and ensured his place in Parliament by encouraging a unanimous vote from his fellow councilmen for Pitt to stand as MP for Bath in 1757. Pitt had purchased No. 7 the Circus in around 1755. In recognition of their friendship and political allegiance, Pitt commissioned Sanderson Miller in 1755 to design a 'considerable Gothick Object which is to stand in a very fine situation on the Hills near Bath. It is for Mr Allen.'

Sham Castle endures, an eye-catcher on the side of Bathampton Down, and can easily be seen from Bath's once fashionable centre near the Abbey. The architectural splendour of the mansion, the fashionable landscape garden, the technology of the tramway and cranes and the celebrities that visited Prior Park – including Henry Fielding (who based his character Squire Allworthy on Allen), Sarah Fielding, David Garrick, Samuel Richardson, William Shenstone, Johan Hayden, Pitt and Lady Luxborough – was an intoxicating combination for Bath's visitors. People regularly climbed the steep incline to catch a glimpse of the Enlightenment in action.

Allen responded by opening the gardens to the public every Thursday afternoon. The area was filled with steps, ornaments and statues – all to show the beauty and adaptability of Bath stone and to encourage commissions. Dr Richard Pococke, Bishop of Meath and later of Ossory, noted in his diary for 15 October 1754 that he had visited Allen's gardens:

> … which are laid out in wilderness, with a piece of water in the middle, from which there is a decent, on each side of which are beautiful meadows arising up the hill; on one side is a new Gothick building, higher up is a statue of Moses with his hand striking the rock, and below it a beautiful cascade falls down about twenty feet; a little higher is the building of the Cold Bath. The centre of the gardens commands a fine view of Bath. I took a ride round by Combe to Hampton Down … Part of this ride was in the walks and woods which Mr Allen has made for ten or twelve miles round, taking in Hampton and Claverton downs.

Allen's second wife was Elizabeth Holder, and in 1742 Allen acquired the full title to Bathampton Manor from Elizabeth's brother, Charles. In 1758, Allen purchased William Bassett's old manor, Claverton, an estate that comprised

1,300 acres. It too had once been owned by the Holder family. Allen was reinstating his wife's manorial standing. The Allens continued to live at Prior Park, although they visited Claverton weekly and had a tree-lined road built to link the two properties, including the Avenue that now leads to the University of Bath campus. The Reverend John Collinson described the area in 1791:

> The upper part of the road being through a fine plantation of firs and forest trees on each side. The summit of the hill is adorned with wood, disposed in a manner that bespeaks the taste as well as the munificence of Mr. Allen; whole extensive and noble plantations are the pride and ornament of the surrounding country.

Henrietta, Lady Luxborough, recorded that Allen pointed out the fir trees he had planted. As Christopher Pound explains, by the middle of the eighteenth century, Scots pines and other firs had become fashionable after the Duke of Cumberland's Culloden campaign of 1745. On the top of Claverton Down, Allen's plantation of firs covered many acres. The firs have now been mostly removed, the large groves now only commemorated by Firs Field at Combe Down.

Claverton Down, through which Allen's road passed, was notorious for highwaymen, especially at the top of Brassknocker Hill where coaches and carriages had to make the sharp turn to go down the steep hill. Robbers took advantage as the vehicles slowed to make the manoeuvre. A quick look at the local newspaper during this period shows regular references to robberies by footpads or highwaymen at Claverton Down. Mr Ashman, a Bath musician, was robbed at pistol point. Farmer Harris Junior of Keynsham was attacked coming off Claverton Down close to Brassknocker by two footpads with pistols and cutlasses. And Mr and Mrs Whalley, travelling in a chaise from Bradford, were robbed by highwayman on Claverton Down. The area was also popular with duellists and it was this notoriety that Jane Austen played on in *Northanger Abbey* when John Thorpe takes Catherine Morland for a drive to Claverton Down.

Allen's purchase of Claverton Manor also included a 2-mile racecourse (now incorporated within the National Trust's Skyline Walk). The crowds were not renowned for their good behaviour, but Allen did not deny them their traditional pleasures – perhaps because Pitt often had horses entered. The local *Journal* for 1758 issued a warning:

> Whereas Ralph Allen, Esq. hath permitted his Down to be used for the next Races; it is to be presumed no Person will think himself treated with severity if he has an Action brought against him for doing any Damage to the Plantations on the Down, or the Walls thereof. A Watch will be set at each Plantation; and after this Notice, every Person who shall trespass will be deemed wilful Trespassers, and prosecuted as such.

> If any Person hath a Dog, that he wants to be shot or hanged, if he will produce him on the Down his Wish shall be gratify'd, Persons being hired for that Purpose from this time 'till the Races are over.

Despite its questionable reputation, however, Allen obviously felt a deep attachment to the area. Allen's clerk of works, Richard Jones, recorded in his unpublished autobiography that he visited the churchyard with Allen shortly before he died to pick out a spot for his 'vault and monument'. Allen said that he desired 'to be buried as privately and decently as possible, without pomp, in the churchyard at Claverton'. He died on 29 June 1764, aged 71.

Despite his success and extensive property portfolio, Allen was very conscious of remaining true to his origins. He would have realised the benefit of his acquaintances' regular and public declarations of his benevolence and modesty. Henry Fielding wrote that Allen's 'house, his furniture, his gardens, his hospitality … were intrinsically rich and noble without tinsel, or eternal ostentation'. Charles Yorke, son of Lord Chancellor Hardwicke, concurred, 'The elegance and judgement with which art has been employed, and the affectation of false grandeur [has been] carefully avoided' at Prior Park.

Pitt wrote to Allen's widow:

> In Mr Allen, mankind has lost such a benevolent and tender friend as, I fear, not all the example of his virtues will have power to raise up to the world his like again. Admiring his life, and deploring the shortness of it, I shall ever respectfully cherish his memory, and rank the continuation of the favourable opinion and friendship of a truly good man amongst the happiest advantages and the first honours, which fortune may have bestowed upon my life.

※ ※ ※ ※ ※

Bath became increasingly popular. Its more relaxed social rules encouraged socialisation over a more diverse demographic. In 1734, Abbé Prévost reported in *Pour et Contre* (a literary periodical):

> We shall find there at all times, Beauties of all ages who come to show their charms, young Girls and Widows in quest of Husbands, Women who seek Solace for Ones they possess, Players making or becoming dupes, musicians, Dancers, Actors, growing rich on the pleasure for which others pay, and sharing it with them; finally, Dealers in all kinds of Jewels, delicacies and gallantries, taking advantage of a kind of enchantment which blinds everyone in these realms of enjoyment to sell for their weight in gold trifles one is ashamed of having bought after leaving the place.

The unprecedented development of Bath – its amusements, facilities, lodging houses, urban landscape, entertainments, and roads – made it the most fashionable resort in the United Kingdom next to London. Visitors came from America and from all over Europe. In 1763, for example, the newspaper recorded the arrival of Count de Borzfkinkzi, Senator of Poland, Count Sandersleben and Baron Erdmansdorf (of modern Germany), Baron Feldheim, Countess de Boufflers (1724–1800) of France, and Baron Newman:

> Tis neither town nor city, yet goes by the name of both: five months in the year 'tis as populous as London, the other seven as desolate as a wilderness … In a word, 'tis a Valley of Pleasure, yet a sink of Iniquity; nor is there any intrigues or debauch acted in London, but is mimick'd here.

Bath has always celebrated its notable patrons, residents and natives, including George Frederick Handel (1685–1758) who took the waters for his rheumatism. The gifted composer, William Herschel (1738–1822) came to Bath in 1766 to try his fortune as a professional musician. He was later joined by his youngest sister, Caroline (1750–1848), and they lived together at No. 19 New King Street. The siblings developed a passionate interest in astronomy and it was in Bath that they discovered the planet Uranus. William also made discoveries about the Milky Way and Saturn. Caroline discovered eight comets. In 1782, William was awarded the title of King's Astronomer and went on to build a series of huge telescopes, including one which, at 40ft (12m), greatly impressed George III.

In 1760, George II died and was succeeded by his grandson, George III (1738–1820). George III became the longest reigning monarch, outlasting all his predecessors (although both Queen Victoria and Queen Elizabeth II would both exceed his reign). He was probably the most popular of all the Hanoverian kings, despite losing the American colonies and being considered 'mad'.

Eight

SATAN'S HEADQUARTERS:
LATE GEORGIAN

Bath, unfortunately, was a victim of its own success. What had made it fashionably exclusive and safe yet liberating became eroded by the many thousands who took the opportunity to visit Bath in the latter years of the eighteenth century. The season now lasted from September to May. The number of houses increased by 45 per cent between 1780 and 1793 alone.

Matthew Bramble, Tobias Smollett's grumpy and gouty character in *The Expedition of Humphry Clinker* (1771), vividly expresses this change and his displeasure at having to share Bath with the masses who are, in his opinion, less sophisticated and either 'new' money or gold-diggers (the irony, of course, is that he and his party are hardly nobility):

Every upstart of fortune, harnessed in the trappings of the mode, presents himself at Bath, as in the very focus of observation – Clerks and factors from the East Indies, loaded with the spoil of plundered provinces; planters, negro-drivers, and hucksters, from our American plantations, enriched they know not how; agents, commissaries, and contractors, who have fattened, in two successive wars, on the blood of the nation; usurers, brokers, and jobbers of every kind; men of low birth, no breeding, have found themselves suddenly translated into a state of affluence, unknown to former ages; and no wonder that their brains should be intoxicated with pride, vanity, and presumption. Knowing no other criterion of greatness, but the ostentation of wealth, they discharge their affluence without taste or conduct, through ever channel of the most absurd extravagance; and all of them hurry to Bath, because here, without any further qualification, they can mingle with the princes and nobles of the land. Even the wives and daughters of low tradesmen, who, like shovel-nosed sharks, prey upon the blubber of those uncouth whales of fortune, are infected with the same rage of displaying their importance; and the slightest indisposition serves them for a pretext to insist upon being conveyed to Bath, where they may hobble country-dances and cotillions among lordlings, squires, counsellors, and clergy. These delicate creatures from Bedfordbury, Butcher-row, Crutched-friers, and Botolph-lane, cannot breathe in the gross air of the Lower Town, or conform to the vulgar rules of a common lodging-house; the husband, therefore, must provide an entire house, or elegant apartments in the new buildings. Such is the composition of what is called the fashionable company at Bath; where a very inconsiderable proportion of genteel people are lost in a mob of impudent plebeians, who have neither understanding nor judgement, not the least idea of propriety and decorum; and seem to enjoy nothing so much as an opportunity of insulting their betters.

Thus the number of people, and the number of houses continue to increase; and this will ever be the case, till the streams that swell this irresistible torrent of folly and extravagance, shall either be exhausted, or turned into other channels, by incidents and events which I do not pretend to foresee.

Some of the most iconic illustrations from this period are Thomas Rowlandson's (1757–1827) satirical 'comic drolls', called the *Comforts of Bath* (1798). The series was originally known as *Matthew Bramble's Trip to Bath*.

Smollett, in turn, said his novel had been greatly influenced by Christopher Anstey's (1724–1805) hugely successful *The New Bath Guide* (1766). Anstey's

Thomas Rowlandson: The Artist's Studio, Plate 6, Comforts of Bath, 1798. (Bath Central Library/Bath in Time)

poem was delivered in five editions in its first year of publication and eventually ran to eleven. These three humorous, though mocking, works of creativity illustrate perfectly how the reputation of Bath had turned around inexplicably in a few mere decades.

The population of Bath when Richard 'Beau' Nash arrived was around 2,000; at his death it was 10,000 and by 1800 it had risen to 34,000. Wood's architecture set a pattern which other architects followed and helped to create the unified city that we know today. Almost all of Bath was created by local men who had started out as builders, learning the trade as they went along, as opposed to researching classical architecture on a Grand Tour to Italy, or under the guidance of an established Palladian academic. Other than the period leading up to and during the American War of Independence (1765–83), when speculative building ceased, Bath was a town of huge expansion.

There were three major building booms (1725–58, 1762–64 and 1783–93), leading commentators such as Smollett to describe the city as 'a rage of building'. Horace Walpole claimed that he detested Bath, writing that he thought the new buildings 'look like a collection of little hospitals – all crammed together, and surrounded with perpendicular hills'. The artist Thomas Gainsborough wrote to Richard Stevens MP in 1767, 'I believe Sir it would astonish you to see how the new buildings are extending in all points from the centre of Bath'.

Key areas of expansion were on Barton Fields and Lansdown and across the river at Bathwick. Brock Street, which leads west from the Circus, was laid out by John Wood the Younger (1728–82) from 1763 and, just like Gay Street, serves as an understated link between two architectural masterpieces. The Woods had immense skill for both town planning and the capacity to create an emotional response from the built environment. Just as you cannot truly appreciate the magnificence that awaits you as you trudge up Gay Street, so the placement of Brock Street hides the impact of the Royal Crescent until it suddenly bursts upon you.

John Wood the Elder had intended to have short roads radiating from his Circus, but his son decided to elongate Brock Street and build the Royal Crescent (1767–75) at the end. Architectural historian Walter Ison wrote that the Crescent is 'the greatest single achievement in the whole field of our urban architecture'. Whereas Queen Square and the Circus form enclosed architectural spaces, the Royal Crescent embraces the surrounding landscape with its wide open sweep. There is no question that the Royal Crescent represents a momentous pinnacle in British architectural history, but this is the Elder's temple to the moon, and whilst it is undoubtedly his concept and design, the understated elegance of the building and the dramatic augmentation of the natural landscape setting is the triumph of his son.

Reece Winstone: Royal Crescent, Bath, A Gordon Fraser Card, *c.* 1940. (Author's Collection)

The Royal Crescent comprises thirty houses of identical frontage, over 49ft (15m) high. The decoration is extremely simple, especially when compared to the Circus. It consists of a giant order of 114 Ionic columns, each 20ft (6m) tall. The central house, now the Royal Crescent Hotel, has columns flanked in pairs, as do the end corners on houses No. 1 and 30. The curvature of the elliptical geometry was increased towards each end of the crescent so that the façades of the two end houses face each other. These façades then continue round each corner to form handsome end pieces.

The foundation stone for No. 1 Royal Crescent (now a museum) was laid in May 1767. Most of the houses were finished by 1774, and all were finally occupied by September 1778. Just as at Queen Square and the Circus, each of the houses on the Royal Crescent was built speculatively and sporadically over a number of years. Wood's position as architect and surveyor ensured that each individual builder complied fully with his design so that each house perfectly occupied its place on the ellipse. It is a remarkable achievement.

Each conveyance stated that the builders should copy No. 1 for external decoration, height, roofline and position of the chimneys, etc. Wood was entitled to make two site visits a year 'to view, search and see the state and condition of the repairation'. He specified white paint for both the windows and doors –

innovative at this time when most developments were painting woodwork brown. The finest ashlar stone was used for the fronts, whilst rubble stone was seen to be adequate for the backs (a common expression was 'Queen Anne at the front, Mary-Ann at the back'). The interior plan was up to the individual builder or initial leaseholder, meaning that some houses were fitted out with exquisite and expensive detailing, whilst others were completed with stock mouldings.

The builder also had to pave a breadth of 12ft (3.5m) in front of their plot 'with the best sort of stone of the pennant kind … and shall … raise the same one foot above the pitching of the coachway and border the same with a deep good strong course of pitching stone'. Bath was acclaimed for its pavements – raised up above the general mire, they allowed for the company to parade safely and cleanly. The builder also had to pay a share for the building and upkeep of the pedestrian pathway between the Circus and the Royal Crescent. Finally, each builder agreed that the house they completed would not be let to tradesmen who might carry out any 'noisesome, noisy or offensive trade' such as melting tallow, baking, stone cutting, slaughtering or brewing.

The residents' lawn in front slopes down towards a ha-ha – an ingenious invention that contains the livestock but does not spoil the view. This is probably its first urban use (it is generally agreed that the first occurrence of a ha-ha in Britain was at Stowe, Buckinghamshire). Part of the condition of sale was that trees were not allowed to exceed 8ft (2.5m) in height and no buildings were to block the view, otherwise Wood had the right to 'wholly reduce to the ground' any contravening obstruction. There are still no buildings that block the front prospect.

In 1779 Elizabeth Montagu, the celebrated hostess and writer, was mortified that there was not a house available on the Royal Crescent and 'was obliged to content [herself] with one in the Circus'. She later moved to No. 16 Royal Crescent where she enthused about 'the beautiful situation [which] cannot be understood by any comparison with anything in any town whatsoever'.

※ ※ ※ ※ ※

By the 1760s, Bath's Assembly Rooms were seen to be old-fashioned, too small to accommodate the increasing numbers of visitors, and – now ironically – too far away from the chic part of town. In 1765, the Corporation invited John Wood the Younger and Scottish architect Robert Adam to submit plans for a new assembly room. It was a further three years, however, before the Corporation accepted a revised plan from Wood.

To finance the build, Wood set up a 'tontine' subscription, whereby the shares of those who died were added to the holdings of the survivors, with the last man standing inheriting everything. He opened the list in November 1768 and within five months had raised £14,000 from fifty-three shareholders. The total cost of the build was £20,000, making it the largest investment in a single building in Bath during the eighteenth century.

The foundation stone was laid on 26 May 1769 and the sumptuous interior was finished in 1771. Essentially a U-shaped building, it contained a ballroom which could house up to 800 dancers, a tearoom and the octagon (for gambling); a further card room was added in 1777. Sedan chairs could be kept out of the rain and tucked away from view in the colonnade along the north side of the ballroom. Pedestrians used the main entrance, whilst those who arrived by carriage alighted at the north-west and south-west doors. These provisions ensured the seamless arrival and departure of the hundreds of guests.

The Rooms were opened on 30 September 1771 with a Ridotto (a combination of a dance and musical concert). The master of ceremonies (MC) was Captain William Wade, the great nephew of General Wade. For the first six years he acted as MC for both the Upper and Lower Rooms. However, he was forced to leave Bath in 1777 when John Hooke Campbell, Lord Lyon of Scotland, named him in a divorce suit.

Indicative of the Lower Rooms' diminishing status, subsequent MCs aspired to the position at the Upper Rooms – a number (including Richard Tyson, James King and James Heaviside) all moved from the Lower to the Upper Rooms. In 1797, Caroline Powys compared King's ball at the Lower Rooms unfavourably with Tyson's at the Upper Rooms, her main complaint being the comparably cramped accommodation which 'made the croud [sic] very disagreeable indeed'.

Many of Jane Austen's characters attended events at the Assembly Rooms, although Lady Dalrymple in *Persuasion* had no interest because the middle classes dominated the Rooms, so she preferred attending and hosting private parties. In 1780, Fanny Burney wrote that she and her company took pains to avoid 'the showy, tonish people who are only to be seen by going to the Rooms, which we never do'. Matthew Bramble luridly described the 'compound of villainous smells, in which the most violent stinks, and the most powerful perfumes, contended for the mastery'. 'Imagine', he commanded:

a high essence of mingled odours, arising from putrid gums, imposthumated lungs, sour flatulencies, rank arm-pits, sweating feet, running sores and issues, plasters, ointments, and embrocations, hungary-water, spirit of lavender … musk; besides a thousand frowzy steams, which I could not analyze. Such, … is the fragrant aether we breathe in the polite assemblies of Bath.

The higher ranks of society started to entertain at home, something that had been outlawed during Nash's tenure.

※ ※ ※ ※ ※

The topography of Bath's seven steep hills was one of the greatest challenges that faced the city's Georgian developers. It was both costly and treacherous to create level sites for building. Whilst John Wood sliced into the side of Lansdown to create the Circus, other developers stepped their terraces up the steep inclines of Bath.

On Lansdown Road, Belmont (originally Bellemont Row), for instance, is a terrace of twenty houses built between 1768 and 1773. The larger rooms are situated at the back to make the most of the prospect. It was often the case that sites were chosen because of the views they afforded, despite the difficult and costly nature of the extensive retaining walls and vast vault systems required before building the actual dwellings could start. At nearby Camden Crescent, nature proved too difficult to tame. As building neared completion in 1788, a landslide swept away the last five houses at the eastern end. The crescent was never finished and, if you look, you will see that the central pediment is not actually in the centre.

As Bath continued to develop northwards, so the rugged nature of the landscape made the continued devotion to the Palladian architectural style practically impossible. Built in 1789–93 by John Palmer (1738–1817), Lansdown Crescent illustrates this change in taste by taking full advantage of its picturesque surroundings. A series of serpentine terraces follow the contours

Lansdown Crescent, Bath.

Oct.   1812

Lansdown Crescent and All Saints Chapel, 1812. (Bath Central Library/Bath in Time) of the hillside and abandon the formal layout of earlier developments, such as at Queen Square.

The steep approach to the crescent has meant that the setting has remained pastoral – sheep still graze in the field at the front. It would never have been possible to transform this area into a formal lawn such as at the Royal Crescent. Lansdown Crescent thus fulfils the sublime requirements of the Picturesque Movement and has been described as 'the pinnacle of the Georgian suburban dream of *rus in urbe* [countryside in the town]'.

Originally the picturesque quality of this development, financed by Charles Spackman, was made even more explicit by the establishment of All Saints Chapel (1788–94), a Georgian Gothic proprietary chapel also designed by Palmer. The dramatic change in ground level on the site meant that when viewed from Lansdown Crescent the chapel was tucked away in a neat hollow, but when viewed from the south or High Common the chapel provided a spectacular eye catcher enhanced by its isolation and height against the backdrop of Lansdown Crescent and neighbouring Somerset Place. Sadly the chapel was gutted during the Bath Blitz of April 1942.

Thomas Warr Attwood (1733–75) was a member of the building committee that sat for thirteen years choosing a new design for the guildhall. He was the City Surveyor and so was able to steer building policy in directions which gave him, as official architect, endless opportunities to acquire profitable contracts. He not only built for the Corporation, but his position enabled him to acquire leases of city property and then develop them as a private builder, effectively giving himself the contracts. He built the Paragon (1769–71) and Oxford Row (*c.* 1775) in this manner. He also built the new prison in Bathwick, in what is now known as Grove Street. Attwood received the Corporation's approval for his design for the new Guildhall in 1775, but he was killed on site when a floor collapsed on him. Thomas Baldwin, his former assistant, had his plans accepted by the city the following year.

Baldwin became City Surveyor and went on to design Somersetshire Buildings on the east side of Milsom Street in 1782 (the site of the old poor house). In 1746 the Corporation had leased land to Daniel Milsom (a wine cooper) to enable development that would link Bath's upper and lower towns. Negotiations over access through the city walls meant that it was in fact his son, Charles, who embarked on the development in 1761. Milsom Street was originally built as lodging houses, but it quickly became Bath's luxury retail quarter. Even London struggled to compete with the choice and quality of the fine goods to be found in Bath. Out of season it was said you could fire a musket down Milsom Street without fear of scaring anybody but a dog. As Bath's popularity grew, however, so did the industry of its day-to-day running. The street criers, who nosily competed with each other, had become such a nuisance by 1784 that the Corporation decided they should be banned, pushing trade exclusively to the shops and market stalls.

The River Avon acted as a barrier to expansion. Whilst Bath grew rapidly, advancing north up the steep slopes of Lansdown, so prime real estate lay undeveloped just across the river. On behalf of his wife Frances, Sir William Johnstone Pulteney (1729–1805) instructed architects Robert (1728–92) and James (1732–94) Adam to design a bridge. Pulteney Bridge was built in 1769–74 and is unique in having been designed with shops as an integral part of the original concept. There is some suggestion that the bridge was built just to provide easier access to the Bathwick Meadows, but the ornate design, choice of architects and inclusion of integrated business premises makes this seem highly unlikely. Nevertheless, the building of the bridge cost far more than Pulteney expected, it was therefore vital that the land be developed. In 1777, the Adam brothers were invited to submit plans for the 600 acre estate, but their scheme was probably too expensive, especially at a time when the demand for new buildings was diminishing – '1778 to the year 1783,' wrote a local surveyor, 'by reason of our dispute with America, our army and navy being then on service, the seasons at Bath were so little frequented that houses in Bath were greatly reduced in value.'

In 1782 Frances died, leaving the entire Pulteney fortune to her only daughter, Henrietta Laura (1766–1808), subject to a life's income for William. Together, father and daughter commissioned Thomas Baldwin to draw up new plans, and work eventually began in 1788. After the Woods, Baldwin had the most influence on how Bath took shape.

Baldwin's more economical development for Bathwick New Town proceeded rapidly, with 105 ninety-nine-year leases granted between 1788 and 1793. The land was levelled, and the grand buildings constructed over a vast vault system that raised them above the flood plain. Just how impressive this engineering work was can easily be determined when you look up at the raised level of Johnstone Street from the Recreation Ground. It is also macabrely illustrated by the demise of Mr Smithett, a cellar man at the Bear Inn, who stepped off the pavement in Johnstone Street in January 1792 and fell 20ft (6m) to his death.

Baldwin designed a scheme of crescents, squares and streets radiating off from the central spine of Great Pulteney Street (1788). His work began with Laura Place, where four streets of irregular widths meet, the grandest being Great Pulteney Street, described as Bath's most impressive thoroughfare.

It divides to form a lozenge shape around Sydney Gardens and was intended to join up again and continue in the same magnificent way as Upper Pulteney Street. Baldwin planned eight terraces of houses fronting the road and gardens,

Great Pulteney Street, postcard, 1930s. (Author's Collection)

but only the fourteen houses of Sydney Place were completed to his design. Halfway up Great Pulteney Street, on the left, is Sunderland Street, only one house long, but it was intended to lead to an impressive residential area to be called Frances Square after Pulteney's wife. On the right are three more incomplete roads, namely Johnstone, Edward and William. They were designed to lead to Great Annandale Street, which would have run parallel to Great Pulteney Street.

However, disaster struck. The speculative development of Bathwick was largely financed by Messrs Bayly, Sons, Gutch and Cross, trading as the Bath City Bank, one of the two leading Bath banks that crashed in 1793. In the wake of the French Revolution, war broke out between France and England instigating a surge in interest rates. Creditors called in their loans, the banks crashed and the wave of bankruptcies was like a cataclysmic game of dominoes. Baldwin was amongst those ruined, and in 1794 was forced to sell both his home on Great Pulteney Street and all its contents.

Despite the heavy losses, Bath remained optimistic of a return to the boom years and many alternative plans for finishing the Bathwick Estate were instigated, but other than New Sydney Place, completed by John Pinch in 1808, there was no significant residential development between 1793 and 1810.

Despite Bath's rapid expansion during the eighteenth century relatively little development occurred within the city walls. Contemporary accounts complain of the narrowness of the lanes, traffic congestion and historic buildings obstructing natural routes around the city centre and on to the upper town. The passage to the Cross and Hot Baths, for example, was via a narrow dog-legged lane. Wood deplored 'the little dark dirty narrow passages' in order to reach the baths, 'as though the citizens were ashamed of the hot waters, their staple commodity'.

The Bath Improvement Act (1789) gave the Corporation powers to enlarge the Pump Room, improve the baths and enter into compulsory purchase contracts should they need to in order to widen Cheap Street and Stall Street, and create Union Street, which – as its name suggests – integrated the old and new towns coherently for the first time via Stall and Milsom Streets. A number of older properties, including the yard to the Bear Inn, were removed to facilitate these improvements.

As City Surveyor, it was Baldwin who was engaged to undertake the work – in actual fact, much of his plan had been approved and work had started the previous year. His plan involved the complete rebuilding of the Pump Room and the King's Bath complex, the creation of a new suite of baths and five new streets: Bath Street, Beau Street, Hot Bath Street and Nash Street. That the entire project, except for Nash Street, was achieved says much for the Corporation's determination to keep Bath profitable at this time.

The first element to be built were the colonnades facing Stall Street, and each section is divided into nine equal bays by ten Ionic columns. The north segment is open, allowing access to the west front of the Abbey. The southern segment

Grand Pump Room, postcard posted in March 1928. (Author's Collection)

is closed and provided access to the New Private Baths (1788–89) (this would become the entrance to the King's and Queen's Baths and is now one of the entrances to the Roman Baths Museum). The triangular pediments feature two sphinxes on either side of a wreath, surrounding the head of Hygeia in profile.

Next was the erection of the Grand Pump Room. John Harvey's original Pump Room was almost immediately too small. The building was remodelled and extended during the first half of the eighteenth century, but Baldwin advocated a total new build. Although completed by John Palmer, Baldwin started the project in 1791. He was dismissed in 1792 because he refused to show the Corporation his account books (he was declared bankrupt the following year).

The inscription over the entrance is Greek for 'water is best' and, as was fashionable at this time, there are a number of Greek Revival stylistic attributes to the design. The Grand Pump Room was opened by the Duchess of York, and nearby York Street, created in around 1806, was named after Frederick Augustus, Duke of York, who had also attended the opening. By the end of the eighteenth century the Pump Room was merely a place to go to meet people, as with Mrs Allen and Catherine Morland in Austen's *Northanger Abbey*. However, the Sunday crowd was intolerable to them. In fact none of the main characters in *Persuasion* visited the Pump Room.

Bath Street, originally Cross Bath Street, with its Ionic colonnades and crescent-shaped termini, was laid out in 1791 by Baldwin as a new link between the Cross Bath, amenities on Stall Street and the new Grand Pump Room. Baldwin's scheme was built 'for the honour and dignity' of Bath, although the improvements did not show their advantages immediately to everyone. Fanny Burney wrote on 8 September 1791 that Bath 'is so filled with workmen, dust, & lime … Even the streets around the Pump room are pulling down for new Edifices, & you can only drink from their choice stream, by wading through their chosen mud'.

※ ※ ※ ※ ※

By the 1790s Bath was welcoming as many as 30,000 visitors a year, and a typical day had not changed. The visitors bathed, drank the waters (2 quarts, or eighteen glasses), worshipped, visited the coffee houses, went to a concert or saw a play, and engaged in a dance or a game of dice or cards. Between about 10 a.m., when the company left the Pump Room, and 3 p.m., when most people retired to their lodgings to dine, however, people needed to fill their time. A look at contemporary letters and diaries shows that people enjoyed walking, especially on the Parades, taking a carriage ride, visiting the libraries, shopping and visiting artists' showrooms (they also, naturally, sat for a portrait).

At one time, Bath boasted 160 artists – mostly portrait or miniature painters. There was good business to be had. Commentators such as Daniel Webb spoke of the Englishman's unrivalled passion for portraits, whilst Thomas Bardwell noted in 1756, 'It is well known, that no Nation in the World delights so much in Face-painting, or gives so generous Encouragement to it as our own'.

Britain was obsessed with portraiture and few eighteenth-century painters made a living away from the portrait business. Thomas Gainsborough (1727–88), who spent fourteen years in Bath, spoke of 'picking pockets in the portrait way'. He started out charging 5 guineas a head, but eventually charged 40 guineas for a half-length portrait and 100 guineas for a full-length one. To put this in some context, the average wage for a labourer in the 1750s was £20 a year. Gainsborough's approachable personality and lively conversation also attracted sitters as, very often, it was the fear of boredom that put many potential sitters off having their portrait painted. He was also quick, so reducing the sitting time. On the other hand Robert Edge Pine (c. 1730–88), in Bath from 1772 to 1779, who had his studio and show room at Hetling Court, off Westgate Buildings, found his career was hampered by a 'morbidly irritable' temperament. He is perhaps now more famous for opening the first artists' showroom in Philadelphia, USA, in 1786.

Visiting artists' studios became part of the daily routine in Bath and artists started to set aside rooms in which the public could view works they owned and others they had painted. The 'shew' rooms also acted as drying rooms for the oil painting commissions. Gainsborough showed old masters alongside his own work, inciting the public to favourably compare the two. Artists tended to charge for entrance, some provided refreshments and others entertainment. Horace Walpole described a morning he spent at Thomas Beach's (1738–1806) house at No. 2 Westgate Buildings, in 1781:

> A little private concert, in the picture rooms of Mr Beach of Bath. Amongst the performers were the celebrated Mr Salomon, Sig. Tenducci, and Miss Guest … A fine light and shade being thrown upon the paintings, every one found himself surrounded, as if by magic, by a number of his acquaintances, breathing in canvass … About fifty ladies and gentlemen formed the audience; and, in such natural shapes did the pictures look upon, and seem to listen to us, that it was difficult to persuade ourselves they were not auditors also.

The artist William Hoare (1707–92) was in Bath from 1738 until his death in 1792. Richard Graves praised Hoare as 'not only the most virtuous, friendly and inoffensive of men, but one of the best classical scholars both in Greek and in Latin with whom I was ever acquainted'. This was a huge compliment as one's knowledge of the Classics dictated your social acceptance during the eighteenth century. Before the eighteenth century, the names of non-court painters would not have been known, their status the equivalent of any other tradesman or craftsman. Hoare, alongside Gainsborough, was one of the founder members of the Royal Academy, but by staying in Bath Hoare appears to have played very little part in the institution's administration.

One of Gainsborough's more renowned group portraits from his Bath period is *The Linley Sisters* (c. 1772), now in Dulwich Picture Gallery. Gainsborough, also an accomplished musician, was a friend of Elizabeth and Mary's father, Thomas. Thomas Linley was the organist at Margaret Chapel on Brock Street (he was also a shareholder in the enterprise that built the chapel). Thomas and his wife, Mary, had eight children, they were all accomplished musicians and the family was known as 'The Nest of the Nightingales'.

Their eldest daughter, Elizabeth (1754–92), was a fine singer and a renowned beauty. The Bishop of Meath said that she 'formed the connecting link between angel and woman'. George III was also known to admire her. Her love life, however, was complicated and scandalous. She broke off her engagement to Walter Long, a 60-year-old Wiltshire landowner, in 1771, reputedly because she was having an affair with married family friend, Captain Thomas Matthews.

Richard Brinsley Sheridan (1751–1816), the writer and politician, wrote that Elizabeth sang 'like an angel'. Obviously infatuated, he helped her to escape from Bath. Initially she intended to enter a convent in Lille, France, but Sheridan declared his love for her and the two were secretly married near Calais in 1772. (That marriage was illegal and so they married again in London in April 1773.) The elopement greatly angered Matthews, who wrote a number of insulting letters to Sheridan and published an advertisement in the *Bath Chronicle and Weekly Gazette*.

Sheridan challenged Matthews to a duel in London. Sheridan won and, although Matthews apologised, he continued to cause trouble. This naturally could not go unchallenged and a second duel was fought, this time at Kingsdown near Bath. Matthews proved the stronger, and in an ungentlemanly fight he struck Sheridan in the neck several times with the broken tip of his sword whilst strangling him. Sheridan was left dangerously ill. Public sympathy was with Sheridan and Matthews was never seen in Bath again.

Delia's Grotto on Harrison's Walks can still be seen today below North Parade Bridge. It predates Sheridan and Elizabeth's romance, but is thought to have been where they met. The name refers to Sheridan's play, *The Rivals*. Delia is the pseudonym adopted by Mrs Malaprop in her correspondence with Sir Lucius O'Trigger, who thinks the letters are actually coming from the beautiful Lydia.

Bath also attracted a number of important academics and authors, many of whom wrote about the city. Catharine Macaulay (1731–91), the historian, lived in Bath for four years from 1774. Frances, or Fanny, Burney (Mme d'Arblay, 1752–1840) stayed at No. 14 South Parade; she wrote the novel *Evelina* in 1778, when aged 25. Her characters visit Bath, where they are particularly surprised by the lack of decorum shown in the baths. The novel won instant popularity and was praised by Dr Johnson. Two years later she visited Bath and was welcomed as an important champion of contemporary literature. Her diary is a wealth of source material on the characters and social life of the later eighteenth century, when Bath's fashionable heyday had passed. Although Burney dismissed much of the clientele, she was an admirer of Bath and noted its elegant houses and beautiful streets. Fanny and her sister also stayed at No. 19 New King Street on one of their frequent visits to Bath. She is buried at Walcot Church.

The artist, botanist and educationalist, Mary Delany (1700–88) was a regular visitor, her second husband, Dr Delany, died in Bath in 1768. And the educationalist Hannah More (1745–1833) retired to Bath, living on Great Pulteney Street. Because their friends knew Bath it was an easy subject for their correspondence, leaving future historians with a rich inheritance.

From 1772, Lady (Anna) Miller (1741–81) and her husband, Sir John, held fashionable literary soirées fortnightly during the season at their home, Batheaston Villa. Anstey was a regular attendee and contributor to these events, which encouraged guests to bring with them poems on a prearranged topic. The poems were then ceremoniously placed in an ancient Roman vase brought from Frascati. Once judged, Lady Miller crowned the winner with a wreath of myrtle. Walpole ridiculed these assemblies for being elitist, vain and unscholarly. In response to the given subject, 'The Ancient and Modern Dress and Manners of the English Nation compared', Anstey, who had moved permanently to Bath in 1770, penned *An Election Ball. The Imitation Ode*. Anstey drew inspiration from the lavish ball held by Sir John Seabright in 1775, to celebrate his return to Parliament as a member for Bath.

Anstey's satire was written in the form of poetical letters from Mr Inkle, who has accompanied his daughter Margery (Madge) to Bath, to his wife who remained at home in Gloucester. The poem focuses on Madge, who is thrilled that she has been invited to the ball. She is determined to appear like a lady of the highest fashion and so creates an outlandish headdress. To an old ginger wig she adds dripping, flour, jewellery, a cushion, fruit, flowers and all sorts of other things she can find. And, rather than the more normal ostrich feathers, Madge tops off her headdress with the rump of a live cockerel. It is so big she finds it difficult to even get in the sedan chair that arrives to take her to the ball. Nevertheless, once at the ball, her ridiculous headdress is greatly admired by the fashionistas and she is asked to dance by Billy Dasher, a macaroni (a fashionable fop or dandy). Madge's great admirer, Mr Squirt, becomes jealous and 'accidentally' pours thick

So to please his revenge, he pretend'd to stoop
And on poor Billy Dasher dispos'd of his soup.
And Soup a la Reine so exceedingly rich is,
It fasten'd like Glue to his flesh-colour'd breeches,

Alas! how my soul was prophetic of Evil!
Oh! I wish that old Barnaby Buzz al y Devil!
Assure as you live, that conceited old prig
The candle knock'd down on poor Margery's wig?

John Sneyd: Illustration to Christopher Anstey's *An Election Ball*, 1815. (Bath Central Library/Bath in Time)

soup over Dasher. In the resulting fracas, a candle is knocked over and sets light to Madge's headdress and completely ruins her outfit. Dasher challenges Squirt to a duel and Marge retires from the ball embarrassed and deeply disappointed.

With the sudden death of Lady Miller, Anstey lost his muse. He became friends with Fanny Burney, who found him 'shyly important and silently proud'. He joined the committee of the Mineral Water Hospital and was key to the successful appeal to enable the building of the attic extension. Through his friendship with Hannah More, Anstey found his muse again and produced a number of important poems in the last decade of his life – although nothing on the scale of *The New Bath Guide* or *An Election Ball*. He did, however, write a poem in Latin in praise of Dr Jenner and his work to find a vaccination against smallpox.

The great tragic actress Sarah Siddons (1755–1831) lived at No. 33 The Paragon. Her performances in 1775 had not been well received in London; however the Bath audience loved her. She first performed at Bath's Theatre

Royal on Old Orchard Street in October 1778, in the *Provoked Husband*, *School for Scandal* and *Bladud*. Her performance as Elvira, the following month, won her the accolade 'as the most capital actress that has performed here these many years'. On the back of her success in this city she was invited back to join the company at the Drury Lane Theatre, London, by David Garrick. Although he never performed in Bath, Garrick (1717–79) did visit at least four times to take the waters, staying at Mrs White's lodging house on North Parade. Garrick enjoyed Bath, describing to Hannah More in May 1775, 'I do this, & do that, & do Nothing, & I go here and go there and go nowhere – Such is ye life of Bath & such the Effects of this place upon me – I forget my Cares, & my large family in London, & Every thing'.

※ ※ ※ ※ ※

Before Nash suppressed the carrying and using of swords, duels were fought in the Orange Grove, where Webster died, and afterwards at the Dell, in what was to become Royal Victoria Park. Richard Sheridan and Captain Thomas Matthews fought their duel at Kingsdown (near Box) in 1772. What is said to have been the last legal duel to be fought in England took place on Claverton Down in 1778 between Captain Rice and Vicomte du Barré. Du Barré was killed and is buried in Bathampton Churchyard. Rice got off with a lighter punishment than the murder he was charged with by proving du Barré was the instigator and provided the weapons. Although duelling was banned in Bath, it was still fashionable for visitors to take fencing lessons or watch displays.

One such spectacle was performed by Charles-Geneviève-Louis-Auguste-André-Timothée d'Éon de Beaumont (1728–1810) at the Lower Assembly Rooms in 1796. Chevalier d'Éon, as he was more commonly known, came to Bath in December 1795 in order to give a series of demonstrations of the Art of Defence. He stayed until March 1796. He was a notorious character: a French diplomat, spy and soldier who had fought in the Seven Years War. He had successfully infiltrated the Russian Court, disguised as a woman. Later, when he had been sent to London to help negotiate the Treaty of Paris, he deserted his post. He returned to France with a pardon from Louis XVI, but came back to England at the start of the French Revolution. For thirty-three years from 1777, d'Éon dressed as a woman and claimed that his parents had forced him to live as a boy. Doctors who examined his body after he died stated that they would have assigned him male.

In later life, he made his living from teaching and giving exhibitions of his sword skills, sometimes he wore his military uniform, sometimes he dressed in female attire. He fascinated the public and almost a year before he visited Bath

Chevalier d'Éon de Beaumont, 1728. (Author's Collection)

the *Bath Herald and Gazetteer* published an article entitled *Concise account of Chevalier d'Éon*. The following January he displayed *A Grande Assault D'Armes*. 'A true representation of an attack and defence in single combat, sword in hand with an English gentleman. Mademoiselle d'Éon choose to dress as a Captain of the Dragoons for this display'.

Mademoiselle d'Éon was a friend of the radical (and bawdy) politician John Wilkes (1725–97). Wilkes notoriously became infatuated with the married Maria Stafford after meeting her in Bath in January 1778 – Emmanuel Green published his love letters to her in 1918. Stafford almost compromised herself, but was saved by the timely intervention of a friend. Rebuffed, Wilkes criticised her for keeping up 'a foolish prudery which the present age is too refined to relish or approve'. Wilkes' friend Thomas Potter, whilst accusing him of leading him astray, was very keen that Wilkes leave his humdrum life in Aylesbury and travel to Bath with him as long as 'life and spirit and wit and humour and gaiety but above all if the heavenly inspired passion called lust have not deserted' him. Bath's licentious reputation had ripened to such an extent that it was the favoured destination for a debauched 'stag-do'. Potter and Wilkes were also friends with Pitt.

When Allen helped Pitt win his seat at Bath, Pitt's seat at Okehampton was won by Potter, which left Potter's Aylesbury seat to Wilkes. Sadly, this quartet's mutual co-operation was tested by Pitt and Allen's public falling out in 1763 over George III's treaty with France. (The King agreed to end the Seven Years War by signing the Peace of Paris.) As a loyal subject, Allen had congratulated the monarch on an 'adequate peace'. He was supported by sixteen fellow councillors, but Pitt objected to Allen's message as he did not support the end of the war and disliked the term 'adequate'.

Allen was also criticised for his motives; wartime economy is notoriously unstable and few investments were being made towards building projects. Running naval battles with the French in the English Channel also made it more difficult for Allen to transport his stone from the port of Bristol around to London, or to the Continent. Allen was therefore seen to be keen for the war to end to aid his business interests; he became the butt of a political satire, *The Knights of Baythe, or the One Headed Corporation*. A companion print, *A Sequel to the Knights of Baythe, or the One Headed Corporation*, shows Wilkes drawing aside a curtain to show the antics of the Corporation of Bath, with the words, 'I'll shew them in their proper colours'.

Wilkes used his weekly publication, *The North Briton*, to criticise the King's pro-treaty speech and the prime minister, Lord Bute's 'betrayal' through what Wilkes considered an overly generous peace with France. Wilkes was accused of libel and a warrant was issued for his arrest.

�֍ �֍ �֍ ✖ ✖

After centuries of religious power struggles the early Georgians were at best apathetic towards organised religion. The influx of visitors put pressure on Bath's parish churches and the majority were enlarged, refurbished or rebuilt. The working classes, even if they could afford the cost of a pew, found their churches full during the season. The Reverend Penrose complained that 'a stranger cannot get a sitting under half a crown at time, or a guinea for the season'. This situation was alleviated by the opening, in 1798, of the Free Church (Christ Church) on Julian Road. Yet burials were expensive too, and all 'except the rich and great, are carried, when dead to the churchyards of Widcombe or ... Bathwick'. The Catholic community was swelled by those fleeing the French Revolution, and although Bath's Catholic Mission had been burnt down during the Gordon Riots in June 1780, by 1793 the *Bath Chronicle* was comfortable to report on the service held for King Louis, after his beheading, by the French refugee clergy and nationals 'who have here found a shelter from the distractions in their own unhappy country'.

The south-west, in general, was tolerant of a number of Nonconformist religions towards the end of the eighteenth century. In Bath, Philip Thicknesse wrote that worshippers of all modes of faith were offered the greatest freedom. Some religious leaders were attracted to Bath because of its wayward reputation. 'The hardships of bathing,' wrote historian R.S. Neale, were 'sweetened by the knowledge that it was accompanied by amatory dalliance, sexual titillation and open prostitution'. John Wesley (1703–91), the Methodist evangelist, felt compelled to visit Bath over eighty times, which made Nash very uncomfortable about the effect his preaching would have on the city's pleasure-seekers. George Whitfield (1714–70) preached here in 1739, followed by Charles Wesley in 1741, when he announced that 'Satan took it ill to be attached in his headquarters, that Sodom of our land, Bath'.

Selina, Countess of Huntingdon, built a chapel on the Paragon in 1765, where John Wesley preached in 1766. No matter where Lady Huntingdon found herself, no matter what her company, she would insist on the conversation being turned upon religion, the terrible sins of those present, the hopelessness of their future state as compared with hers, her own former sinfulness and present righteousness, her virtue in contrast to her companions' lack of virtue and her religion.

※ ※ ※ ※ ※

Bath breweries did a fair trade, mainly due to the number of visitors to the town – most households homebrewed, but that was not possible during a visit to Bath. The largest brewery was probably the Northgate and Long Acre Breweries. A brewery was established in the Camden Works (now the Museum of Bath at Work) on Morford Street by 1753, to supply the growing upper town. It was known as the Tennis Court Brewery because the building had originally been a royal tennis court. Another brewery is recorded on Westgate Street, situated where the Grapes public house remains. The building has one of the most impressive seventeenth-century plaster ceilings remaining in Bath. The road was widened in 1720, which accounts for the later ashlar façade disguising this much older building.

Visitors, though, expected to be able to order beers that they were used to and so many London brews could be found in Bath, especially Porter. Other types that travelled well were the pale ales from Staffordshire, Taunton and Dorset. During the many wars with France, beer was promoted as the patriotic drink for the British.

There were at least five distilleries in Bath, too, to satisfy the visitors' demand for spirits. National sales of gin were at an all-time high in 1742 at 7.16 million gallons. In 1788, however, the magistrates announced that they would not be granting licences to the retailers of spirits in an attempt to crack down on 'the worst of all nuisance – the petty gin-shops'. In 1781, *The Bath Evening Chronicle* lamented that in Stall Street alone there were thirty inns, alehouses and gin shops. The peak for licensed houses in Bath was 1781, when 176 are known to be operational.

※ ※ ※ ※ ※

Horse racing had taken place in Bath since at least the time of Charles II's visits. Meetings at Claverton are recorded from the 1720s, and from 1723 they were run by the Corporation, who had taken the lease. There does not appear to have been any racing at Claverton during the 1760s, although there was a three-day meet at Lansdown in 1765. The meets tended to focus around September and October, kick-starting the season, but that did mean that if there had been a dry summer the going could be too hard at Claverton with the stone not far from the surface; this is probably why Lansdown – another plateau – became more favourable. It could also attract a larger audience, being closer to Bristol. A three-day meet was held at Claverton in 1770, but from 1784 Lansdown took precedence and since 1811 (bar the two world wars) the racecourse has operated continuously.

※ ※ ※ ※ ※

As we have seen, Sydney Gardens was not the first Vauxhall, or pleasure, garden in Bath, but it was the largest and most successful; in fact, its 12-acre span made it the largest outside of London. Naturally the desire for urban expansion elsewhere in Britain has seen the loss of almost all other such historic open spaces. Bath's decline in popularity paradoxically secured this area from extensive redevelopment.

Designed by Charles Harcourt Masters (1759–c. 1817), the pleasure gardens were central to the scheme to create the Pulteney Estate in Bathwick. Based on the popular entertainment venues of Vauxhall, Ranelagh and Marylebone in

Sydney Gardens, Bath, 1801. (Bath Central Library/Bath in Time)

London, Vauxhalls – or pleasure gardens – were an important aspect of both seventeenth- and eighteenth-century British culture. They were commercial enterprises, and for an entrance fee provided a wealth of marvellous distractions and curiosities. Sydney Gardens became the focus of Bath's fashionable visitors at the height of its popularity in the late 1700s. A contemporary described the gardens as being one of 'the most prominent, pleasing, and elegant features' in all Bath.

Even the cutting of the first sod, in September 1793, was a theatrical spectacle. An oak tree was planted on the site of the new gardens, cannons were fired and a barrel of strong beer was given to the spectators. Hosiery businessman John Gale was the first proprietor when the gardens opened on Monday, 11 May 1795. Initially the gardens featured two bowling greens, two swings, exotic trees and shrubs and refreshment facilities. Gale oversaw the addition of a further swing, a grotto, a labyrinth and a new tavern.

The labyrinth, which opened before August 1795, was an object of the greatest curiosity. It was 'twice as large as Hampton Court's, with ins and outs measuring half a mile'. At the centre was the reputed health-giving Merlin's Mechanical Swing, designed by John Joseph Merlin (1735–1803), whose portrait was painted by Gainsborough. Merlin was a musician and clock-maker from Flanders; he also invented roller-skating. It cost 6*d* to swing, but no swinging was permitted on Sundays.

In April 1799, Mr J. Holloway took over as proprietor and further attractions were added including supper boxes, music, gravel paths for promenading, breakfasts and galas, illuminations and fireworks, a ride and serpentine paths, a trapeze and a Hermit's Cottage. The gardens were 'so fantastically wrought by nature … so happily intersected by concealed art, that a lengthened tour may be made without retracing the same path'.

From the beginning Harcourt Masters had planned a 'space for fireworks', and from 1796 the legendary Giovanni Invetto provided regular dazzling displays. Advertisements exalted Signor Invetto's 'ingenious skill to produce new and astonishing effects'. An evening's entertainment at the gardens would normally commence with the gardens opening at 5 p.m., followed by a musical concert at 7 p.m., and culminating with fireworks at 10 p.m. During a gala evening the gardens were lit up with lamps and transparencies. For instance, the loggia, below the orchestra balcony, featured a backlit transparency of Apollo.

The first gala was held in the summer of 1796 and was attended by a staggering 4,000 people. These more extravagant festivities were often staged to celebrate national events, such as the birthday of a member of the Royal Family. A gala held in August 1798 to celebrate the birthdays of George, Prince of Wales (later King George IV) and Frederick, Duke of York, was attended by 'fashionable parties from Bath' who were joined by 'numerous parties from Bristol'.

Four years after the gardens had opened, in 1799, Sydney House (now the Holburne Museum) was completed and provided a gateway to the gardens, as well as further facilities. The original design for both garden and the house was by Thomas Baldwin, but after his bankruptcy the commission fell to his pupil, Charles Harcourt Masters. Masters advertised for builders to tender in the *Chronicle* in December 1795.

Sydney House provided coffee, tea and card rooms and, on the first floor, a ballroom. In the basement was the Sydney Tap, a tavern for the coachmen, sedan chairmen and servants, who were not allowed to use the gardens. It was important to keep them on hand, however, so patrons could ensure their prompt return journey to their lodgings situated, more likely, in the upper town. At the rear of Sydney House was a canopied two-storey balcony that could accommodate a 100-piece orchestra and, on either side, arching wings of supper boxes. Before the house was built, and because music was such a key feature of the garden's attractions, there had been a moveable orchestra. Contemporary advertisements indicate that horns and clarinets were played every Thursday evening.

The 1793 crash thrust Bath into a depression as speculative builds failed and builders went bust. The city had grown too quickly and was too big to sustain itself, and it could no longer be seen as an exclusive resort. The trendsetters looked elsewhere: to Cheltenham, Tunbridge Wells or the rising seaside resorts. Additionally, a change in medical opinion is illustrated by Sir Walter Scott, who lived in Bath for about year when he was a child. The purpose was to try and cure his lameness. Although he wrote fondly of his months in the city, he did not believe the waters had provided any benefit to him. Later he spent a season at Sandy-Knowe, 'where it was thought sea-bathing might be of service to my lameness'.

In 1772, a house was advertised as not being finished in the normal or common state, 'but in the most substantial and fashionable manner; they are calculated for the reception of a genteel and large family, and are not completely ready to be inhabited'. Just as brand new houses are offered today with bathrooms, kitchen units, carpets, curtains and tiles, the delight being you can just move in, this illustrates that Bath was now trying to attract permanent residents. The houses were larger too, and therefore able to accommodate a full family, with servants, for far longer periods than the usual seasonal visit of six to eight weeks.

Nine

REGENCY REINVENTION

The end of the eighteenth and the turn of the nineteenth centuries was a period of great social and political unrest in Britain. The American Revolution (1776–83) was quickly followed by the French Revolution (1789–99) and naturally countless individuals greatly feared a revolution in Britain, whilst others actively encouraged it. Both France and America had spoken about liberty and the rights of man.

In November 1789 Richard Price (1723–91), the Nonconformist minister, gave a sermon that commemorated the Glorious Revolution of 1688, in which he concluded that the upheavals in France were the dawn of a new republican era that he championed should be enthusiastically adopted in Britain too:

> Behold all ye friends of freedom … behold the light you have struck out, after setting America free, reflected to France and there kindled into a blaze that lays despotism in ashes and warms and illuminates Europe. I see the ardour for liberty catching and spreading;… the dominion of kings changed for the dominion of laws, and the dominion of priests giving way to the dominion of reason and conscience.

Radicals believed in democracy and the rights of all men (although not necessarily all women) to play an active part in politics. The loyalists feared any change and believed that Britain's constitution was robust and reliable. Thomas Paine's *The Rights of Man* (1792) was a rallying cry in support of the French Revolution and an answer to Edmund Burke's *Reflections on the Revolution in France* (1790). Burke was a loyalist and he and his followers believed the concept of the 'rights of man' were extremely dangerous and destabilising. One-time Bath resident, Mary Wollstonecraft, was the first to respond to Burke's publication with *A Vindication of the Rights of Men, in a Letter to the Right Honourable Edmund Burke; Occasioned by His Reflections on the Revolution in France* (1790).

The country was split, but the anti-French feeling, fear of a war with France and the outrage at what was happening during France's Reign of Terror (1793–94), when thousands of people were executed by their fellow French citizens, meant the loyalist cause had increasing support. Many liberals, such as William Wordsworth, were disgusted by these events in France and their politics changed forever.

Despite not having the vote, not owning property, surviving on low wages and terrible conditions, huge numbers of people from the lower classes joined 'Loyal Britons' societies. The Loyal Bath Association had 7,000 members in December 1792. They considered themselves to be extremely patriotic, in support of the King and, importantly, fervently anti-French. Thomas Paine was declared a traitor and his effigy was burnt in towns and cities across the country. The *Bath Chronicle* reported the burning of Thomas Paine effigies at Norton St Philip, Kingsdown, Corsham, Keynsham, Lacock, Hemington, Atworth, Marshfield and Beechen Cliff during late December 1792 and throughout January 1793. At Saltford, however, some 'rogue [had] carried off the effigy before the hour of conflagration'. Paine was forced to flee to France.

Towards the end of the eighteenth century Bath's population modified, and rather than a destination for revelry and recreation it became instead a place to take up permanent residency. Bath's allure as a fashionable resort was fading, mainly due to the new craze for sea bathing at locations such as Brighton, and an increasing admiration for the smaller, more discrete spas such as Cheltenham. Despite Bath's decline as a resort, its population continued to grow during the early years of the nineteenth century – by 1831 it stood at 50,802.

What is interesting is that the census shows that there was now a larger proportion of older and female residents. Bath had become a destination for genteel retirement, which needed domestic servants and shop assistants to support it. Robert Southey declared in 1807, 'It is plain that Bath has outgrown its Beauty'. These new residents sought a different type of accommodation, often away from the tightly packed central area, and even away from the once highly prized Palladian terraces of the upper town. What was desirous now was the villa house on the edge of the city – where city and countryside meet. The quest for the *rus in urbe* can therefore be seen to have continued beyond that created by Palmer at Lansdown. And, as John Wood had prophesied in 1742, Bathwick was favoured as the place in which to build your individual home:

Many of the Citizens of Bath have already beautified [Bathwick] Village by their little Places of Retirement in it, so nothing is more probable than that the higher Lands of the whole Lordship will soon be enriched with nobler Villas, and the lower Grounds be covered with such Structures as will augment the Body of the City, and become the chief Beauty of Bath in respect to her Works of Architecture.

Cartography was notoriously time-consuming, and having engaged in an expensive survey and engraving, publishers wanted to ensure that their maps remained relevant for as long as possible. For this reason maps and plans of Bath continued to show Baldwin's intended series of radiating streets and crescents across the Pulteney Estate for the next forty years. For example, *The City of Bath Map* of 1812 has 'intended buildings' printed over the top. Although, perhaps this also tells of Bath's continuing optimism for a return to the boom years.

※ ※ ※ ※ ※

A victim of the infamous bank crash was John Eveleigh. On 23 November 1793, *The Bath Herald and Register* published a notice from Harry Elderton, a Bristol solicitor, in which he set out the details of Eveleigh's bankruptcy and the procedure by which creditors should prove their debts. Eveleigh, an associate of Baldwin's, was an architect, builder and merchant who, at the time of his bankruptcy, was involved in two ambitious building projects in Bath.

The first was Bailbrook House, situated on the slopes of Little Solsbury and built for Denham Skeet, a lawyer from Buckinghamshire. In 1790 Skeet contracted Eveleigh to 'provide articles and materials of every description for building and completely furnishing such house and offices'. Skeet agreed to advance Eveleigh 'any reasonable sums of money that he might be in want of the better to enable him to perform his said undertaking'. In total, Skeet advanced nearly £13,500. After the crash, work on the house justifiably slowed and in 1795 James Beale and Laurence Field, surveyors at Bath, were appointed to value the house. Once this was added to the value of the unused materials and the costs Eveleigh had paid for directly, a balance of nearly £5,000 was owed – to Skeet. Skeet therefore joined Eveleigh's other creditors.

Simultaneously, Eveleigh was involved in one of the more impressive developments Bath had seen. By late 1790 he was improving with William Hewlett a plot of 20 acres along the London Road. There he planned a Vauxhall garden 'laid out with taste and elegance for the reception of nobility, gentry and the public in general'. The development was to include a hotel, saloon with organ, hot houses, a temple with chimes, swimming baths, two bowling greens, a labyrinth, Merlin's swings and cave, a grotto, accommodation for angling, fishponds, pleasure boats, a meadow for fashionable Alderney cows, alcoves, boxes, retreats, pleasant and rural walks with lamps and an aviary. Eveleigh's plan included the building of 143 handsome houses by subscription, with the hotel and entrance to the gardens at the centre.

On 24 June 1791 the foundation stone for Grosvenor House was laid 'amid the firing of cannon and a liberal treat of beer'. Grosvenor has been described

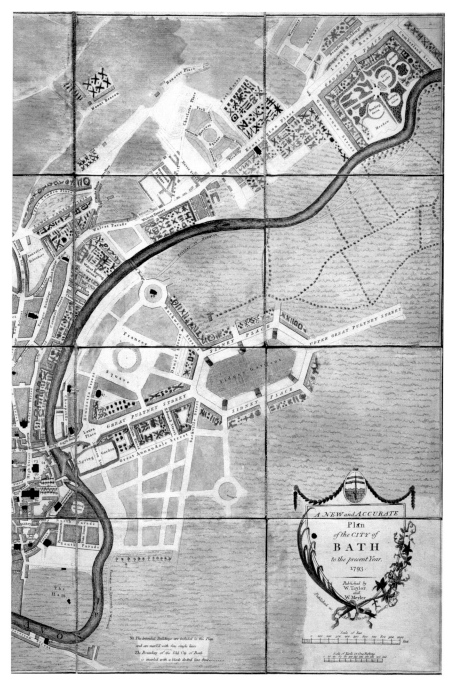

W. Taylor and W. Meyler: Detail of the planned Pulteney Estate, Sydney Gardens to Grosvenor Gardens, 1793.
(Bath Central Library/Bath in Time)

as one of the most exciting buildings in Bath and certainly its gentle sweep and lavish decoration, including the bearded icicle man keystones, make it instantly recognisable. By 1792, however, Eveleigh was struggling to find funds. As an incentive he offered subscribers of £100 an annual ticket for two to the gardens. Few could have predicted the financial crisis, but Eveleigh more than most had overstretched himself. Contemporary reports speculate that he had laid out nearly £30,000 at Bailbrook and the Grosvenor Vauxhall. Added to his worries were the rumours that William Pitt had identified him as a former government official in Jamaica; a position he lost after an investigation into his financial record keeping.

Alongside other bankrupts Eveleigh was required to surrender himself to the commissioners on 25 and 26 November and 24 December 1793, at the Argyle Coffee House, Argyle Buildings, to make a full disclosure of his estate and effects. Creditors were instructed to attend the second meeting and have proof of their debts. In November 1793 Eveleigh was forced to sell, at a loss, his share in the unfinished Grosvenor. This was followed in April 1794 by an auction of 'a large quantity of dry seasoned timber, of various kinds and dimensions, scaffold planks and poles, cisterns, ladders, barrows, a stone carriage, and other numerous building materials' representing unused materials from the Grosvenor build. The eighty-four lots raised just over £130.

Skeet continued to expend on Bailbrook, making piecemeal progress until January 1799 when he engaged Peter Hill, an upholsterer from London, to furnish the house in readiness for auction the following year. Hill found that he, too, could not complete the project and by 1801 he was declared bankrupt and as a consequence spent time in Fleet Prison. Skeet eventually sold Bailbrook in 1802 to Valentine Jones, a merchant and official in the West Indies. The £7,000 raised was immediately swallowed up by the debts to tradesmen and loans Skeet had taken out to ensure Bailbrook's completion.

Despite the heavy losses Bath remained optimistic of a return to the boom years. At Grosvenor, *The New Bath Guide* for 1801 declared that 'in Grosvenor Gardens is now erecting a spacious hotel with a delightful garden of near 14 acres, laid out with great taste for summer and winter amusements'. In fact, the gardens failed due to the low-lying site that was often misty and occasionally flooded. They were abandoned shortly after 1810. The unfinished state of the hotel and houses was noted in 1819, ultimately only the hotel and forty-one houses were ever completed.

John Pinch the Elder (1770–1827) also made his name in Bathwick, taking over after Baldwin's bankruptcy. He is one of the few Bath based architects to successfully rebuild his business after the crash. The sites Pinch worked on in Bathwick and at Lansdown were often sloping and he utilised a distinctive decorative device of 'stepping up' the string course and cornice to link the individual terraces harmoniously. As the surveyor to the Bathwick Estate, Pinch was responsible for a number of developments at this time and together they illustrate the transformation from the Palladian terrace, through a less formal Classicism, to the expression of a taste for Picturesque irregularity.

Pinch designed New Sydney Buildings (1804–8), a partial fulfilment of Baldwin's intended architectural frame of Sydney Gardens. At the foot of Bathwick Hill he created a spectacular example of late Georgian Gothic in the form of St Mary the Virgin Church. Stepping up Bathwick Hill is Raby Place, an elegant terrace of eighteen houses (1818–25) where Pinch's distinctive ramped cornice unites the individual houses. Sion Hill Place is his masterpiece. Completed in 1820, it really is the last of the fine speculative terraces built in Bath; what followed was individual and semi-detached villas. Pinch was responsible for a number of these on Bathwick Hill, but as the hill rises steeply and becomes more rugged and striking it is his protégé, Henry Edmund Goodridge (1797–1864), who fully developed the potential of the suburban villa.

The creation of suburban villas, placed pictorially in the landscape, was not a revolutionary concept. A villa was a more informal and, therefore, more personal retreat than the grand country house or town residence. Andrea Palladio, the sixteenth-century Italian architect who influenced Britain's passion for Palladianism, designed a number of such places in the 1500s; as did John Wood, who designed Jerry Peirce's Lilliput Castle (1738) on the outskirts of Bath, Belcomb Brook, near Bradford-on-Avon (1734), and Titan Barrow at Bathford (1748).

The construction of the great terraced crescents in Bath relied on investors and speculative builders; the developer needed phenomenal expertise in surveying, management and finance. It was, of course, far easier and cheaper to build a single building for a single client. The suburban villa, surrounded on all sides by its own garden, afforded the resident privacy, improved air quality, the delight in planting out their immediate environment and an awareness that they were an integral part of the new 'romantic' movement.

Goodridge created a series of Greco-Italianate villas in the 1830s and 1840s with names such as Fiesole, Montebello (now Bathwick Grange) and Villa Bianca (now Casa Bianca), ensuring the link with Italy, a country to which he travelled regularly. A number of the properties included Greek Revival detailing, illustrating how eclectic the national architectural style had become. In its original form, Goodridge's own home – Montebello – conformed with the ideals of the Picturesque – an asymmetrical house utilising different roof levels, towers and chimneys to accentuate the variety of the architectural concept. Rather than be enslaved to the rules of Palladianism, these villas show that tastes had changed.

Here, the full potential of the natural landscape was exploited and the exertion of individualism through variety was prized. On Bathwick Hill, therefore, we have in architectural form the national influence of more eclectic styles, the realisation of the Picturesque and the manifestation of Bath's changing status, both economic and social.

Goodridge is now more readily associated with the work he undertook for the wealthy art collector, William Beckford (1760–1844). Beckford moved to Bath in 1822 and leased and owned Nos. 19 and 20 Lansdown Crescent and No. 1 Lansdown Place West. In the 1820s he built a bridge to connect the last two properties and reputedly left No. 19 empty to ensure peace and quiet. The parapet is decorated with green oxidised copper palms in gadrooned urns. Beckford then leased and purchased land from behind the Crescent to the top of Lansdown Hill, 1 mile away. Here he commissioned Goodridge to design him a retreat, where he could study and house his precious collection of prints, paintings, art objects and rare books. Beckford's Tower (now a museum) was completed in 1827. The retreat comprised luxuriously decorated rooms and a spiral staircase of 154 steps leading to the belvedere. The tower rises 120ft (36.6m) and is crowned with an octagonal lantern decorated with columns gilded in gold leaf.

※ ※ ※ ※ ※

Whilst eighteenth-century Bath was built by locals, the nineteenth century is characterised by the more prestigious contracts going to outsiders. For example, the Theatre Royal, the first to receive a royal warrant outside London, was moved from Old Orchard Street to Sawclose in 1805. The theatre, considered to be 'the most compact and elegant of provincial theatres', was designed by London architect, George Dance the Younger (1741–1825) and built by (local) John Palmer. The theatre opened with a production of Shakespeare's *King Richard III*.

The Tepid Bath, which was added to the Hot Bath in 1829, was designed by another London architect, Decimus Burtin, but again the work was carried out by a local architect, this time George Philip Manners (1789–1866).

Bath artist Thomas Barker engaged Sir John Soane's creative partner, architect Joseph M. Gandy (1771–1843) to design Doric House (1818), which included a 30ft gallery in which Barker displayed his paintings. In 1825 he painted an enormous fresco of *The Massacre of the Sciotes by the Turks* on one of the gallery walls. And Walcot Methodist Chapel was designed by the Reverend William Jenkins (1815–16), although architecture was his second career choice, he was another Londoner.

One of Bath's most extraordinary buildings was the National School, designed by John Lowder (a local) and, sadly, demolished in 1896. It looked like a spaceship had landed near Abbey Gate. The school was begun in October 1816 and was ready to welcome schoolchildren in 1818. The building, which could hold 1,000 children, comprised a polygon of thirty-two sides, 80ft (24.4m) diameter and 20ft (6m) high for the boys' schoolroom, whilst the girls' room was circular and 54ft (16.5m) in diameter. The whole building was erected without the aid of scaffolding and became known as the Rotunda.

❈ ❈ ❈ ❈ ❈

Although he had reigned longer than any of his predecessors, King George III suffered debilitating bouts of illness. In 1788–89 and again in 1801 he was found not fit to rule. He may have had porphyria, the blood disease medical historians believe Queen Anne may also have had. Consequently, in 1811, his son the Prince of Wales (1762–1830, later George IV) became Regent. The debt-ridden Prince was a socialite, a notoriously heavy drinker and a compulsive gambler. He would have fitted in well with Bath society of the previous century, but fashions had changed and the Prince favoured Brighton instead.

Medical opinion recommended that sea bathing and sea air were extremely beneficial for a number of ailments, and Brighton was particularly popular due to its proximity to London. By 1801 it was the largest resort in Britain. The Prince first visited Brighton in 1783, when his doctor advised that sea bathing may help his gout. In 1785, he secretly (and illegally) married the Roman Catholic Maria Fitzherbert. The following year he rented a farmhouse in the Old Steine area of Brighton where the couple could live discreetly away from the prying eyes of the royal court in London.

The Prince employed Henry Holland to enlarge the building. He also bought up the land surrounding the property to guarantee some privacy. In 1803–08 he built a riding school and stable, designed in the Indian style by William Porden. And between 1815 and 1823, the Prince engaged John Nash to redesign the property into the Royal Pavilion. The palace is an eclectic mix of highly exotic decorative styles including Indian, Chinese and Islamic. To unify the façade, however, the surfaces were rendered and painted to look like Bath stone.

Other resorts, such as Weymouth, where George III visited from 1789 and Ralph Allen had owned a property; Ilfracombe, where as early as 1788, it was noted to be 'remarkably full of genteel company … from most parts of the country'; and spa towns such as Leamington Spa and Tunbridge Wells, which had competed with Bath (and often shared masters of ceremonies, musicians, artists, fan painters, etc.), now overtook Bath.

Cheltenham particularly benefitted from Bath's decline. The Saxon town had reinvented itself after the discovery of a source of medicinal spring water in 1716. However, its development was painfully slow. Cheltenham was unable to compete with the hot waters of Bath. After George III visited in 1788, Cheltenham's luck changed. By 1821 the town could boast 2,416 houses and 13,388 inhabitants, a vast increase from 710 houses and 2,000 people at the turn of the century.

Other towns were also catching up with Bath architecturally. Both Edinburgh and Buxton could now claim their own classical crescents and squares and, even in London, where the fashion for Palladianism had started, they looked to Bath when deciding on the layout of Regent's Park. Bath became a modest place to retire to, where a modest title and wealth gave you great eminence. It was a place to be someone, but at an affordable price. This is demonstrated in Austen's *Persuasion*, in which Walter Elliot moves his family to Bath where he will be able to keep up appearances, but at far less cost than in London. Marketing concentrated on Bath's gentility and convenience:

> The city of Bath has so considerably increased in size and number of its inhabitants, that it has become one of the *most agreeable* as well as *most polite* places in the Kingdom; owing chiefly to the elegant neatness of its buildings, and the accommodations for strangers, which are superior to those of any city in Europe.

Entertainment continued to be offered by the Assembly Rooms, the theatre and the races. There were also travelling novelty shows, of people and animals – effectively 'freak shows'. Madame Tussaud (1761–1850) visited in November 1831 with celebrity portraits in wax. There was a greater emphasis on scientific demonstrations and discussion.

This change in attitude is perfectly illustrated by the Corporation's decision not to rebuild the Lower Assembly Rooms (Harrison's) after they were destroyed by fire in 1820, but to build a scholarly institution instead, in 1824, to a design by George Allen Underwood (1793–1829), surveyor to the county of Somerset, as the Bath Literary and Scientific Institution – the forerunner to the Bath Royal Literary & Scientific Institution (BRLSI) at Queen Square. In 1838, Captain Roland Mainwaring proclaimed that by establishing the institution, 'Bath stands redeemed from the imputation of being a city devoted to pleasure and dissipation'. Lindsey's Assembly Room was demolished in around 1820 to make way for York Street.

Romanticism also had an influence on the places people wanted to visit. Through the ideologies of individualism and liberalism, emotional responses to the power and beauty of nature – or sublimity – were pursued. On one level the movement was a counter-response to man's increasing attempts to control and tap the potency of nature through industrial exploitation; but also, at a time of the Napoleonic Wars (1803–15), extremely nationalistic.

The fear of an invasion by Napoleon's 'Army of England' was palpable and fervid. The long-running war (which came hot on the heels of the American War of Independence and the French Revolution, and coincided with Britain fighting in India, Russia, Haiti and Sri Lanka), alongside an urgent need for increased homeland defences, was expensive. This meant higher taxes, rising inflation and skyrocketing food prices. The population of Britain was poor, hungry and scared. Unemployment also rose because of wartime trade restrictions and the increasing use of labour-saving machinery. Many men, married or not, were forced to join up rather than starve. Those who left their families to fight could only hope that their parish would provide their loved ones with charitable relief and keep them alive until their return from war. Times were desperate and miserable in Britain at the turn of the nineteenth century. No wonder the Prince Regent was seen as a frivolous and ignorant spendthrift.

For those with money, travel in Europe was greatly hampered, and as a result the aesthetic qualities of the rugged windswept beaches and mountains of Britain became ever more attractive. In 1823, John Constable wrote of Italy:

> Oh dear. O dear. I shall never let my longing eyes see that famous country … Am I doomed never to see the living scenes – which inspired the landscape of Wilson & Claude Lorraine? No! But I was born to paint a happier land, my own dear England – and when I forsake that, or cease to love my country – may I as Wordsworth says 'never more, hear Her green leaves russel, Or her torrents roar'.

Some historians, such as Linda Colley, insist that British identity was forged during this period. The poetry of Samuel Taylor Coleridge, John Keats and William Wordsworth, alongside the paintings of J.M.W. Turner and John Robert Cozens gave Britons an opportunity 'to transcend their troubles and their circumstances', or so the Romantics thought.

❋ ❋ ❋ ❋ ❋

After 1815, Europe opened up again and now a far wider demographic, including the new middle class based on industrial wealth, could travel. The end of the Napoleonic Wars did bring stability, but Bath's boom years were over. Its purpose as a purely medical spa came to dominate.

Rear Admiral Lord Horatio Nelson (1758–1805) stayed on at least five occasions. He initially came to recuperate from illness and battle fatigue after the raid on San Juan Castle in 1781. His treatment consisted of massage, bathing and taking the waters. He visited again, shortly after his marriage to Fanny Nisbet, so he could meet her Bristol relatives. After 1793, Fanny settled in Bath whilst Nelson was away fighting. Bath, like many other towns, awarded Nelson the Freedom of the City in 1797, following his capture of two Spanish ships.

Satirical prints became synonymous with this period of huge political and social upheaval. 'These prints,' writes John Harvey, 'were potent propaganda, they could laugh at nightmares or engender and swell them … [they] lampooned everyone … [and] taken together, the massive picture-show they make [shows] the tireless self-contemplation and self-mockery of a society exploding with wealth and pain.'

Most satirical prints were produced by London publishers as single-sheet prints (either etched or engraved) and later hand coloured; they did not appear in newspapers as they do today. Print and book sellers would cover their shop windows entirely with cartoons and a common activity was to visit the High Street to view the latest additions. Print shops would also put portfolios together, which were lent out as amusing diversions to guests at a house party. Charles Williams (c. 1797–1830), was one of the principal satirists of the day. He worked almost exclusively for Samuel W. Fores of Piccadilly, London, between 1799 and 1815.

The Little Green Man. Or The Bath Bugabo. Or the Widows Terror (1802) is typical of the age and, although strangely compelling, the story behind the scene has been lost in time. The troubled 'Little Green Man', who provokes such accentuated fear and loathing in the three Bath ladies, is captivating. The man in question was one Henry Cope, a gentleman well known in both Bath and Brighton at the turn of the nineteenth century. Undoubtedly an eccentric, he was thought to have committed suicide in 1806. Clifford Musgrove's research for his publication *Life in Brighton* (1970), however, showed that although Cope had indeed thrown himself from his window in 1806, he had not died.

The extravagance of the Prince of Wales and his circle, which included Beau Brummell, and the increase in the moneyed class, meant it was important to get noticed and be memorable. The younger members of society adopted characteristics that allowed them to stand out from the crowd. For instance, Mr Crampton, one of the Prince of Wales' friends, was well known for his incredible ability to jump and somersault – even over horses. Another way was to have a coloured or flamboyantly dressed carriage, and to dress outlandishly was especially popular. Some adopted one particular colour for their carriage, horses and dress. Mr Mellish favoured white, Lord Petersham brown, whilst the Honourable Tommy Onslow chose black.

Henry Cope's idiosyncrasies, however, led to his notoriety in both Bath and Brighton as the 'Little Green Man'. The Brighton *Annual Register* of 1806 described him in detail:

Charles Williams: The Little Green Man or The Bath Bugabo or the Widows Terror, 1802. (Bath Central Library/Bath in Time)

He dressed in green pantaloons, green waistcoat, green frock [coat], green cravat; and though his ears, whiskers, eyebrows and chin were powdered, his countenance, no doubt from the reflection of his clothes, was also green. He ate nothing but green fruits and vegetables, had his rooms painted green, and furnished with green sofa, green chairs, green tables, green bed and green curtains. His gig, his livery, his portmanteau, his gloves and his wigs were all green. With a green silk handkerchief in his hand, and a large watch-chain with green seals, fastened to the green buttons of his green waistcoat, he paraded every day on the Steyne.

The Steine, or Steyne, was a broad, grassy thoroughfare in Brighton, popular for promenading. Cope was a regular visitor and became known as the 'The Green Man of Brighton' – although we now know he was equally known as 'The Green Man of Bath'! *The Lewes and Brighthelmstone* [historic name for Brighton] *Journal* noted that 'the Green Man continues daily to amuse the Steyne promenaders with his eccentricities'. A later contributor to the *Journal*, who signed himself 'Quiz', sent in a poem about Cope:

> A spruce little man in a doublet of green
> Perambulates daily the streets and the Steyne.
> Green striped is his waistcoat, his small-clothes are green,
> And oft round his neck a green 'kerchief is seen.
> Green watch-string, green seals, and, for certain, I've heard,
> (Tho' they're powered) green whiskers, and eke a green beard.
> Green garters, green hose, and, deny it who can,
> The brains, too, are green, of this green little man!

Another writer recorded that Cope 'sometimes … wore a huge cocked hat with gold tassels. He was surrounded with company, who expressed their surprise at the size of his hat: … He is the gaze of Brighton.' Another commentator described him as always being on his own, and walking very slowly. He would stop and look at every lady he passed, but he was not courteous, as he 'never honours us even with a smile. If notoriety be his object he has fully succeeded, as the windows are filled with ladies whenever he passes.'

The ladies' concern and distress in *The Bath Bugabo* is as much to do with Cope's eccentricity as it is with their own worry that the evil spirits, thought to possess the mad and troubled, could fly out and seize them. As Roy Porter tells us, 'the deranged were [thus] feared and shunned'. Williams satirises the anxiety Cope aroused, believing it to be out of hand. The title of 'bug-a-bo' means something that is an object of obsessive, exaggerated fear or anxiety. The three widows (dressed in black) scatter frantically, proclaiming (in turn), 'O Lord the Monster', 'O dear the Monster', and 'The Monster, the monster'. By including posters on the buildings in the background, detailing the Hot and Cold Baths, Williams has instantly shown that the scene is in Bath.

In his *A Peep into the Pump Room, or the Zomersetshire Folk in a Maze* (1818), Williams captures the boundless excitement experienced in Bath during the visit of Queen Charlotte, who came to take the waters in November 1817. The wife of George III, Charlotte was 73 years old and quite infirm at the time of her visit – she died the following year. According to the author Hester Lynch Piozzi (1741–1821), 'The illumination was more gaudy than I ever saw London exhibit; and a prodigious expense was incurred by subscription to pillars, arches, and I know not what beside. The mayor and corporation put on new dresses the cooks prepared a magnificent repast'. The visit was cut short by the news that the Queen's granddaughter, Princess Charlotte, had died in childbirth.

Charles Williams: A Peep into the Pump Room or the Zomersetshire Folk in a Maze, 1818. (Bath Central Library/Bath in Time)

In Williams' view, the Pump Room is seen crowded with people straining to catch sight of Queen Charlotte, who is sat facing the pump with a glass of Bath water in her hand. The Duke of Clarence (later King William IV), in naval uniform, is seen leaning on the back of her chair. Queen Charlotte is surrounded mainly by ladies who were anxious to be received by royalty. Williams shows the company offering different solutions for her stomach ache, including brandy and 'Old Tom' (gin). The mayor, John Kitson, who had the honour of giving Queen Charlotte her first drink of the Bath waters, is seen saying, 'Three seconds more will produce a motion'. Williams' audience would have known the Pump Room and so he was careful to remain faithful to the location, including the tall arched windows and statue of Richard 'Beau' Nash. This print, however, mocks Bath and the town's leaders, who relished any sort of royal patronage as a sign that the town was on the up again.

❋ ❋ ❋ ❋ ❋

In 1830 William IV succeeded his brother, George IV, and Lady Rivers, a descendant of Robert Gay, leased further land to the Bath Corporation to create Royal Victoria Park, one of the earliest public parks outside London. It was designed by Edward Davis and included a circular carriage drive, dells, a serpentine lake and Gothic cottages. It was opened by Princess Victoria on 23 October 1830 – she was only 11 years old, and it was the first to be named in her honour. Pedestrians could use the park for free, but those who rode or drove carriages had to pay a subscription. Although it provided a free open space in Bath, wardens ensured the middle and upper classes had exclusive rights, as they removed anyone who was deemed unsightly or unclean.

This was extremely provocative at a time of great social and political unrest which would soon lead to the 1832 Reform Act. There had been growing discontent amongst Britain's working classes. The Corn Laws of 1815, which kept the price of corn artificially high, but maintained jobs by preventing the market being flooded with cheap foreign corn, still left hundreds of thousands of people desperately hungry. They may still have had employment, but the wages were too low to pay for the bread.

The electoral system was corrupt and unrepresentative – the new, highly populated industrial centres had the same parliamentary representation as a rural village in Cornwall. Bath was what was termed a 'rotten borough', in that it sent two Members to Parliament, but only thirty men, out of a possible 50,000 who should have been eligible to vote, were allowed to vote for them. Working conditions were harsh and pay was low. Riots occurred in Manchester, Birmingham and Bristol, in which about seventy people lost their lives.

The first election after the Reform Act was in December 1832. Bath's three candidates for two seats were Major General Charles Palmer – extremely confident of the people's loyalty to him after serving Bath since 1808; John Roebuck, a radical; and Henry Hobhouse, who described himself as a reformer, but was actually a Tory in disguise.

One of the more contentious issues at the beginning of the nineteenth century was still the question of slavery. Bath, like any other town or city in Britain, had benefitted from the slave trade. From the residency of one of England's wealthiest plantation owners, William Beckford, to the sugar on your table. Sugar was as important to the economy as oil is today. Other imports that relied heavily on slave labour were tobacco and cotton. Raw cotton, imported mainly from America, was worked in the cotton mills of Lancashire, and the resulting cloths were then exported to Africa in exchange for slaves. Between 1730 and 1745 Bristol was the world's leading slave port and the city's wealth was largely built on the trade. An estimated 500,000 Africans were carried into slavery in ships that sailed from Bristol, only 14 miles from Bath.

Bath was one of the era's most fashionable towns for the elite, the majority of whose fortunes would have been linked with Britain's transatlantic trade.

Most large estates had directly benefitted from slavery; just within the Bath region there is Badminton House, Dyrham Park and Oldbury Court. William Wilberforce, credited with the abolition of slavery in Britain, lived in Bath for a time and his committee, the Society for Effecting the Abolition of the Slave Trade, regularly held public meetings in the city. About 300,000 people across Britain showed their support for the abolition by refusing to have sugar in their tea or to eat sweetened desserts. Many others signed petitions. In fact, far more people called for the end of slavery than were allowed to vote.

The Abolitionist movement was gaining momentum and in 1807 the British Slave Trade Act was passed. This brought an end to the legal trafficking of slaves within the British Empire, although an illegal slave trade continued long afterwards. It was not until 1833 that slavery within the British Empire was abolished altogether with the Slavery Abolition Act.

Hobhouse favoured a more moderate approach, declaring that 'a partial abolition should be made at once and be continued on such a scale as not to risk the welfare of the slave or the planter'. An admirable approach if it wasn't for the fact that his statement came sixteen years after the Slave Trade Act, and was thus indicative of his antiquated attitude. Roebuck, on the other hand, demanded an immediate and total abolition.

The Reform Act had increased Bath's electorate to one in three adult males (as opposed to one in five in more typical boroughs). To get their policies known the candidates held public meetings, more intimate dinners, distributed leaflets and displayed posters across the city. Hobhouse's campaign was the victim of a satirical poster that announced the arrival of 'Mr Henry Van Hobson Housen and his Tory menagerie', a reference to a travelling menagerie that had visited Bath earlier that year advertising a 'Great Baboon, Howling Hyena, Harmless Viper, Largest Ass'.

On 14 December 1832, the mayor counted up the votes and declared that General Palmer and Roebuck had won the majority (Hobhouse was only ninety-eight votes behind Roebuck).

Sadly, the 1832 Reform Act did not bring about the level of reform the people hoped for with only about 18 per cent of the total adult male population of England and Wales allowed to vote. Nor did it enforce a secret ballot. The 1833 Factory Act failed to impose the promised maximum ten-hour working day. The 1834 Poor Law Amendment Act effectively made poverty a crime by increasing the threat of being sent to a union workhouse, despite the ever rising unemployment rate leaving people little choice but to be desperately poor. Chartism was seen as a more hopeful and effective movement.

Chartism had its origins in William Lovett's London Working Man's Association of 1836. Perhaps because Bath's fortunes had so dramatically

Tory Menagerie,

A.D. 1833 **WHITE LION YARD.**

Mr. Henry Van Hobson Housen

Having ascertained that the very thin attendance of Company at his Menagerie is caused by the intolerable stench arising from some of the Reptiles contained in the Exhibition, he respectfully informs the Inhabitants of this City, that he intends offering a few of the most useless and disagreeable of these Animals for Sale by

Public Auction,

On the 31st Instant, unless previously disposed of by the

COMMON HANGMAN.

The following may serve as a Specimen of the most dirty and offensive of these Reptiles

THE

Hermaphroditical Surgico Doctoro,

A very insignificant Creature, presented to the Proprietor by GEORGE, KING of the Chimney Sweeps.

THE

Diavolo de Lionelio de Atkinio,

PRINCE OF THE SATYRS.

A particularly disagreeable Savage. The Proprietor feels extremely anxious to dispose of this Brute, as he is paying One Guinea per day for his maintenance.

The Thick Skullio Jobio Sealyo,

An Amphibious Animal, noted only for his stupidity and dirty tricks.

The Squeakyo Bartlottio,

Or *Little* Mermaid.

This Creature will be easily known from its Companions by the very masculine feminine Frontispiece it displays, and is supposed to *paint* itself every morning.

THE RASCAL RAT,

Noted for sneaking in a certain *Orchard*, will prove a very advantageous bargain to the Purchaser, being admitted by all classes to be a very fit Ornament for the

SHERIFF's PICTURE FRAME.

Several others will be offered, and the Proprietor earnestly solicits the attendance of an enlightened Public, who will no doubt appreciate the full value of them.

Henry Van Hobson Housen (Hobhouse): Satirical Election Poster 'Tory Menagerie', 1833. (Bath Central Library/ Bath in Time)

dropped, alongside the economic decline of the neighbouring cloth towns of Bradford-on-Avon, Trowbridge, Melksham and Frome, there was a strong and early following of Chartism. A Working Man's Association was established in Bath as early as 1837.

Bath's Chartists, who had their offices on Monmouth Street and were led by George and Samuel Bartlett and Alderman James Crisp, were very active with regular meetings, petitions, marches and rallies. Across the country, Chartists believed in the 'Six points of the People's Charter', which were:

A vote for every man over 21 years of age.
A secret ballot (instead of the system for voting in public, which left people open to intimidation and bribery).
A Member of Parliament did not have to own property, opening up the position to a far greater demographic.
MPs would receive a salary, enabling those without a private income to stand.
Equal voting constituencies.
An election every year for Parliament.

It would take until 1918, but eventually full manhood suffrage was achieved, along with secret voting and payment of MPs. The only demand not implemented was the call for annual elections.

✳ ✳ ✳ ✳ ✳

In 1839 G.S. Gibbes wrote:

Bath is not a city of trade. No manufacturer worthy of notice is carried on within its limits, nor is it the resort of commerce ... Bath is best fitted for the retirement of individuals with independent incomes, whether small or large. For those past the meridian of life, its quietness, beautiful neighbourhood, and warmth of climate, particularly recommend it ... Trade in Bath consists principally in the sale of articles connected with the refinements, rather than the necessities of life.

Bath could not compete with the likes of Manchester, Birmingham or Leeds, but it is wrong to believe that there was no industry here. Manufacturing in Bath employed half of the male and a good proportion of the female population. These businesses tended to be established by the river, and since the navigation of the Avon opened in 1727 Broad Quay had been a hive of activity. There were numerous stone yards, coach builders and maltsters alongside the oppressive smells of the brewers, soap boilers and steam dyers.

Larger industries were also represented, such as the world-famous iron founders Stothert & Pitt, founded in the 1780s, which developed their first foundry on Newark Street before moving to the south side of the river. George Stothert moved to Bath from Shropshire in around 1774 to work at Thomas Harris's ironmongers. The company benefitted from the last building boom, and George took control of Harris's company. In 1795, George Stothert was registered as 'Ironmonger, Smith, Brazier, Tin Man, Plane Makers, also operator of a Manufactures Register and Supplies of all kind of stove grates'. His business interests and services were wide enough to keep the company buoyant during the 1793 crash, but not so thinly spread to have been owed money by the many hundreds of bankrupts.

By 1796 Stothert was the local agent for a range of products engineered by Abraham Darby's Coalbrookdale Co. It was Stothert who supplied the Coalbrookdale cast-iron bridges that span the canal in Sydney Gardens. In 1815 the company set up its own foundry alongside the original ironmongery in Horse Street, possibly because of the newly opened Coalbrookdale Co. warehouse in Bristol, but also the improved economic situation with the end of the Napoleonic Wars. George Stothert the Elder retired from the business in September, leaving his son, also George, in charge.

In 1805 De Montalt Mill, near Combe Down, was established on wood once owned by Ralph Allen and his heirs, Lord and Lady de Montalt, who were annual visitors to Bath in the late 1780s and early 1790s. It was a paper mill operated by the firm of Bally, Ellen & Steart, and originally produced high-quality writing paper and the sketching paper used by artists like Turner and Constable, as well as paper for banknotes issued by provincial banks. The mill was noted for its overshot wheel, 56ft (17m) in diameter, fed by a large pipe supported on pylons, bringing water from a reservoir to the north-west. By 1834 the mill was producing gutta-percha, the rigid natural latex produced from the sap of *Palaquium* trees. The papermaking side of the business was subsequently removed to Wookey Hole.

The Bath Gaslight & Coke Company was one of the first works to make gas from coal when it opened in 1818. The 13-acre site was on the outer limits of the city, and the original cylinders were small and enclosed in wooden sheds. As time went on the city expanded westwards and the cylinders got much larger. The huge structures were soon a very controversial feature of Bath's skyline. The gasometers were all decommissioned and the site, which also included Stothert & Pitt's Victoria Works, was redeveloped for housing and business by Crest Nicholson as the Bath Western Riverside. The holders generated gas for Bath's streetlamps, another aspect that the Corporation used in order to promote living in or visiting Bath.

People of note still came to Bath and it seems that the city still provided great inspiration to an impressive array of writers and commentators. Charles Dickens visited Bath as a young journalist and his characters in *The Pickwick Papers* (1836) discuss the unique taste of the Bath waters, whilst Thomas Hardy's Cain describes Bath to his companions in *Far from the Madding Crowd* (1874), stating that the residents never needed to light their fires as 'the water springs up out of the earth ready boiled for use'.

By locating scenes from novels in Bath, authors were assured that their readers would know of the place, whether they had visited it or not, whilst adding an element of familiar realism to their works of fiction. Equally, a character's association with Bath, especially from the 1780s to 1820s, instantly projected an indication of their wickedness. For example, Wickham's depravity in *Pride and Prejudice* is alluded to when he goes to amuse himself in Bath, leaving his wife at home. Another dishonest Austen character, Augusta Hawkins in *Emma*, is associated with Bath and thus the reader is to understand that her character is questionable.

On 8 September 1816 Percy Shelley, his lover Mary Godwin and her step-sister Claire Clairmont arrived at Portsmouth from Le Havre. Claire had persistently pursued Lord Byron and, in a moment of weakness after his bitter divorce, he had made Claire pregnant. Byron knew himself to be weak enough to love 'anything on earth that appeared to wish it'. Knowing that London would be a difficult place in Claire's condition, Shelley decided that they should go to Bath instead. He arranged for Mary and Claire to occupy discreet lodgings at No. 5 Abbey Churchyard, whilst he went to London. It was decided that the Shelleys would winter in Bath. In a letter to Bryon, Shelley paints a domestic scene:

> We are all now in Bath, well and content. Claire is writing to you at this instant. Mary is reading over the fire; our cat and kitten are sleeping under the sofa; and little Willy is just gone to sleep. We are looking out for a house in some lone place; and one chief pleasure which we shall expect then, will be a visit from you.

Mary took drawing lessons whilst in Bath and she and Shelley studied chemistry. Bath's leading position in modern science was one of the attractions of the city and Mary made great progress with her novel, *Frankenstein*. The three of them walked up to the Royal Crescent to view the solar eclipse, but it was cloudy and Mary amused herself watching the many cheerless people with burnt glass. (Incidentally, Mary Godwin's mother was Mary Wollstonecraft.)

'The father of English geology', William Smith (1769–1839) surveyed the landscape surrounding Bath whilst working as a coal and mineral prospector.

What he discovered there led him to understand the order of the earth's strata. He famously dictated his findings at his friend, the Reverend Joseph Townsend's house on Great Pulteney Street in 1799. The work he did in Bath would form the basis of his 1815 map, *A Delineation of the Strata of England and Wales, with Part of Scotland; Exhibiting the Collieries and Mines, the Marshes and Fen Lands Originally Overflowed by the Sea, and the Varieties of Soil According to the Variations in the Substrata, Illustrated by the Most Descriptive Names.*

Prime Minister Benjamin Disraeli (1804–81) visited with his friend, Lord Lytton, in the January of 1833. He complained about their lodging house being in an unfashionable part of town, but he made progress with his novel *Alroy*. Disraeli later purchased No. 8 Brock Street in 1861.

William Wordsworth visited for three months in 1841 and stayed at No. 12 North Parade, and his daughter was married at St James's Church.

Possibly Bath's most famous past resident, however, is Jane Austen (1775–1817). The Austen family's first visit to Bath appears to have been in November 1797 when they stayed with Jane's aunt and uncle, the Leigh-Perrots, who were winter residents. Mr Leigh-Perrot was Jane's maternal uncle. In 1799 his wife was arrested and charged with stealing a card of white lace from a milliner's shop in Bath. The value of the lace was high enough to categorise her offence as a capital crime, which usually demanded death by hanging if found guilty or, more likely in this instance, exile in Botany Bay. She was imprisoned for eight months before she came to trial, where she was fortunately acquitted on 27 March 1800.

Perhaps to be of support to their relatives, and because Austen's brother Edward came to take the waters for his ailing health, the Austens took lodgings at No. 13 Queen Square in 1799. 'We are exceedingly pleased with the house; the rooms are quite as large as we expected,' wrote Jane to her sister, Cassandra:

> Mrs Bromley is a fat woman in mourning, and a little black kitten runs about the staircase. Elizabeth has the apartment within the drawing-room;… it is settled for us to be above, where we have two very nice-sized rooms … I like our situation very much;… and the prospect from the drawing room window, at which I now write, is rather picturesque, as it commands a perspective view of the left side of Brock Street, broken by three Lombardy poplars in the garden of the last house in Queen's Parade.

In May 1801, Jane and her mother were again staying at No. 1 The Paragon with the Leigh-Perrots, whilst they searched for a suitable home. 'We know that Mrs Perrot will want to get us in Axford Buildings (near the Paragon), but we all unite in particular dislike of that part of the town, and therefore hope to escape.' By the end of the month, the Austens had rented No. 4 Sydney Place, built by Thomas Baldwin in 1792, where Jane's father, George, and elder sister, Cassandra, joined them. The family moved to No. 27 Green Park Buildings in the autumn of 1804. 'When my uncle went to take his second glass of water,' wrote Jane to Cassandra, 'I walked with him, and in our morning's circuit we looked at two houses in Green Park Buildings, one of which pleased me very well' (Mr Leigh-Perrot was taking a course of the waters as a cure for gout).

After the death of her father in January 1805, Jane, her mother and sister found their income sharply decreased and they became reliant on Jane's brothers, Frank and James. Frank and another brother, Charles, were serving in Nelson's navy. The Austens moved to No. 25 Gay Street.

George Austen was buried at St Swithin's, Walcot, on Saturday, 26 January 1805. Jane's parents had been married there in 1764. The Austens' last address in Bath was on Trim Street. After Frank Austen had saved enough money to marry his fiancée, Mary Gibson, it was decided that they should set up home in Southampton with the three Austen women and their orphaned friend, Martha Lloyd. Jane left Bath for Clifton first, on 2 July 1805, with no regrets but, as she wrote later, with 'happy feelings of escape'.

Between 1801 and 1804 Jane Austen lived at No. 4 Sydney Place, near Sydney Gardens. She had attended events at the pleasure gardens since she moved to Bath in 1799. Her letters record that there was 'a public Breakfast in Sydney Gardens every morning, so that we shall not be wholly starved!' Public breakfasts certainly took place every Tuesday and Saturday. There were also occasional benefit breakfasts, such as the one held for Martha Hewlett in 1798, who had been left in distress with three infants. Austen enjoyed the fireworks and illuminations, taking her sister Cassandra to a display on 4 June 1801, but unlike the majority of the garden's patrons, she was not a fan of the musical events.

Further enhancements to the gardens over the years illustrate not just technological advances, but also society's changing tastes and interests, especially in science. From 1802 there were occasional tethered hot air balloon ascents. A cascade was added in May 1810, a watermill in 1825, and the supper boxes were replaced with an aviary and a cosmorama in 1824. The popularity of the Vauxhall, however, declined alongside Bath's own.

In 1836 John Pinch the Younger (1796–1849) added an attic storey to Sydney House, and it became a residential hotel and cold water spa. After 1853 the Bath Proprietary College took over until the lease ran out and the council sold the building in 1913 to the trustees of the Sir William Holburne (1793–1874) art collection. The alterations to adapt the property to a museum were undertaken by Sir Reginald Blomfield (1856–1942), and the Holburne moved from its premises in Charlotte Street, Bath, where it had been since June 1893, in 1916.

Sir William Holburne (1793–1874) was born in Bath to a Scottish family. He fought with the navy during the Napoleonic Wars. So did his elder brother Francis, but he died in 1814. Therefore it was Thomas (known as William) who succeeded to the title of 5th Baronet of Holburne of Menstrie on the death of their father in 1820. He lived with his three unmarried sisters for the rest of his life at No. 10 Cavendish Crescent. He undertook the Grand Tour in 1824–25 and gradually filled his house with paintings, miniatures, bronzes, gemstones, cameos, silver and silver-gilt objects, ceramics, books and prints. A century on, Holburne's collection can still be seen at the museum in Sydney House.

❋ ❋ ❋ ❋ ❋

Canal fever was sweeping the country during the second half of the eighteenth century. Britain's prowess as an industrial nation with potential and impetus to trade on both a national and international level was significantly enhanced by its expanding network of canals. The Kennet and Avon Canal completed the critical communications and trade link between London and Bristol. Work began to the designs of consultant engineer John Rennie the Elder (1761–1821) in 1794, and was completed in 1807. The canal cost £16,666 per mile, but quickly turned a profit. Attempts had been made since at least the 1500s to navigate the Avon, which – as we have seen – were eventually successful in 1727. Serious schemes to link the Thames and Avon are recorded from the 1600s.

The River Kennet at Newbury and the Thames at Reading were made navigable between 1715 and 1723 under engineer John Hore. The benefits to the businessmen in the west from bridging the gap between Bath and Newbury was unquestionable, but the Kennet and Avon Canal was one of the later systems introduced. The proprietors of the Avon Navigation offered to sell their interest in the river to the Kennet & Avon Canal Co. (K&ACC) in 1793, but the K&ACC obviously did not appreciate that control of the Avon was the key to success and turned the offer down. Two years later, when the K&ACC offered to purchase the Avon Navigation their offer was refused. Instead the K&ACC bought up shares when they became available, taking control in 1796.

Whilst the canal was completed by 1807, the Caen Hill flight of sixteen locks at Devizes took a further three years. During the interim period a tramway lifted barges up the steep incline. No one can deny how impressive the Caen Hill flight is, but the whole trade link is a phenomenal testament to the engineering achievements of our Georgian ancestors.

Just around Bath we have the Claverton pumping station, with its steam-driven beam engine, which pumped water from the Avon to the canal. Originally there was a further pumping station at Widcombe, but that has long since gone. Dundas Aqueduct, near Limpley Stoke, carries the canal over the River Avon. It too was built by Rennie, with chief engineer John Thomas, between 1797 and 1805. It is named after the first chairman of the Kennet & Avon Canal Company – Lord Amesbury Charles Dundas. The aqueduct, built of Bath stone, is nearly 460ft (140m) long, with three spanning arches. In 1951, it was the first canal structure to be designated as a Scheduled Ancient Monument. The Somersetshire Coal Canal (SCC) joined the Kennet and Avon Canal at Limpley Stoke in 1805; today this is the only section of the SCC that survives.

Just up the canal (towards Bradford-on-Avon) is another impressive construction by Rennie and Thomas, the Avoncliff Aqueduct (1797–1801). This structure dominates the hamlet of Avoncliff and, like Dundas, carries the canal over the Avon. Unfortunately, its central spanning arch sagged immediately after construction and it is understood that Rennie regretted using stone. It has since been discovered that the stone used was not of the best quality and Avoncliff has required almost constant maintenance over the last 200 years.

Originally the canal was to join the river at Bathampton, but the fear of seasonal flooding making the route impassable led to the decision to carry the canal on to Bath. As the canal reaches Sydney Gardens it passes through a short tunnel, followed by a further tunnel that passes under Cleveland House, the former canal office of the K&ACC. There is a gap in the roof of this tunnel, and legend has it that it leads to the cellars of Cleveland House, through which letters could be exchanged.

The canal cuts across the eastern corner of Sydney Gardens. Part of the agreement to allow the K&ACC access through the Gardens was that the canal company was required to beautify its passage. The ornamental ironwork and chinoiserie pedestrian bridges, which remain to this day, were designed by Rennie, made in Coalbrookdale from cast and wrought iron and supplied by Stothert & Pitt. In the age of the Enlightenment the canal was seen to be adding to the Gardens' appeal. The canal then joins the River Avon at Widcombe.

❊ ❊ ❊ ❊ ❊

King William IV (1765–1837) only reigned for seven years; he had not expected to succeed, being the younger brother. He served in the navy and was in New York during the American War of Independence; there was even a plot – approved by George Washington – to kidnap him. He served under Nelson in the West Indies and the two were good friends. Due to the Royal Marriages Act (1772), no descendant of George II could marry without the consent of the monarch or the Privy Council. William instead chose to live with his Irish actress girlfriend, Mrs Jordon (Dorothea Bland), and had ten illegitimate children with her. As it started to become obvious that he might ascend to the throne (neither of his two older brothers had produced a legitimate heir), William married Adelaide of Saxe-Meiningen, but their two daughters died in infancy. William was, therefore, the last Hanoverian monarch and the Crown passed to his niece, Victoria, the daughter of his younger brother, Edward.

Ten

ASIA MINOR AND NUISANCE NEIGHBOURS: VICTORIAN BATH

At the beginning of the nineteenth century Bath was the tenth largest town in the country with a population of 33,000, which rapidly increased to 50,802 by 1831, and then more slowly, only reaching around 55,000 in 1851 and declining to about 49,000 in the 1890s. This is in stark contrast to any other major town in Britain at the end of the century. The population *was* increasing, however, in the satellite parishes of Twerton and Weston for instance, but these areas did not come under the administration of Bath until later.

Industry, churches and parks may be a simplistic summary of the Victorian era in general, but it does provide a useful résumé of Bath. After the unprecedented boom of the city during the 1700s, Victorian Bath was not so different from any other metropolis in Britain at this time. Unlike the histories of these other areas, Bath's nineteenth-century legacy is often eclipsed by its Roman and Georgian stories. When it does get told, the narratives often focus on the seedier side of life. This is probably as a counter to Bath's own marketing during the 1800s, which tried desperately to focus on the genteel and ignore the problems of crime, poverty and disease.

For example, in 1832, the Bath Board of Health decided not to release the daily totals of cholera victims to the Central Board in London for fear of the damage it would do to the city's reputation just before the start of the winter season. The local newspaper, nevertheless, carried details of the outbreaks elsewhere in the country, for instance in Sunderland, Liverpool and London.

Another example, as Graham Davis has shown, was that one of the attractions used to entice potential polite residents were the low rates paid by Bathonians. A consequence of this was a lack of civic investment in slum clearance and the provision of decent working-class housing. This public relations illusion was further enhanced instead by the extravagant expenditure on public amenities such as the Guildhall extension (1893–97), Concert Room (1895–97), the Roman Baths Museum (1897) and the Victoria Art Gallery (1897–1900), all designed by Scottish architect John McKean Brydon (1840–1901).

The social structure of Bath during the nineteenth century was, nevertheless, different to other booming Victorian towns. It had become home to the older, retired gentlefolk living off their tolerable incomes. One critic, writing in *The World* in 1876, described both Bath and Cheltenham as being:

> … a kind of Asia Minor; so thickly do old Indians congregate [there … we do not] find many of the men who take the largest and keenest interest in life. There is a leisurely and conventional air about them, a tone of the invalid and dilettante. Generals and Admirals abound; a perceptible portion of the inhabitants have retired on pensions … many simply came to [Bath] to die, and take their twenty or thirty years about it.

Seven years earlier, Charles Dickens had teased Bath for looking 'as if a cemetery full of old people had somehow made a successful rise against death, carried the place by assault, and built a city with their gravestones, in which they were trying to look alive, but with very indifferent success'.

To support the elderly residents, Bath's population included a disproportionate number of young women, who found work as domestic servants and – Bath's greatest employer – in retail. James Jolly, and his son, Thomas, opened their flagship department store, the Bath Emporium, in 1831. It was extended in 1834 and again in 1879, and continues to occupy Nos. 7–14 Milsom Street. The interior retains a number of exquisite Victorian and Art Nouveau architectural details.

Bath did support some industry, as we shall see later, but to nowhere near the extent of other Victorian conurbations and, as a consequence, the majority of working-class men left Bath (or never came in the first place) to seek work elsewhere. The retired population, however, supported a higher than average professional class of bankers, lawyers, doctors and clergy.

This decorous image also helped Bath put some distance between its rowdy Georgian semblance of gambling, drinking, sex, parties, frivolity and pleasure. Much was made of abstinence, with organisations such as the Bath Temperance Association, founded on 15 June 1836, erecting the Rebecca Fountain in June 1861. Bath was described in 1864 as 'probably one of the most religious cities in the kingdom'. The extent of chapel and church building during the 1800s would support this, but what is perhaps lost to us now is the range of division, not just in denomination, but also in the classes who attended.

For example, Bath catered for Catholics with the Catholic Apostolic Church on Guinea Lane, built by George Phillips Manners (1789–1866) in 1841, and St Mary's Roman Catholic Church by Archibald Mathias Dunn and Charles Francis Hansom on Julian Road, built between 1879 and 1881. St John the Evangelist on South Parade (1861–63) was also by Hansom. Christ Church on Julian Road,

J. & J. Dutton: St John's Roman Catholic Church, c. 1868. (Private Collection/Bath in Time)

by John Palmer (1798), was a Free Church erected primarily for working-class families who could not afford the pew rents elsewhere. A cemetery and prayer room in Combe Down served the small Jewish community from 1812.

Nearby, at Claverton Down, T.B. Slick and S.S. Reay's Gospel Hall was built in 1896–97. The Hay Hill Baptist Church was built by Wilson & Willcox in 1869–70. John Wood's St Mary's Chapel, which was lost when Chapel Row was widened in 1870, was replaced (a little further down from the corner with Queen Square) by Holy Trinity Church, also by Wilson & Willcox (1872–74). It was originally dedicated to St Paul, but with the loss of Holy Trinity, built by

John Lowder (1820–22) on James Street West, during the Second World War, it was rededicated. On Charlotte Street, which runs parallel to Chapel Row, is the former Moravian Chapel by James Wilson (1844–45). Moravians were Protestants originating from Germany.

On the opposite side of the street was Goodridge's Elim Pentecostal Chapel (formerly the Percy Chapel) built in 1854 for a breakaway congregation from the Argyle Chapel in Laura Place. James Wilson (1816–1900) also designed St Stephen's Church on Lansdown Road (1840–45), whilst Manners completely rebuilt St Michael's on Broad Street (1835–37). He also added the pinnacles, turrets and flying buttresses to the Abbey in 1833.

Later in the century, Sir George Gilbert Scott (1811–78) undertook a further restoration of the Abbey, including taking the fan vaulting into the nave in 1863–67. Scott also built St Andrew's, behind the Royal Crescent, between 1869 and 1873. The spire was completed in 1878, making St Andrew's Bath's tallest building. It too suffered a direct hit during the Bath Blitz of April 1942 and was eventually demolished in 1957.

Church building and remodelling was certainly prolific, especially in the 1830s, with almost one a year erected. Yet, not all religious buildings were so revered by the Victorians. Part of John Wood's development of Brock Street included Margaret Chapel, where Thomas Linley played the organ. The body of the interior measured 73ft by 60ft, plus the altar recess which contained a painting by a Bath artist called Williams, depicting *The Offerings of the Magi*. Contemporary accounts describe the chapel as being 'light, spacious and elegant'. During the first half of the nineteenth century the chapel was still functioning, with divine service every Sunday at 11.15 a.m. and 3 p.m. It could seat 900 and had 200 free seats. In the 1830s and 1840s the Reverend was William Hutchins, who lived at Winifred House on Sion Hill.

By 1846 Reverend Henry Widdrington, as rector of Walcot, had as part of his responsibilities ministerial duties at the re-sanctified Margaret's Episcopal Chapel. Within thirty years, however, the chapel had fallen out of use, and in 1878 was converted into a skating rink. It was called the People's Hall in 1884, and Jason Steers is recorded as the secretary. In 1898 the chapel was renamed the Brock Street Hall, with Steers still running it. He took advantage of the 'golden age of bicycles' and was now offering cycling lessons too.

A revival in 1905 saw the chapel's rebirth as the Trinity Presbyterian Church under the ministry of Reverend Campbell. The church continued to function until 1921, when it was again put to a secular use as Tilley, Culverwell & Parrott Auction Galleries. The Presbyterian church briefly made a comeback in 1929, but by 1930 Margaret Chapel was once again the Brock Street Hall and being used for badminton. Ultimately the interior was completely destroyed during the

Bath Blitz of April 1942 and the shell of the building was eventually cleared away a few years later.

❋ ❋ ❋ ❋ ❋

With the coming of the railway many hoped that Bath's fortunes would be reversed. The Corporation invested heavily in the spa, introducing all the latest technology. Before the railway, the Kennet and Avon Canal allowed goods to be transported from London to Bristol in just four days. The canal was a massive investment, but it only enjoyed twenty-five years of prosperity before the railway arrived.

The railway at least provided plenty of jobs during the construction work of 1839–41 and the prospect of work attracted even more of the poor and working classes to Bath. However, after the railway was finished there was little to support this increasing population.

The opening of the Great Western Railway in 1841 transformed passenger travel to Bath. In 1835 the average coach journey between London and Bristol took fourteen hours. Isambard Kingdom Brunel (1806–59) aspired to create the fastest and smoothest journey across the country, linking London Paddington to Bristol Temple Meads. To guarantee stability at the speeds he hoped for, Brunel adopted a broad gauge of 7ft (2m). On 30 June 1841, with the completion of the Box Tunnel (between Bath and Chippenham), the train journey took just four hours.

For the Victorians the railway was a beautiful invention, and Brunel showed this universal pride through the attention he gave to every detail, from the goods sheds to the brackets on the lamp posts. He also believed that the railway would enhance Sydney Gardens as it cut through the pleasure grounds. The impact of the Great Western Railway, however, was very severe, destroying the labyrinth and effectively cutting the Gardens in two. In order to try and compensate, in the 1860s the grounds were laid out with a bandstand, croquet, archery and lawn tennis, reflecting the changing leisure interests of the public. The Gardens, which had been separated from the Sydney Hotel in 1855, became the responsibility of the local council in 1912. As a municipal park the remains of Bath's most prominent pleasure garden have been open and free to all for 100 years.

The railway also robbed the canal of its trade – ironic when one considers that the railways could not have been built without the versatility of the canal system to ship materials to the often isolated track construction sites. 'God's Wonderful Railway' approaches Bath in a majestic sweep as it crosses and re-crosses the Avon over a series of bridges. The viaduct, with its battlemented details complete with turrets and heavily moulded Gothic doorways, is in stark contrast to the station building. Bath Spa Station is in the Jacobean Revival style, with mullioned windows, a first floor oriel window and faced in Bath stone – it seems more at home in Bath than the viaduct. A grand approach to and from the station was laid out with Manvers Street and Dorchester Street, but sadly it was butchered later with ad hoc development. As the track continues on to Bristol it crosses the river again via Skew Bridge. At Twerton a number of mill workers' cottages had to be demolished for another viaduct, and the occupants were rehoused in homes created within the railway arches.

A second station, known as Queen Square Station, was built in 1869–70 as a terminal for the Midland Railway from Birmingham. It was built on the fringes of the Green Park development at a cost of £15,625, and served a 10-mile branch line from the main Bristol to Birmingham line at Mangotsfield. From 1874 it was also used by the Somerset & Dorset Railway Company. Travel between the south coast and the north of England flourished and in 1910 the Midland Railway introduced a through service between Manchester and Bournemouth called the 'Pines Express'. It ran until September 1962. The station was a masterpiece of mid-Victorian railway architecture. A glazed and ornamental cast-iron *porte cochère* enhanced the entrance, which led through the hall to an iron-framed single span roof covering the platforms and track. The fine ironwork led to the station being called the 'mini St Pancras'.

The railway encouraged visitors and as a consequence a number of large, purpose-built hotels started to transform the cityscape. Within living memory, the view from the Abbey's west front, through the Pump Room colonnade, on to Stall Street was dominated by an imposing High Victorian hotel.

The area is now partly occupied by Primark, but in its day the Grand Pump Room Hotel was a signifier that Bath was fighting back as a tourist destination. The intention was to give the middle-class visitor to Bath's medicinal waters the same advantages that the Mineral Water Hospital offered the poor. The local joint stock company of proprietors believed that a well-appointed building, filled with every domestic comfort, would encourage the much-needed revival in the spa's fortunes. Such a hotel, it was hoped, would once again raise the prestige of Bath and win back visitors who had been attracted away by other, mainly European, watering places and thereby save Bath from further economic decline.

The site, which once housed Bath's oldest recorded inn – the White Hart Hotel – was given by the Corporation to the scheme because it adjoined the site of the new baths they were about to erect. The White Hart, immortalised by Charles Dickens in *The Pickwick Papers* (1836–37), dated from at least the turn of the sixteenth century, when it was passed down through the Chapman family, many of whom became mayors of Bath. From the seventeenth century the White Hart Hotel was Bath's largest coaching inn, and as such a landmark it was referred

J. & J. Dutton: The Grand Pump Room Hotel, *c.* 1870. (Bath Central Library/Bath in Time)

to often in literature and correspondence. As part of the Bath Improvement Act (1789) the inn received a new, more fashionable façade in 1791. However, the hotel's business was destroyed almost overnight when in 1841 the railways traversed west and replaced the stagecoaches. The White Hart struggled on until 1864, when it finally closed its doors.

The competition to design Bath's new hotel was won in 1867 by William Willcox (*c.* 1838–1923), the business partner of James Wilson. Willcox's design, in the French Renaissance, or Modern French style, was formed around three sides of a courtyard. Across the open side was a screen with a large pedimented entrance intended to reflect the entrance to the Pump Room opposite. With a vermiculated rusticated ground floor and engaged Corinthian columns, Willcox's design was both impressive and confident. The final version, however, was not

as extravagant and details such as the screen were not included. Despite this, few could say that the hotel did not impress quality and luxury on Bath's middle and upper-class visitors. Modern French had become a popular style for grand new hotels at this time, characterised by their multi-storeys and broken skylines of mansard roofs, chimneys and dormers – functional aspects more normally hidden behind parapets in neoclassical Bath were now celebrated as an integral stylistic characteristic.

Completed for £27,000, the Grand Pump Room Hotel was formally opened on 16 June 1869 with a banquet hosted by the mayor and attended by 150 guests. The entrance steps were guarded by two stone lions, which now reside in the grounds at Sion Hill Campus of Bath Spa University. The entrance hall and grand staircase, comprising mahogany handrails over cast-iron balusters and set into Bath stone bases, led to the 107 rooms. The hotel boasted a swimming pool (50ft (15m) long and 27ft (8m) wide) – the Corporation's New Royal Baths; a lift large enough to accommodate a wheelchair; ladies' coffee room and drawing room; a public coffee room, which occupied the whole of the northern wing; and a large billiard room.

The fixtures and fittings were of a high standard with walnut furniture, Kidderminster and Brussels carpets, mantelpieces made from dove marble and relieved by red Devon, and elegant gasaliers. But probably most important was the fact that the hotel could provide direct access to the baths 'by means of an internal doorway and electric lift'. 'Hitherto, guests have been compelled to journey between their hotels and the baths through the open air, with the attendant risk of catching cold.'

The New Royal Baths, built with Corporation money, had opened in 1867:

> Everyone who sees the beautiful suite of baths adjoining the hotel … sees also what the city has gained in this respect. Conveyed by a lift from bedroom floors, the patient is not subject to hazardous and comfortless exposure, while the variety of baths, suited to various forms of complaint, is a great advantage … at the end of a spacious corridor, was added a swimming bath of magnificent proportions surrounded by dressing-rooms; the architecture of the entire building being worthy of the ancient city.

The immediate period did see a gradual increase in demand and family hotels multiplied. In 1889, after the advice of Dr Henry Freeman, surgeon to the Royal Mineral Water Hospital, Douche and Massage Baths were built on the corner of York and Stall Streets. They were an instant hit with Bath's visitors.

The Grand Pump Room Hotel was an immediate success, and could claim patronage by many famous names including Rudyard Kipling and the actors George Arliss, Edward G. Robinson, Sir Ralph Richardson and Leslie Howard.

Willcox and Wilson were instructed to extend the hotel in 1872, and were employed again in 1890–01 to make alterations.

During the rebuilding of the Pump Room in 1790, part of the loose blocks forming the pediment of the Temple of Sulis Minerva had come to light, causing a flurry of excitement and interest. Little was done, though, until the White Hart Inn closed in 1864. James Irvine, a keen antiquary and clerk of works to Sir Gilbert Scott who was engaged on the restoration of the Abbey, knew of the 1790 finds and believed that the body of the temple must lie under the site of the White Hart. Irvine embarked on exploratory excavations. They weren't phenomenal, but modern-day archaeologists have started to appreciate the value of his finds.

Irvine enthused the City Surveyor, Major Charles Edward Davis, and in this way Davis was introduced to the great Roman outfall drain, which led him to discover and excavate the Roman reservoir between 1878–79. And in 1880 Davis was uncovering the Great Bath. A committee was set up and funds raised. The Queen's Bath was demolished in 1885, and beneath it – to the south – the Roman circular bath was discovered. In 1892 the Pump Room extension was intended to make sense of the Roman exhibits and provide a new concert room to relieve the overcrowding. A vaulted roof should have covered the baths, as it would have been and as Davis intended, but party politics kept Davis out of the competition to design the architecture. Instead the baths are open to elements with a really inappropriate and out-of-scale colonnade.

Photochrom Co. Ltd: Roman Baths, 1900s. (Author's Collection)

J.M. Brydon, a London architect, won the competition. The extension was complete by 1897. Brydon had already enlarged Baldwin's Guildhall by providing two new wings set back from the main front. He used an open Tuscan colonnade with pierced balustrade which is reminiscent of Sir Francis Stonor's balustrade that enclosed the King's Bath. Around the terrace are statues of Roman dignitaries by George Anderson Lawson (1832–1904).

These incredible discoveries reignited interest in Bath, the spa and – importantly – Bath's significant Roman past. The Corporation appreciated how important this groundswell was and went all out to provide better visitor facilities. Within a decade the number of bathers had risen by 68 per cent.

❋ ❋ ❋ ❋ ❋

As a dignified and temperate city, Bath disguises a far more habitual picture of a Victorian city. Like numerous other urban regions, Bath had areas of terrible overcrowding and insanitary conditions. These slums tended to be in close proximity to the river. Avon Street and, to the south of the river, the low-lying land of the Dolemeads (colloquially known as 'Mud Island') was particularly poor. It had still been pastureland in 1788 when advertised in the *Chronicle* as about 18 acres of meadowland. According to Rowland Mainwaring, the 'miserable abodes', which suffered regular and devastating floods, were a 'nuisance … neighbourhood' harbouring 'a colony of vice and dissipation'. Life expectancy here by the 1840s was a shocking twenty-five years.

As we have seen, Bath's popularity and prosperity, its reputation as a saviour of health and charitable outlook has encouraged the poor and needy to travel to Bath for centuries. Previously these groups created their ghettoes across the river in Holloway and Widcombe – now they occupied a very central and very visible part of town.

The Building Act of 1760 specified that the thickness of the party wall of new houses needed to be increased from 2 to 2½ bricks for cellars and from 1¼ to 2 bricks thick for the remaining storeys (or the equivalent in stone). The 1764 Act banned the use of timber in the construction of hearths. Whilst the Act of 1774, which still instructs our building regulations, imposed a minimum standard for working-class housing – it also served to diminish previously built houses to the status of a slum. Works not executed in accordance with the act could be demolished or amended, and the workmen were liable to a fine of 50 shillings and to be 'committed to the house of correction'. The act strove to prevent fire and shoddy construction methods, a consequence of the lessons learnt from the Great Fire of London. A typical terrace built in the mid-eighteenth century was two rooms deep and three storeys high, with entrance, stair and passage along the party wall.

The slums of the Dolemeads, Avon Street and Holloway were notorious. The houses were damp, cramped and unhygienic. The communities were diseased and miserable. Avon Street was considered one of the worst parts, but that may have been because it was incredibly close to the higher quality areas of Kingsmead and Queen Square. Avon Street had been built as middle-class accommodation in 1727, but soon became a through route for horses being led to the Avon for water and for materials being shipped from the city's wharf.

An open letter to the City Commissioners, published in the *Bath Evening Chronicle* in 1777, decried:

> But who, gentlemen, that has any delicacy of taste, can survey the streets of Bath, – the grand resort of the British Nobility and Gentry, without being disgusted with the excrementitious filth with which some of them are spread? – I cannot be supposed to allude so much to the new ... parts of the town; but never, surely, was censure more justly applied, than to the management of some of the old, and in particular Avon street, and the parts adjacent ... Suffer me Gentlemen, here to suggest to you the necessity, the absolute necessity, of a particular attention to those parts of the town where the greatest number of the labouring people crowded together; they are ever apt to take example by each other in degenerating into indecency: Nastiness gradually produces sloth, and debases and corrupts both the body and the mind. By a proper attention to regulations, some plan might be, doubtless, formed for restraining, not only the nasty practice of easing nature on the pavement in almost every corner, but also the equally disagreeable one, of throwing urine and other foul water, from the windows into the streets ... and the almost universal one of throwing cinders and other refuse out before the doors ... And, as some of the owners of houses in Avon Street, have begun to do something in the long-neglected business of repairing the pavement, it is hoped you will give proper directions for removing all the straggling posts, raising the foot-paths, and rendering a narrow street, in which a great number of children are frequently seen, as secure as may be from the many horses which pass and repass to water.

In 1874, John Earle showed that the situation was little better across the river at Holloway. It was the haunt of vagrant vagabonds:

> In proportion as the Squares and Crescents filled with the affluent, the dens of Holloway filled with beggars. This was their camp from whence they watched the visitors who were their prey, and eluded the Corporation who were their natural enemies ... Bath, which enjoyed a pre-eminence in other things, was equally distinguished for its colony of beggars.

Towards the end of the eighteenth century it had become uneconomical for the night soil men to remove the sewage and sell it on to the local farmers. Instead, much of the waste went directly into the rivers, making housing developments near the river instantly less desirable. Lady Nelson wrote from New King Street (adjacent to the slum areas) in 1797, 'the higher you go, the dearer'. Annual rents for New King Street were £90 in comparison to Gay Street, where they were £160. There was, of course, a well-known house of ill repute, kept by Jane Jarvis and Ann White in New King Street, enough to keep any property price down.

During the cholera epidemic of 1832, more than half of those killed in Bath came from Avon Street. One in twenty-five of Bath's population, or 10,000 people, lived in the slums of this district. In 1821 the *Bath and Cheltenham Gazette* described Avon Street as having 'at least 300 people who obtain a living by begging, thieving, or on the miserable wages of prostitution'.

According to Reverend Elwin in 1842, 'Everything vile and offensive is congregated there. All the scum of Bath – its low prostitutes, its thieves, its beggars – are piled up in the dens.' In 1852 the area was described as 'a region of filth, squalor, and demoralisation, where poverty and crime lurk in miserable companionship, and where … they may be said to enjoy, a kind of sanctuary free from the intrusion of respectability'.

Despite this enduring perception of Avon Street as a notorious slum, home only to beggars, thieves and prostitutes, it could at least sustain a school, and a third of the ninety properties are listed in the *Bath Directories* because the residents could claim a trade such as chimney sweep, drover, grocer, mason or fish dealer.

Many of the properties were owner-occupied and lodging houses and pubs still did good business. In 1890, for instance, George Hartnell kept a lodging house at Nos. 16 and 17. The migrant workers, tramps and hawkers found cheap lodgings here. Tenement buildings sprang up, gardens were filled in with courts and workshops, such as New Court between Nos. 59 and 60 and Pickwick Mews between Nos. 20 and 21. The area was overcrowded, damp and unhygienic.

Mrs Mary Neil was landlady of the Fountain, Avon Street's largest pub. There was also the Old Fellows Arms at No. 70, the Shamrock at Nos. 31 and 32, the Lamb at No. 42 and the Garibaldi at No. 10 (John Baker, a grocer, opened the beerhouse in 1864 to note the visit to Bath of the great military unifier of Italy). A couple of these, including the Lord Nelson at No. 2, stayed open for business from the eighteenth until the first half of the twentieth century. No. 14 was a warehouse and at the bottom was Wilcock's Bath City Iron and Brass Foundry.

Artist Robert Cruikshank chose to illustrate a very local theme – with a national reputation – with his *The Buff Club at the Pig and Whistle, Avon Street Bath* (1825). The Pig and Whistle was the colloquial name for the Lord Nelson pub on Avon

Avon Street, *c.* 1880. (Bath Central Library/Bath in Time)

Street. It had started life as the Crown, and then around 1790 became known as the Crown and Thistle, and with that came its rhyming nickname the 'Pig and Whistle'. Tobias Smollett had referred to 'the nymphs of Avon Street' in *Humphry Clinker* and we immediately appreciate the true destitution of Anne Elliott's friend, Mrs Smith, in Jane Austen's *Persuasion* as she lodged in Westgate Buildings, near the river and ominously too close to Avon Street for Anne's father to feel comfortable about her visiting.

The Pig and Whistle was notorious for the depravity of its gin-soaked prostitutes. The pub was frequented by wealthy men, looking for a rollicking good time. Cruikshank's complicated crowd scene shows the full extent of the lurid behaviour with its variety of half-dressed women, excessive drinking, smoking, fighting (strikingly, placed centre stage are two prostitutes engaged in a violent confrontation), spitting and general free-for-all – all whilst the band plays on. One nineteenth-century commentator believed that the authorities continued to grant the premises a licence as it contained, and therefore controlled, the more shameless side of Bath's nightlife. The fear and misunderstanding of the culture of these communities by those who believed they held the moral high ground compounded the problem. By blaming the community for the conditions, and thus the rampant spread of disease, the Corporation felt appeased for not doing anything.

Of course Bath had its share of what the higher social orders called the 'deserving poor'; those who lived good moral lives and through no fault of their own had fallen on hard times. They were seen, therefore, to be more entitled to receive charity. The higher-class moralists had little understanding of the conditions or the communities. They believed that 'thrift, sobriety, education, apprenticeship, church attendance and outward social conformity were,' as Graham Davis neatly summarises, 'the passports to a higher social station'. Bath's charitable side thankfully continued throughout the nineteenth century, with facilities such as the dispensary on Cleveland Place East, built in 1845, which gave medical advice and medicines to the poor, and the Bath Ear and Eye Infirmary (1837) on the London Road, a drop-in centre for the poor.

The Bath Poor Law Union was formed on 28 March 1836 (a consequence of the 1834 Poor Law Amendment Act), and its operation was overseen by an elected board of guardians – forty-one in number, representing the twenty-four constituent parishes of St James, St Michael, St Peter and Paul, Walcot, Bathampton, Batheaston, Bathford, Bathwick, Charlcombe, Charterhouse

Robert Cruikshank: The Buff Club at the Pig and Whistle, Avon Street, Bath, 1825. (Bath Central Library/Bath in Time)

Hinton, Claverton, Combe Hay, Dunkerton, Englishcombe, Langridge, Lyncombe & Widcombe, Monkton Combe, St Catherine, South Stoke, Swanswick, Twerton, Wellow, Weston and Woolley (Freshford was added in 1883). The population falling within the union in 1831 was 64,230. The average annual poor-rate expenditure for the period 1832–35 was £19,928, or 6s 2d per head.

The new workhouse was built in 1836–38 by Manners, to a design by Sampson Kempthorne on a site to the south of the city at Odd Down, between Warminster Road (now Midford Road) and Frome Road. It was designed to accommodate 600 people and cost around £12,300. The workhouse had a hexagonal outer range and a 'Y' shaped inner block of radial wings with a central supervisory hub. The buildings, mostly of three storeys, were faced with Bath stone. At the north of the site was the bakery, which employed the services of two full-time bakers. In addition to producing its own bread, the workhouse had 5 acres of vegetable gardens, orchards and a pigsty, all looked after by the inmates. There was also a shoemaker's shop, an infirmary and a chapel. Unfortunately, by 1845 the workhouse was overcrowded, and a total of 758 adults and 374 children were crammed into accommodation designed for 600.

Despite the cramped conditions, the education of the children seems to have been successful. As well as the standard three daily hours of schooling required by law, the guardians decided that every child should acquire basic skills in knitting, tailoring and shoemaking. The boys also learnt haircutting. In 1846 the inspector of schools, Mr Clarke, reported that he had spent three hours of great satisfaction in the schools of Bath Union Workhouse. The boys were smart, intelligent and well informed. The girls also deserved praise, except in their arithmetic.

In 1905, the workhouse became known as Frome Road House, and later as Frome Road House Poor Law Institution. During the Second World War, an EMS (Emergency Medical Service) hospital operated on the workhouse site. In 1948, with the inauguration of the National Health Service, it became St Martin's Hospital. Many of the original buildings were redeveloped for residential use in 2005.

❊ ❊ ❊ ❊ ❊

The low-lying land in Bath was frequently flooded up until the last century. The local newspapers provide us with a record throughout the eighteenth, nineteenth and early twentieth centuries of normally two per year (winter floods with rainfall or snow thaw and summer floods created mainly by storms and parched land). Naturally some of the floods were far worse than others, but the accounts

The great floods in Bath, Nov.ʳ 13ᵗʰ & 15ᵗʰ 1894.

Friese Greene & Co.: The Great Floods in Bath, 13–15 November 1894. (Bath Central Library/Bath in Time)

are littered with stories of people losing their lives, their livestock and their livelihoods.

In 1823 a man drowned because he was bedridden in his home in the Dolemeads. In January 1841 a terrible flood caused by a sudden thaw saw devastation sweep through areas adjacent to the Avon. Fortunately no one was killed, but there was extensive damage. Residents of Bathwick described how the river had risen at about '10 inches an hour, reaching 20ft at its highest'. The *Bath Evening Chronicle* reported:

The effects of the flood were, as usual, the most severely felt in the Dolemeads where, in consequence of the poverty of the inhabitants, houses with four rooms very generally contain as many families. During the recent severe weather, much misery has been experience by this part of our population. In many of their dwellings there was neither food nor fuel, and but a very scanty supply of clothes and bedding ... On Monday, after the water had left their houses, the inhabitants were seen occupying them wet as they were, without the spark of fire, and exposed to the cold wind, making its way through the broken windows ... We regret being obliged to add that many of the in habitants of the Dolemeads had gone to bed the preceding night in a state on intoxication habitual to them, and had they not been roused ... we should not be now able to announce that no loss of human life took place.

The Avon has flooded regularly here, the levels of which are recorded on the riverside wall of Widcombe footbridge. In addition, when the river flooded it would flush back up the sewer as well as over the riverbanks, flooding the streets and lower levels of the houses on the low-lying land. Bill Cottle, who grew up in Corn Street in the early 1900s, recorded 'rats as big as cats' scampering across his bedroom revisiting the redeposited sewage. In the 1860s there were fifty-three slaughterhouses in central Bath, and they tended to concentrate along the riverfront so that the blood, guts and animal dung could be easily swept into the Avon. Other industries that tended to line up along the river and add to the pollution and stench were the breweries, tanneries, soap boilers and steam dyers.

What 'saved' Bath on the one hand were the plentiful fresh water springs, but on the other, this supply probably condemned the city to having a Corporation who did very little about public sanitation. Even in 1530 John Leland noted that there were lead pipes conveying the fresh water from house to house and place to place. In addition there were the public conduits and fountains enabling anyone to have access to fresh water. Davis redesigned the Ladymead Fountain in 1860 as part of the planned scheme, adopted in May 1850, to erect public fountains. Stephano Pieroni donated an ostentatious hot mineral fountain to the city in 1859. Although pared down over the years, it stood until 1987 on Stall Street, at the entrance to Bath Street.

The Housing the Working Classes Act of 1890 empowered councils to redevelop slum areas. The ground of the Dolemeads was raised up, in some places by over 13ft (4m), in order to avoid the worst of the river rises. New, red brick houses – so unusual in stone-built Bath – were erected between 1901 and 1921 and standards of living were instantly improved.

❋ ❋ ❋ ❋ ❋

Bath, just as every other city in Great Britain, had its fair share of Victorian entrepreneurs. At the age of 14 Jonathan Burdett Bowler (1834–1911) was apprenticed to the City Brass Foundry and Iron Works, working his way up to foreman. Bowler, however, occupied his leisure hours with more work. He repaired, maintained and made mechanical equipment, including leg irons, corset stiffeners, pumps and soda water apparatus. He also kept a smallholding of vegetables and pigs, selling any surplus.

All of his activities brought in enough profit to enable Bowler to establish a property portfolio, leave the foundry and set up his own engineering and soft drinks business. J.B. Bowler & Sons provided a diverse service from soda siphons, house bells and pony harnesses to gaslights. They equally specialised in servicing the equipment used by brewers, public houses and mineral water manufacturers. Bowler briefly entered into a partnership with Walter Edward Annely in 1876, and together they bought and expanded Thomas Bull's mineral water manufacturing company on Corn Street. By November 1877, however, Bowler had taken full control. The mineral water business and the brass foundry were kept as separate concerns, although one or other of the family firms employed almost all of his thirteen children.

The mineral waters were particularly popular, researchers have discovered that the once 'secret recipes' all included a liquid called Twaddle. This consisted of a hundredweight of sugar, 4oz of refined saccharine and 4lb of tartaric acid, stirred briskly into 50 gallons of water. It was added to every drink Bowlers offered, including its lemonade, ginger ale and lime juice. The cordials had delightful names, such as Cherry Ciderette, Orange Champagne, Hop Stout and Horehound Beer. J.B. Bowler & Sons was one of Bath's most successful and prominent Victorian businesses; a prestigious moment must have been when the company was engaged by the Corporation to illuminate the Guildhall for Queen Victoria's Diamond Jubilee in 1897.

Bowler never threw anything away – all spare parts, fittings, bottles, machinery, paper records (bills, receipts and correspondence) were kept. Machines were fixed, just as the firm fixed the machines, cars, valves, steam engines, boilers, lamps and soda siphons of its customers. When the firm closed in 1969 the archive was kept in trust and in 1978 transferred to (what is now called) the Museum of Bath at Work. The museum has evocatively recreated the Corn Street premises. Bowler's previous employer, Wilcock's, who owned the City Brass Foundry and Iron Works on Avon Street, also had a mineral water machinery factory, further workshops on Avon Street and Back Street, and a showroom on Westgate Street.

In the late 1840s, the Carr family from Penrith in Cumbria bought Charles Wilkins' cloth mills at Twerton and coal mine at Pennyquick. By 1860 the company had established an international reputation as producers of high-quality woollen materials and the business expanded with a new mill built on Weston Island. The family owned a number of prestigious properties, including Wood House (demolished 1965), Claverton Manor (now the American Museum in Britain) and Poolemead House (now a centre for the Royal National Institute for the Deaf), and left a legacy of investment and benefaction throughout Bath, but especially in Twerton.

William Harbutt (1844–1921), an art teacher at the Bath School of Art and subsequently at his own art school on the Paragon, invented Plasticine in the basement of his home at No. 15 Alfred Street (near the Upper Assembly Rooms) for use in his art classes in 1897. A growth in demand required a more commercial form of production and so by 1900 an old steam flour mill in Bathampton was utilised. The business expanded, and in 1902 a limited company was formed with William and his two elder sons, Noel and Eric. By 1908, William and his eldest daughter, Olive, were undertaking promotional tours together: they visited Australia, New Zealand, Canada and the United States. Harbutts was taken over by Berwick-Timpo Ltd in 1976 but, very sadly, the Bathampton premises went into receivership in 1983.

Messrs Stothert & Pitt continued to grow during the Victorian era; they took chances and invested in different trades, such as the woollen mills in Twerton and a portable brewing machine. They established a separate engineering company in Bristol for the manufacture of steam locomotives and steamships. The Bristol operation was run by Henry Stothert, and it was this company that Robert Pitt (1818–86) joined as an apprentice. In November 1844, alongside George Rayno, Pitt became a partner in the company. The works expanded and was renamed the Newark Foundry in 1827. The growth of maritime trade and the increasing bulk of cargo led to the expansion of their crane production. It is probably for their cranes that Stothert & Pitt are best known. By 1890 the firm acquired another large factory, called the Victoria Works, on the south side of the River Avon.

Other notable entrepreneurs, industrialists and inventors were based in Bath. John Arthur Roebuck Rudge, who lived at No. 1 New Bond Street Place, was the first Englishman to produce moving pictures by means of photographs on a revolving drum. Nearby, on the Corridor, his friend William Friese-Greene had his studio. He was the inventor of commercial kinematography.

Bath was also the birthplace of Henry Cole (1808–82), the organiser of the Great Exhibition at Hyde Park, London. Alongside Stothert & Pitt, a number of Bath companies were represented amongst the 13,000 exhibits showcasing Britain's industrial strength and leadership. Bath sent forty-six exhibitors (the far larger Bristol sent sixty-five in comparison), including Vezey (carriage maker), Randell & Saunders (industrial stone quarrying equipment) and the cabinet makers Henry Eyles of Broad Street.

Bath's traditional industry of stone quarrying also grew. The canal and then the railway had opened up new markets for Bath stone. The digging of the Box Tunnel (1836–41) for the Great Western Railway (GWR) had shown that there was quality stone still available to the east of Bath and by 1864, 100,000 tons of stone was being exported via Corsham Station.

In a city such as Bath, celebrated for its honey-stone buildings, it is rare to find brick-built properties, but they do exist, for example in Excelsior Street, Westmoreland Street, Avondale Road, Audley Park and the railway bridge on Pulteney Road. There were a number of commercial companies including the Bath Victoria Brick & Tile Company in Oldfield Park (established in around 1890, bankrupt 1952), the Moorfield Brick & Tile Company, established in 1885, and the Morland Brick & Tile Works, which was located at the end of Dartmouth Avenue and Millmead Road with sidings on the Somerset and Dorset railway line.

❋ ❋ ❋ ❋ ❋

The Bath and West Centenary Show at Bear Flat in 1877 was beset with disaster. Hundreds of visitors to the show alighted the train, but the toll keeper on the bridge across the river could not collect the halfpennies quickly enough – there were too many people on the bridge and it collapsed. Ten people died and many more were injured. The *Bath Evening Chronicle* established quickly that the passengers were not unruly and were waiting in an orderly fashion to take their individual turn to pass through the tollgate. One of the victims was John Milborne, a 62-year-old tailor from Yeovil. His badly crushed leg had been amputated as soon as he had arrived at the Royal United Hospital (now the

Workers of the Moorland Brick and Tile Works, Oldfield Park, Bath, *c.* 1900. (Bath Central Library/Bath in Time)

Gainsborough Hotel), and he appeared to be making progress, but suddenly he took a turn for the worse and died a week after the incident on Sunday, 10 June.

Lansdown Fair, usually held on St Lawrence's day, was, according to Pierce Egan:

> A very large fair, and distinguished for the sale of horses and large quantities of cheese; great numbers of cattle and pigs are also brought here. It is a most convenient spot for the numerous assemblage of persons that arrive from Bristol, Gloucestershire, Wiltshire etc. and it proves quite a jubilee day for the country people to enjoy the gingerbread stalls ... and the numerous shows from different parts of England, of every description, to obtain the money from the pockets of the lads and lasses, are not wanting. Lansdown Fair is also notorious for a number of pitched battles which are fought by the pugilistic heroes of Bristol.

There were also Punch and Judy shows, fake exotic animals and human freak shows. It was renowned for being an unruly affair and the location for major criminal damage and intimidation by one of Bath's more notorious criminals, Carrotty Kate. She has probably been remembered because she was a woman (and a redhead).

Towards the end of the 1839 Lansdown Fair, Kate and her gang descended on the site and started to smash up the stalls and steal alcohol and money. They set fire to property until they grew bored and returned to Avon Street. The gang, including Kate, was captured, brought back to the site of the fair and flogged. When they returned again to the city they were met by the police. A further riot ensued, and a policeman was seriously injured. The gang was eventually rounded up, arrested, tried and a number were transported.

※ ※ ※ ※ ※

Bath is world famous for its rugby club, which was founded in 1865, making it one of the oldest clubs in existence. The club did not have a permanent home until it leased a plot of land from the Forester family, the owners of the Bathwick Estate, in 1894. They played at Claverton Down, Lambridge Meadows (where they still train) and Henrietta Park (amongst other locations). The first rugby match was played on the ground later that year. About a quarter of the space the club currently occupies lies over the site of Spring Gardens.

※ ※ ※ ※ ※

John Betjeman believed Major Davis was a 'monster' for giving us the Empire Hotel (1901). The height, architectural treatment and proximity to the Abbey,

Grand Parade and the Empire Hotel, 1930s. (Author's Collection)

River Avon and Pulteney Bridge have consistently been levelled against Bath's second largest purpose-built hotel. Now refurbished as luxury retirement flats with restaurants below, it was the people of Bath who perversely campaigned to save this seemingly loathed building from being demolished in 1991. Love it or hate it, the eccentric Empire Hotel seems to have a special place in Bath's history.

Major Charles Edward Davis (1827–1902) is probably more famously associated with the discovery and excavation of the Roman Baths. According to some reports, his failure to secure the contract to develop the Pump Room and Roman Baths, despite winning the anonymous open competition of 1893, was the final disappointment after decades of fraught relations with the local council. The difficulties lay in Davis' parallel occupation as both Bath's Surveyor of Works for forty years and director of this own architectural practice. Davis and those in local government who supported him were lambasted for what others considered an unethical conflict of interests.

Critics will have you believe that the Empire Hotel was in fact a final act of pompous revenge by Davis on a council who had thwarted his plans and made his professional life a misery. However, Davis had had ambitions to build a hotel in Bath for a number of years. He narrowly missed out on the contract to build the Grand Pump Room Hotel in 1865 (another example of the Council purposefully rejecting Davis' winning designs after he was unveiled as the architect). On at least two other occasions (1875 and 1886) Davis was at the forefront of plans to develop another large purpose-built hotel in Bath. Although they came to nothing, both schemes were sited on city-centre land overlooking the Avon.

Furthermore, although few praise the style of the Empire, it is very iconic of its time. Across the country grandiose and flamboyant hotels were springing up in every major city – the Empire is contemporary with the Langham (1885), Savoy (1889) and Ritz (1905) hotels in London, and the Midland Hotel in Manchester (1898–1903). This type of architectural eclecticism was all the rage at this time. Jacobethan or Old English was seen to be more in keeping with our history than Classicism, and became a preferred national style. Mixed as it is with elements of Queen Anne Revival and a flurry of French Renaissance Revival style, the Empire is Bath's only true example of a High Victorian building.

Davis' other main ambition for Bath was for a new road system along the Avon between Orange Grove and Bridge Street. The building of the Empire was therefore part of a larger scheme which included improvements to New Market Row. Extending over Parade Gardens with the use of a colonnade created the wider Grand Parade roadway we have today. However, whilst the scheme was praised for clearing away the shambles of ill-matched and rundown market buildings, it also saw the demolition of a number of historically significant buildings including Nassau House, the Athenaeum, Grove Tavern, Sun Tavern and Winchester House.

This central site, with river frontage, suggests that this must have been a very valuable building plot. The Council's acceptance of the plans reflects Bath's sadly short-lived upturn in fortunes at this time. Interest was being generated equally by the spa and (rather ironically) by the recently discovered Roman antiquities. Nevertheless this optimism was not shared by all the local ratepayers. In October 1898, Tommy Rot Publishing Co. produced two handbills which sarcastically ridiculed the council's policy of using their rates to fund the building of the hotel.

Similar protests had been made over the council's plans to extend the Guildhall and provide a new art gallery. *Tommy Rot* asserted that the facts and figures provided were misleading. The Council promised that the hotel would boost the local economy, and what every citizen would gain from increased job and trade opportunities would far exceed the £500 a year of ratepayers' money that the hotel was estimated to cost. During a speech at the Cornmarket, Mr Mallet proclaimed that the hotel could accommodate 150 visitors, and these would be mostly millionaires. In response, *Tommy Rot* revealed that this would amount to 7,800 millionaires a year. They therefore asked for a new promotional picture of the Empire with a millionaire in each window, and those awaiting accommodation camping out in the New Market Row – to be renamed Millionaire's Piazza!

Private investment was found in Alfred Holland, an entrepreneur who approved of Davis' designs and wrote to the council, 'I am taking it for granted there are no restrictions as to its height', although Davis did submit drawings of the skyline, showing the divergent gables. The foundation stone was laid on 7 December 1899, and the hotel opened to the public on 28 November 1901.

It is a solid building, extremely well-built, of five storeys with an additional two in the roof and the octagonal corner turret rising to the equivalent of an eighth storey with ironwork on top. An advertisement feature soon after its completion boasts of the building being 'most beautifully appointed', with an inner and outer lounge overlooking the river but protected from draughts. The hotel was heated and ventilated using modern scientific methods, especially advantageous to invalids. 'In addition there are numerous public rooms containing every comfort of modern life.' The hotel's own omnibus met all trains arriving in Bath, and the visitors' servants were facilitated with their own dining and reading rooms.

The response to the Empire has always been mixed. *The Illustrated London News* welcomed the hotel in 1901 as 'the latest addition to [Bath's] splendours'. However, in 1961 Bryan Little likened its 'neo-Jacobean bulk' to being as out of place 'as a gasometer could have been'. Nikolaus Pevsner called it 'an unbelievable piece of *pompier* architecture' and decried its proximity to the Abbey. In 1982, John Haddon, in his *Portrait of Bath*, admitted a certain fondness for it and felt it to be sufficiently far from the Abbey not to be overwhelming. In 2000 Peter Borsay summarised, 'To the post-war generation the principal symbol of Victorian bad taste was the Empire Hotel, an edifice which seemed to epitomise the awful consequences in Bath straying from the straight and narrow path of the classical tradition'.

For our generation the Empire has always stood prominently, challenging our perceptions of classical Bath, and I rather like it for that.

Eleven

PAGEANT, PRESERVATION AND WAR

At the beginning of the twentieth century, Queen Victoria still held the throne, outlasting her grandfather as the longest reigning monarch. Her children had married into the royal families across Europe, leading to Victoria being known as the 'grandmother of Europe'. Sadly this would see cousins pitched against each other during the First World War.

In 1900 only 60 per cent of adult males had the vote and no woman could vote in anything other than a local election. Huge swathes of the population were illiterate, many living in slums. Child labour was still rife and working conditions were harsh. The Empire, however, was strong and dominant, with Britain 'owning' 20 per cent of the world and governing 400 million people. Lord Salisbury, the last peer to be prime minister, was succeeded by his nephew, Arthur Balfour, in 1902. Salisbury's first name was Robert, and the saying 'Bob's your uncle' originates here.

In Bath, as elsewhere, the lower classes made a living the best way they could. No ordinary street seller, Dominico Conio was described as 'the best-known man in Bath' in 1906. His patch was Manvers and Pierrepont Streets where he sold newspapers, mainly *The Bladud* and the *Bath Chronicle*. Of course, what set him apart were the twenty or so guinea pigs he kept. Few people knew Conio by his given name, but he was recognised internationally as 'Guinea-pig Jack'.

He was said to hail from Chiavari, a village near Genoa, and yet his mysteriousness was intensified not only by his lack of English, but also by his marked colloquial Italian. When Conio was interviewed for the *Bath Herald* he insisted that he had learnt the English language within three years of arriving here, although the journalist still struggled to fully comprehend Jack's life story. He talked about travelling around Britain before settling in Bath, and had particularly fond memories of friends he had made in Portsmouth. When asked how long he had been in Bath he replied twenty years, but everyone knew that he had been here far longer. Further investigation revealed that Jack could not count beyond twenty, and so anything that happened in the past could only

Breamore Series:
Guinea-pig Jack, 1905.
(Author's Collection)

ever be twenty years ago! For the same reason, he did not know his age. Some guessed at 90, but in 1906 Laura Chesshyre wrote to *The Bath Herald* from New Zealand saying that she had met Jack when she arrived in Bath in April 1848, and she guessed him to have been about 16 years old at that time. Jack was, therefore, only in his mid-seventies when he died.

Contemporary descriptions regularly refer to 'his cheery though weatherworn face, surmounted by an antiquated peaked cap, also weatherworn, a jacket and trousers evidently not made to measure' and his diminutive figure. He was said to dress in a bright red soldier's coat, and contemporary depictions do show him in a red waistcoat. It was thought that his father had been a solider and Jack himself reputedly returned to Italy occasionally to fulfil his national service obligations, although his reduced stature meant he was never conscripted.

He lived for at least forty years at No. 84 Avon Street. This property was a lodging house run by Sarah and Antonio Pieroni, where Jack recommended the large fire they kept and the glass of beer that they included with his board. Each day Jack went to work with a wire-fronted wicker basket hanging by his side, and contained within were two or three guinea pigs. According to G.H. Reade in *The Gentlewoman* of 1907, 'he looked at you with twinkling eyes, hand on his basket, heart in your pockets'. To passers-by he offered to 'make you perform guinea pig?'. His trick was to retrieve a guinea pig from the small basket and get it to play dead – 'Johnny die queek'. He would then revive them with his cry, 'Wake Up. Bobby, comin'!' – all for a halfpenny. He was particularly remembered for always being courteous whether you gave him a halfpenny or not. His phrase, 'Much oblige to you', appears as the caption to one of the portraits now in the Victoria Art Gallery collection.

Rumours abounded that Jack was actually very wealthy, with a king's ransom stashed under his mattress. He died, however, in poverty, and so the story goes that when he thought he was going to die in the early 1900s he gave his fortune to the Catholic Church. When he regained his health, he was unable to recover his money. This, according to the word on the street, was why the priests took such good care of him when he fell ill again in October 1906. Mrs Mary Ann Wall, a fried fish deliverer from St John's Place and Sarah Pieroni's niece, nursed him throughout the winter, but Conio died of acute bronchitis in January 1907. Wall kept one of his guinea pigs as a memento of her friend, and paid for his funeral. He is buried in the Catholic cemetery at Perrymead.

The patch he worked meant that Jack was the first sight that greeted visitors to Bath coming from the railway station, and 'to the returning visitor or resident to miss Jack was to lose sight of a well-known and familiar landmark'. His celebrity status is revealed by the international coverage of this strange and quirky character in magazines, newspapers and at least one novel; he was even featured in the American *Harper's Magazine*. Not to mention the outpouring of column inches given over to his obituaries.

The Victoria Art Gallery holds three portraits of him. He was photographed, featured on a postcard, and remarkably a porcelain figurine was also made of Guinea Pig Jack. A sketch by C.M. Hodges, appeared in the *Bath and County Graphic* in April 1897. The caption read, 'An Italian "Fancier" in Bath'. When Jack's absence from Bath's streets was noted at the end of 1906, a fan – known only as H.W.B. – sent a long poem he had written about this much loved Bath personality to the *Bath Herald*. The scenario was based on an imaginary conversation between a visitor and a local policeman:

> Who is that quaint little man down the street, sir?
> He with the coat that's too big for his back?
> Not many folk that I happen to meet, sir,
> Haven't some knowledge of Guinea Pig Jack.
> No one that I know can tell much about him,

Yet it's a fact beyond question or doubt,
This wouldn't be just the same place with him,
So many years he's been hanging about …
This is the road as you see, to the station –
He soon found out its peculiar worth …
One thing's as certain as fog in November,
When his time comes there'll be many regrets
Each one who knew him will 'kindly remember'
Guinea Pig Jack, with his papers and pets.

Not bad for an impoverished keeper of guinea pigs.

In 1909 there was a major development in the fight to preserve Bath for future generations. In the face of the council's decision to allow one side of Bath Street to be demolished, a group of pioneers founded the Old Bath Preservation Society. Bath Street, with its Ionic colonnades and crescent-shaped termini, had been laid out by Thomas Baldwin as part of the Bath Improvement Act. In February 1909 it became known that the council had sanctioned a scheme to improve the facilities at the Grand Pump Room Hotel, which fronted Stall Street and abutted Bath Street.

The hotel had been closed for six years whilst negotiations between the council and the new lessee, Waring-White Building Company, were undertaken. In October 1906 an agreement was reached that granted Waring an extended lease on the understanding that £20,000 of structural work was undertaken to adapt 'the whole of the premises including No. 10 Bath Street for use as a first-class hotel; also, the lessee to re-construct the ground floor and basement of Nos. 9, 11 to 14 and 10, Bath Street of sufficient strength to carry the superstructure'. These works would have enhanced the council owned bathing facilities by incorporating a ticket office and entrance to the baths within the hotel complex.

However, at the time No. 10 was privately owned, and seemingly the owner had no intention of selling up. Over the next two years reports were made and modifications to the plans were made accordingly. On 10 March 1908 an agreement between Waring and the council was reached, on the understanding that all works would be completed and the hotel opened no later than 1 July, in time for the Bath Historical Pageant.

The council were openly accused of supporting the demolition in order that they might profit from the increased rates that the extension of the hotel would afford them. Within days, Prebendary S.A. Boyd, rector of Bath Abbey, had issued petition forms and collected 500 signatures. On 1 March 1909 he held a private meeting at Abbey Church House where it was agreed that a deputation would be made to the mayor and council the next day. The lobby group consisted of Boyd, Reverend C.W. Shickle, Reverend H.H. Winwood, General Coningham, Miss English, Miss Hope, Miss Douglas Fox, Messrs W.S. Brymer, T.S. Bush and J.F. Meehan.

As a representative of Bath's citizens, Boyd addressed the assembly:

Having heard of the proposed demolition of the north side of Bath Street, [we] condemn such a proposal as an act of vandalism, and one likely to do great injury to the reputation of Bath … as a place with a character of its own, rich in associations of the Georgian period, and delighting in its traditions of a famous past.

In response, Mr Colmer, chairman of the Corporate Property Committee, felt that 'a great deal of fuss had been made over a little', he did not admire the old style of architecture nor see any beauty in it, and for him 'it would be a great improvement if the whole thing were cleared away'. *The Builder* reported that by approving Waring's scheme the council had 'the discredit of having, for purely commercial reasons, made the first move towards the destruction, architecturally, of the peculiar charm of their unique and beautiful city'.

Boyd and his fellow campaigners galvanised support through the pages of *The Times* and other national newspapers and journals. Over the next few weeks a number of eminent public figures wrote in support of saving Bath Street. Amongst them was Ernest George, president of the Royal Institute of British Architects; Nigel Bond of the National Trust; Lady Balfour; Sir Philip Burne-Jones; Sir Ashton Webb RA; Reginald Blomfield, professor of architecture at the Royal Academy; and D.S. MacColl, art critic and director of the Tate Gallery.

Editorials under such titles as *Bath and the Philistines*, *An Act of Vandalism* and *The Menaced Colonnade at Bath* discredited the council. The council did little to impress when, in its official statement, councillors said that they could not say whether Bath Street should be saved due to its architectural importance because 'they [had been] unable to obtain adequate assistance from modern authorities' in order to reach an opinion and therefore felt able to permit demolition. 'The corporation must accept a difficulty of the position, and they elect to take a course which values more highly the present life and modern interests of the city than a sentiment which in their opinion has been unduly developed.'

Utterly dissatisfied with the council the group resolved to form an association for the defence of old Bath. At a second meeting, held at the Abbey Church House on 5 March 1909, the Old Bath Preservation Society (OBPS) was formed in order to aid the citizens of Bath to maintain their valuable architectural heritage. They would direct attention to places and objects worthy of preservation and foster 'a feeling of pride in the historical, literary and artistic associations that cling round the city'.

On Saturday, 27 March the Assembly Rooms were crowded with attendees of a public meeting convened in support of the preservation of Bath Street. The meeting was presided over by Boyd, addressed by MacColl and Arthur Beresford Pite, professor of architecture at the Royal College of Art, and supported by the committee of the newly formed OBPS. 'Though to-day we cannot always afford the arts of our forefathers, we may at least preserve and seek inspiration from the examples which remain', consider carefully any changes 'which may destroy the unity on which [Bath's] charm depends'.

In the face of such bad publicity and ill will, Waring submitted a modified scheme that retained the whole of Bath Street. The council, however, persisted that the agreed plans must proceed. The town clerk wrote to Waring's solicitor insisting that they 'rigidly adhere to the terms' laid out. Shockingly, towards the end of November, the north side of Bath Street was being prepared for demolition. It did not progress and eventually the OBPS were able to claim a victory.

Over the next twenty years the Society's membership grew to over 1,000, including international supporters. Its resolutions stated that the OBPS offered:

> … no opinion on the relative merits of different styles in architecture; it [took] its stand on the simple fact that 18th Century Bath is generally admitted to have been as a whole the highest and most complete expression of a particular style, possessing its own peculiar grace, beauty, and dignity, and having for us a special value as an essentially English development of Renaissance art. Eighteenth Century Bath also embodied an ideal of town planning which, in combination with the individual beauty of its Circus, Crescents, Streets and blocks of Buildings, has not been surpassed, if indeed equalled, anywhere.

The Society was never rich, and so forthright campaigning was beyond its means. This was pursued by the Bath Preservation Trust, which was formed in 1934 by some of the more proactive members of the OBPS in response to the Bath Bill. At the annual meeting in 1937, Florence Tylee, a founder member and honorary secretary, paid respect to the few who had been inspired by a love of dear old Bath in 1909, 'They could not achieve all that they hoped for, but they sowed good seed, and many things they longed for have since come to pass'. The OBPS continued until the death of Tylee in 1945, the Society then merged with the Bath Preservation Trust who in 1960, by coincidence, had its headquarters at No. 6 Bath Street.

※ ※ ※ ※ ※

One of Bath's most spectacular events – the Bath Historical Pageant – took place between 19 and 24 July 1909. The extravaganza involved thousands of people, united the city and spawned many cross-cultural and international relations, including the Bath American Society. The whole spectacle, including the writing of the eight episodes (plays) which 'told the story … of the most remarkable events which occurred in Bath from the earliest times', was organised in only seven months – a truly phenomenal achievement.

The late Victorian and early Edwardian era saw an increasing interest in Bath's heritage, especially of its Georgian past. This growing sense of importance coincided with the fashion for historic displays: England had witnessed over twenty pageants in recent years, and it was antiquary Reverend C.W. Shickle (a founding member of the OBPS) who initially suggested that Bath should hold its own pageant. He believed that if other places with 'nothing like the claim to historical record as Bath' had enjoyed successful pageants, then so could Bath. This was resonated by author A.M. Broadley when he proclaimed, 'that Bath offered an almost unrivalled subject to both Pageant Master and Pageant Writer'.

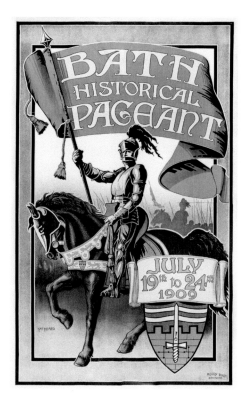

Sadly, support for the project was lacklustre. Critics saw it as 'useless mummery', and a public meeting held on 10 December 1908 at the Guildhall was so poorly attended that there was some doubt as to whether the meeting could be considered truly representative. The main concerns were whether there was enough time to achieve such a large undertaking, especially as little could be done before the plays were penned. Mr Plowman urged that 'the book will have to be written with extreme care … and involve a great deal of antiquarian and archaeological research, as any anachronism would draw attention to the pageant in a way which it would be very desirable to avoid.' In addition

Natheard/Moody Bros: Poster for the Bath Historical Pageant, 1909. (Bath Central Library/Bath in Time)

many questioned the enduring popularity of the pageant, suggesting that it was falling out of fashion. Nevertheless, supporters showed that with pageants planned in London, Plymouth, Bristol, Exeter and Glastonbury in 1909 and 1910, it was obvious that the craze was not waning. Finally, the greatest concern was the cost, especially to city ratepayers – even the Marquis of Bath, who had been offered the position of president of the pageant, wrote that 'from what he had heard there seemed some doubt whether the pageant would be a financial success'.

At the public meeting supporters of the event, led by Chairman Major C.H. Simpson, were determined to reach a consensus to hold a pageant the following summer. Pageants were intended to be both educational and celebratory of a town's past, but they were also undertaken to raise a town's profile and draw large crowds in an increasingly competitive tourist market. A subscription list was to be opened and a guarantee fund formed for the purpose of defraying the expenses incurred. Yet the supporters were confident that all costs would be more than covered by ticket sales. Towards the end of the meeting Reverend C. Hylton Steward proclaimed that if the pageant was to be 'a success they would have to devise means whereby every class of person could be touched, and they must induce people from outside Bath to come and put their shoulders to the wheel'.

Frank Lascelles was engaged as master of the pageant, he was eminently qualified having proved his abilities at Oxford in 1907, as well as organising other towns' pageants such as at Bristol, Carlisle and Rochester. At the time of the public meeting he was in New York managing the pageant there, and had subsequently been invited to run pageants for fourteen other American cities.

Bath's pageant comprised eight main episodes commemorating particular events in Bath's history, starting with the *Dedication of Sul's Temple at Bath, A.D. 160*, written by Cecil T. Carr and finishing with *The Visit of Queen Charlotte to Bath in 1817*, by Broadley. Carr also wrote episode two, *The Sack of Akeman After Dyrham Fight*. Episode three, *The Coronation of King Edgar, A.D. 973*, was prepared by Edward S. Tylee; and episode four, *King Henry VII Visits Bath, A.D. 1497*, was by Reverend J.H. Skrine. Episode five, *Visit of Queen Elizabeth to Bath, A.D. 1574* was by Reverend W.P. Hanks; episode six, *The Battle of Lansdown, A.D. 6th July 1643* was written by Captain C.B. Prowse, and episode seven, *The Glorious Times of Beau Nash and Ralph Allen* was also by Broadley. Curiously for the modern reader, Allen's reputation had so diminished that his inclusion in the pageant line-up was only secured after a local campaign. Literary figures were celebrated throughout, but especially in the final scene where actors portraying a number of authors, including Tobias Smollett, Jane Austen and Charles Dickens introduced their Bath based characters.

The episodes were repeated daily in a covered auditorium in Victoria Park that could hold an audience of 4,000, attended by 150 stewards. The cast alone consisted of over 3,000 local people, with another 500 people in the choir. There were seventy-six members of the orchestra, conducted by Mr A.E. New, and the music was arranged by the likes of W.F.C. Schottler, H.P. Allen and Sir Charles Stanford, who wrote the music for Skrine's *Choric Ode* finale. The many costumes were designed by Nat Heard and Edwin Fagg, and executed under the supervision of Mrs Edwards with hundreds of volunteers. The set, including a wooden replica of the Temple of Sulis Minerva, was also designed by Heard, with assistance from John E. Barker. Each evening saw entertainment at Sydney Gardens, culminating with a 'magnificent fete of unprecedented proportions' and fireworks.

Through sheer determination the organisers were ready for 19 July. The opening ceremony, presided over by the Duke and Duchess of Connaught and Strathearn, consisted of a reception at the Guildhall, followed by a procession through Bath's highly decorated streets, taking in Milsom Street, the Circus and the Royal Crescent before reaching Victoria Park where the inaugural performance took place. Blessed with good weather, the Bath Historical Pageant was a resounding success with critics proclaiming it to be one of the prettiest, most impressive, varied and dramatic pageants that had ever been devised.

This success was recognised a few years later when A.J. Taylor's Minerva's Temple, built to promote Bath at the Empire Exhibition at Crystal Palace in 1911, was re-erected in Sydney Gardens in 1913 to commemorate Bath's spectacular showpiece of civic pride – you can still see it there today.

Other big events in Bath at the turn of the twentieth century included the Bath & West Show at Odd Down in 1912. Visitors were encouraged to view the site with enthusiasm because it could be reached easily by tram and was at least level – more than could be said for the centenary show, in 1877, on the slopes of what is now Alexander Park.

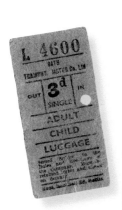

Bath Tramway Motor Co. Ltd: Adult and Child Single Journey Tram Tickets. (Author's Collection)

The greatest advancement for inner-city travel was indeed the introduction of the electric tramway in 1904. The trams provided increased opportunities – in terms of housing and work – to Bath's neighbouring villages, Twerton, Weston and Combe Down. The former brick-clad Bath Electric Tramways Depot on Walcot Street, built in 1903, closed in 1939 with the cessation of the service. BBA Architects sympathetically converted the tram shed into a complex of apartments, business units and a restaurant in 2000–02.

One of the world's greatest tragedies also touched Bath. A luxurious White Star Line ocean liner struck an iceberg on its maiden voyage, sinking within hours, and still with many souls on board. *Titanic* was built at the Harland and Wolff shipyard in Belfast, and was the largest and most opulent vessel of its time. She left Southampton on 10 April 1912 and was expected in New York six days later. The sheer sumptuous magnitude of *Titanic* made this transatlantic crossing extremely prestigious; leading to the wealthy elite of the day clamouring to fill her first-class cabins. *Titanic* has come to represent this era – the disparity between the classes in terms of rights, wealth and prospects; the arrogance of man, and our great fall from grace with the tragic loss of life. Our ways of understanding the world, our personal identities and our future hopes had all changed by the end of this decade.

America lost members from its most prominent families, probably one of the most significant being Colonel John Jacob Astor IV (whose personal fortune amounted to $87 million in 1912), the industrialist Benjamin Guggenheim, and Isidore Straus, the founder of Macy's department store. Over 1,500 people perished, the majority of whom died from hypothermia, rather than death by drowning. The high death toll was quickly blamed on the lack of lifeboats, although *Titanic* actually carried more than the minimum required by the Board of Trade at this time.

Although there were no Bath millionaires on board, two Bathonians were known to have been travelling on the great liner. One of the victims that fateful night was Edwin Charles 'Fred' Wheeler, a second-class passenger who boarded at Southampton. He was the personal valet to George Washington Vanderbilt II (1862–1914).

Wheeler was born in Bath in 1886, and his early life tells of the seedier side to our city. As a child Edwin lived at No. 1 Peter Street with his father, Frederick, a tailor, his mother, Emma, and younger sister. They shared the house with numerous others, including Mary Godfrey, a widowed feather cleaner, and Maria Randell. Randell is recorded as a spinster and laundress, living with her four children – Edith, James, Ernest and Annie. It is probably fair to assume that Maria was a prostitute. Peter Street ran down from the junction of Westgate Buildings, Lower Borough Walls and St James Parade, to Corn Street which, along with Avon, Milk and Little Corn Streets had become part of the notorious slums of Bath, where prostitutes and petty criminals thrived. Peter Street had been developed speculatively from the mid-1760s by Thomas Jelly and his partners, Henry Fisher, a mason, and Richard Jones an ironmonger. Jelly is better known for his work at the Kingston Baths (1763–66) and King Edward's School on Broad Street (1752–54).

Wheeler had done well to leave Peter Street behind him and find such a good position with a wealthy American family. The Vanderbilts had been booked to sail on the *Titanic*, but changed their minds at the last minute, supposedly as a response to a premonition had by Vanderbilt's sister-in-law, Susan Stuyvesant Dresser. Unfortunately it was too late to stop Wheeler, who was accompanying their luggage. Wheeler's body, if recovered, was never identified.

Across the world newspapers covered this momentous tragedy, including those in Bath who were especially concerned with the story of Edwina 'Winnie' Celia Troutt, who mercifully survived. Edwina was born in Bath on 8 July 1884, to Edwin Charles Troutt, the proprietor of the Lyncombe Brewery at No. 40 Claverton Street, and Elizabeth Ellen. The Lyncombe Brewery was a beer house which had opened in around 1870, the family moved next door in 1895 and her father worked as a carpenter. Most breweries had cooperages attached, so it is not surprising that he had two trades. They moved in 1896 to Newark Street. Edwin Troutt is recorded initially as a brewer and then by 1908 as a carpenter. One cannot help but feel the family's fortunes had changed, as Newark Street lay very close to the slums that Wheeler had known.

From 1907 Edwina had been living and working in New Jersey and Massachusetts, perhaps seeking a more prosperous future than Bath was able to offer her. She returned briefly to her family in 1911, but then booked a crossing on the *Oceanic* in order to reach her sister, who was living in Auburnhale, Massachusetts, and nearing the end of her pregnancy. Due to the coal strikes, Edwina, like some others, was transferred to the *Titanic*. She travelled second class from Southampton and shared cabin 101 on E Deck with two other single ladies – Susan Webber from Cornwall and Nora Keane of Limerick.

Edwina recalled that as *Titanic* was considered 'unsinkable' the call for lifebelts was received as a joke; it was not until they saw the lifeboats being lowered that people started to appreciate the peril they were in. She described the heart-rending screams as couples had to part – women and babies being bid to board the lifeboats first. Yet, she also described the situation as calm and gentlemanly, with no one panicking. She was initially reluctant to board a lifeboat, saying it was 'wicked to save the single girls first', but when she was asked to rescue a gentleman's baby she felt happier about taking her place in the lifeboat.

Edwina lived out her life in America, mainly in California. She died on 3 December 1984 in Redondo Beach, having celebrated her 100th birthday that July.

Of the 2,207 on board only 712 survived, the victims were mainly third-class passengers and crew, although numerous men from all classes were lost. *The Times* played tribute, writing:

The Titanic – the greatest thing we have yet produced – lies at the bottom of the ocean, a useless mass of lumber; but at the moment of her destruction the men on board of her rose superior to their fate. They put the women and children into the boats quietly and in order, without regard to their own safety, and stood by ready to meet whatever might befall.

※ ※ ※ ※ ※

The campaign to win universal male suffrage had been fought hard throughout the nineteenth century. Progress was made under the 1867 Reform Act, but it was not until the Representation of the People Act in 1918 that all men over the age of 21 were granted the right to vote. Female suffrage, however, lagged far behind both the franchise of men in the UK, and the franchise of women in other countries, including areas of Australia and the United States. The 1918 Act did extend the right to vote to women over 30, but only if they met the minimum property requirement.

The National Union of Women's Suffrage Societies was founded in 1897 and led by Millicent Fawcett (1847–1929). In 1903, Emmeline Pankhurst (1858–1928) founded the Women's Social and Political Union (WSPU), which was far more radical and militant. Suffragettes chained themselves to railings, undertook criminal damage and protested vehemently. Sadly, Emily Davison died after throwing herself under the King's horse during the Epsom Derby in June 1913. Many of these women were imprisoned, it is estimated as many as 1,000, mainly for public order offences. They lobbied to be considered as political prisoners, but when H.H. Asquith's Liberal government refused this, they went on hunger strike.

Eagle House, in Batheaston, served as a refuge for the suffragettes between 1908 and 1912. Colonel Linley Blathwayt, his wife Emily and their daughter Mary provided a sanctuary in which the women could recuperate after they had been imprisoned; many having also been force fed. One such activist was Lady Constance Lytton (1869–1923), who stayed at Eagle House in 1910.

She remembered that whilst on hunger strike in Walton Gaol, Liverpool:

Two of the women [wardresses] took hold of my arms, one held my head and one my feet. One wardress helped to pour the food. The doctor leant on my knees as he stooped over my chest to get at my mouth. I shut my mouth and clenched my teeth. The sense of being overpowered by more force than I could possibly resist was complete, but I resisted nothing except with my mouth. The doctor offered me the choice of a wooden or steel gag; he explained that the steel gag would hurt and the wooden one would not, and he urged me not to force him to use the steel one. But I

Colonel Linley Blathwayt: Suffragettes Lady Constance Lytton and Annie Kenney, 1910. (Bath Central Library/ Bath in Time)

did not speak nor open my mouth, so after playing about for a moment or two with the wooden one he finally had recourse to the steel. The pain of it was intense; he got the gag between my teeth, when he proceeded to turn it much more than necessary until my jaws were fastened wide apart, far more than they could go naturally. Then he put down my throat a tube, which seemed to me much too wide and was something like four feet long. The irritation of the tube was excessive. I choked the moment it touched my throat until it had gone down. Then the food was poured in quickly; it made me sick a few seconds after it was down and the action of the sickness made my body and legs double up, but the wardresses instantly pressed back my head and the doctor leant on my knees. The horror of it was more than I can describe. I had been sick over my hair, all over the wall near my bed, and my clothes seemed saturated with vomit. The wardresses told me that they could not get a change [of clothes] as it was too late, the office was shut.

Those who stayed at Eagle House were encouraged to plant a tree in Annie's Arboretum, named after the suffragette Annie Kenney (1879–1953). Annie was one of the few working-class suffragettes who rose in the ranks to become one of the leading figures within the WSPU. Alongside Christabel Pankhurst, Annie was at the heart of a more public and militant approach to the campaign.

Miserably, most of the arboretum was destroyed in the 1960s to make way for a housing estate. We are fortunate, however, that Colonel Blathwayt was a keen photographer and captured images of all the suffragettes who stayed at Eagle House, particularly as they were planting their trees. All three members of the Blathwayts kept diaries, which are now preserved at the Gloucestershire Record Office. Suffrage was eventually extended to all women over the age of 21 in 1928.

✳ ✳ ✳ ✳ ✳

The Edwardian era (the reign of Edward VII, 1901–10) is often seen as an idyllic and innocent time; one of positive prosperity and serene semblance. The 'Age of Innocence' only being fragmented by the onset of the First World War. This is far from a full or true picture. The upper classes possibly enjoyed a leisurely time of endless summer afternoons playing tennis and taking tea on the terraces of their luxurious flower gardens, but in fact the country was deeply divided and unsettled. Living and working conditions for the majority of the population were poor. There was no national insurance until 1911, no old-age pension until 1908, no state benefits, as we would understand them today.

And so, with the right to vote being extended, more of the working classes had a voice and became increasingly politicised. The Labour Party was founded in 1900, but in Bath, working-class men seemed content to be represented by the Liberal Party. There were no known socialist organisations established in Bath before the First World War. Historians believe that places such as Bath experienced far less class conflict because the poor were often subsidised by the charities supported by the wealthier residents; the prevailing domestic and retail occupations brought the classes into regular daily contact (unlike the factory workers of the industrial northern cities); and there were tangible opportunities for upward social mobility in towns such as Bath.

Elsewhere, this was a period of great unrest and social anxiety. There were issues at home with the suffragettes and socialists, and an increasing number of general strikes because the miners, railway workers and transport unions had joined together in 1914 to protect against the industry owners cutting costs by bringing in non-union labour. The power of the House of Lords was reduced in 1911, after they had vetoed Lloyd George's People's Budget in 1909. Problems abroad, especially in Ireland, with the Irish Nationalists demanding Home Rule and supported by the Liberal Party, pitched against the Ulster Protestants, supported by the Tories. In South Africa we were fighting the Boer War (1899–1902), a very contentious conflict that divided the country, especially when conditions in the British-held concentration camps became public.

Edward VII was succeeded by his second son, George V (1865–1936), in 1910. George's first cousins were Tsar Nicholas II of Russia and Kaiser Wilhelm II of Germany. The term the Great War had been used to describe the Napoleonic Wars, but now we associate it with the First World War (1914–18). The trigger for the war was the assassination of Archduke Franz Ferdinand of Austria by Yugoslav nationalist Gavrilo Princip in Sarajevo on 28 June 1914. A month later, Austria–Hungary declared war on Serbia and subsequently Russia mobilised in support of Serbia.

Germany invaded neutral Belgium and Luxembourg in an attempt to conquer France. Britain immediately reminded the Germans of Belgium's neutrality, as agreed in a treaty of 1839. Some believe that the German commanders did not think Britain would enter the war when we were so distracted and stretched by industrial action and the troubles in Ireland. Germany ignored the treaty, because they knew that their best chance of victory over France was to attack via Belgium.

Britain declared war on Germany on 4 August 1914, joining forces with France, Belgium and Russia. Despite Britain's domestic conflicts, the majority of people rallied behind the government. The suffragettes ceased their activities and campaigning during the war and, initially, the Irish Nationalists and Unionists banded together and joined the British forces. The elders of Bath, as everywhere else, urged the local young men to step forward and take the King's shilling and go to war.

Britain had relatively few men trained for military action. Other European countries could mobilise millions, but we could only scrape together about 700,000. Lord Kitchener appealed for men to join up, and patriotism and pride led to over 1 million volunteers in less than six months. But the infrastructure to house, clothe and train these men had not been established and Bath's once fashionable lodging houses and hotels became the makeshift billets for many of these new recruits.

There was increasing pressure to join up, various marketing campaigns helped create an atmosphere of distrust and disrespect of those who didn't go to war. The Order of the White Feather was an organisation that saw women hand out white feathers, a symbol of cowardice, to young men not in uniform. Of course, the women were not able to identify those men in reserved occupations and they had become so pugnacious that the government had to issue identity cards to those men serving the country from the home front. This, however, did not help those who had been found unfit to serve.

Over 11,000 men joined up from the Bath area. When the war was not 'over by Christmas' and the number of causalities was reaching into the hundreds of thousands, so conscription was introduced in 1916. Private owners volunteered their properties for use as hospitals after an appeal by the Duke of Sutherland.

Mrs Percival Huth, of Freshford Manor, made No. 9 Lansdown Place West available to the Red Cross and the Earl and Countess Temple offered the south wing of Newton Park (now the home of Bath Spa University), which became a St John Ambulance hospital with accommodation for twenty-three patients.

The Royal United Hospital was founded in 1915 as a war hospital and opened in April 1916. The Mineral Water Hospital had been treating the war wounded with muscular trouble and the hospital at Newton Park had been operational for a year, but this new hospital would have 500 beds in ten fifty-bed huts. By the end of the war that number had almost tripled to 1,300 beds.

The first patients, comprising about 100 injured men, arrived on Easter Monday 1916. Soldiers in hospital received no pay and so local civilians would donate a few luxuries to individual men. Bath continued to look after convalescing ex-servicemen after the war, and the city provided entertainment for 1,000 wounded troops on Armistice Day in 1920.

Anti-German feeling and suspicion was understandably widespread. In 1917, George V changed the Royal Family's name from the House of Saxe-Coburg and Gotha to the House of Windsor. The owners of Horstmann Gear Company in Bath were the victims of unfounded accusations that they were German sympathisers. The company was contracted to make key military items for the Ministry of Munitions, and the accuser suggested that they were sabotaging the war effort by producing shoddy goods. Horstmann retaliated, pointing out that

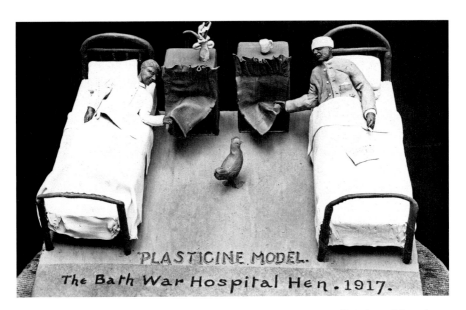

Viner postcard: Plasticine model of the Bath War Hospital Hen, Combe Park, 1917. (Bath Central Library/ Bath in Time)

the family had been in Britain since the nineteenth century and members of the family were fighting for the Allies. They took the perpetrator to court, won their case, and thankfully the business did not suffer unduly.

A number of Bath businesses were engaged with producing equipment for the war effort. Carr Mills produced the fabrics for thousands of military uniforms. Stothert & Pitt Co. developed one of the earliest tanks in 1916; they also provided dock and harbour equipment for the Royal Navy and ammunition and minesweeping apparatus.

The advancement in aircraft engineering is probably one of the First World War's more lasting legacies. The Royal Air Force was formed in April 1918 with over 22,500 aircraft. These early planes were made of wood and a number of cabinet makers in Bath were utilised for their production, including W. & T. Lock's in Twerton and the Bath Cabinet Makers' Company based in Bellott's Road, which expanded and became the Aircraft Flight Works.

A document prepared for Lloyd George in 1922 and published by Andrew Swift in 2005 gives details of Bath's significant contribution to the war effort. Over 3,000 men and women were employed in the production of munitions and shells, aircraft and mine sinkers, gauges and precision tools, torpedo propeller shafts and floors for tents. In addition to the Bath companies mentioned above, Horstmann Carts Ltd, Aldridge & Ranken and Jacob Long & Sons Ltd were also noted for their significant contribution.

The sister ship of the *Titanic*, the *Lusitania*, was sunk by a German U-boat in 1915 with the loss of 1,198 civilian lives, two of whom were heading for Bath, and 128 of whom were American. At the beginning of the war, the United States had adopted a policy of neutrality and tens of thousands of American citizens were caught unawares whilst travelling in Europe in August 1914. President Woodrow Wilson continued to trade and do business with Europe as a whole, but did make significant financial loans to Britain and France to aid their war efforts. News of the atrocities in Belgium started to turn American opinion against Germany. The sinking of the *Lusitania*, followed by Germany's approach to Mexico offering a military alliance, compelled America to declare war on Germany on 6 April 1917 and on the Austro-Hungarian Empire on 7 December 1917.

A number of American soldiers were stationed in Wiltshire and made day trips to Bath. In July 1918 the US troops were invited to take part in a civic reception. They marched through the city, had lunch at the Guildhall and attended a church service in the Abbey. Afterwards a baseball game was played on the Recreation Ground. Bath also played host to soldiers from Canada and Australia.

The American-born artist, J.A.M. Whistler (1834–1903) stayed in Bath on occasions during the last two years of his life, lodging at No. 7 Marlborough Buildings. His pupil, the great British impressionist Walter Sickert (1860–1942), stayed in Bath during the summers of 1916 and 1917, when he painted scenes from the city – most famously Pulteney Bridge. He became a patron of Bath College of Art and lectured there every Friday night. For the last four years of his life he settled at St George's Hill, Bathampton.

Like any town, city, village or hamlet in Britain, Bath suffered devastating losses during the First World War. Swift's research shows that 1,808 men from the Bath area were lost in the Great War, serving in over 120 different regiments. Added to these losses were those who died due to the influenza epidemic in 1918. At least 121 people died in Bath from the flu, or complications associated with the illness, and the majority of the victims were aged between 15 and 35.

❋ ❋ ❋ ❋ ❋

The First World War did bring about more rapid reform. The enfranchisement of women was primarily due to the important work they had undertaken in the munitions factories, trade unions were legitimised and working conditions were improved. Post-war, however, saw an increase in unemployment. The World Depression affected the industrialised nations during the late 1920s and early 1930s.

The 1926 General Strike was triggered by the proposal to cut the wages of the miners, but increase their working day. The coal mining industry was struggling and the owners needed to make cuts. The leader of the miners, A.J. Cooke, coined the rallying cry, 'Not a penny off the pay, not a minute of the day'. King George showed greater understanding of the workers' plight than the Conservative prime minister, Stanley Baldwin. The King urged Baldwin to 'try living on their wages before you judge them'. The government broke the strike by encouraging middle-class volunteers to help run services like the buses and trams.

In 1927 the Trade Disputes Act made general strikes illegal. Great Britain was driven off the gold standard in 1931, but the economic collapse was far more deeply felt in Britain's industrial north than in the southern and western counties. By 1930 unemployment had more than doubled, from 1 million to 2.5 million, and the value of exports had fallen by 50 per cent. The situation stabilised for places like Bath far sooner than elsewhere in the country, mainly because the city has never relied solely on industry for its prosperity. It is from this period that the north–south divide was born.

Between the wars, Bath was much the same as it had been before the conflict. The four main hotels remained open and there were still enough health-seeking visitors to keep the city buoyant. A guidebook from the 1920s claimed:

Bath has its value as a health resort, particularly to invalids in the winter time; for the air is peculiarly sweet and fresh, and the encircling hills protect the city from cold winds ... It is justly claimed that scarcely any other English town is graced with suburbs so bracing as these air-swept heights. In a recent year 1921 the death-rate was at the remarkably low figure of 10.3 per 1000.

This description really could be from any period in Bath's history.

What did change was a far greater level of commuting from Bath to office and factory work in Bristol. Between the wars the Corporation built about 2,000 houses around the city's edge, providing the suburban environs, whilst the private sector built a further 2,000. The first major council estate was at Englishcombe Park (1920). Further houses were built at Larkhall and Southdown. The largest housing project was the Fosseway Estate, developed in 1930–31. The population remained steady at around 68,600.

Entertainment was limited, there were still concerts in the Pump Room and three cinemas – but one of these was in the Assembly Rooms. As Bath had fallen in popularity, so the Rooms became more and more redundant. The Rooms had played host to public readings by Charles Dickens and concerts by Johann Strauss before becoming a cinema. In 1931, a grant from local businessman Ernest Cook, founder of the Thomas Cook Company, allowed the Society for the Protection of Ancient Buildings (SPAB) to purchase the property. SPAB gave the Rooms to the National Trust who, in turn, rented them to the Bath City Council on the understanding that they would restore the building to its former glory. The Rooms reopened in 1938.

Residents and visitors could still enjoy the open spaces of Victoria and Hedgemead parks. Alice Park, which commemorates Alice MacVicar, the wife of Mr H.M. MacVicar who, a year after his wife's death, donated a 9-acre field next to his house for the provision of a park. Philosophies about providing safe and active spaces for children were influencing the design and provision of parks at this time and in keeping with these new ideas, Alice Park was divided into areas of park and areas of playing fields. The western part was railed and designated for the use of children under 14, with cricket and football pitches. There were also tennis courts and interesting planting to attract the adults. Designed by Sir Geoffrey Jellicoe (1900–96), the park also had paddling and boating pools, swings, a roundabout and a see-saw. A Keeper's Cottage, also designed by Jellicoe, housed the resident park keeper. Alice Park opened on 28 May 1938 and was available every day, but not until 2 p.m. on a Sunday.

Bath was ahead of the times when in 1925 and 1937 the Local Acts tried to control the designs of new buildings and the alterations of the old ones. The 1937 Act listed worthy architectural buildings built before 1820. The majority of the new buildings built in Bath during the 1920s and 1930s adopted a mock/revived Georgian style. These included the old Post Office Building by the office of works (1923–27) or the Co-operative Wholesale Society Building on Westgate Buildings (1932–34).

Bath can, however, claim a small yet highly significant number of early twentieth-century buildings. These were built on the outskirts, never within the central 'Georgian' area. In 1909 Charles Voysey (1857–1941) designed Lodge Style in Combe Down for T. Sturge Cotterell, the owner of the local stone quarry and mayor in 1930. Giles Gilbert Scott, grandson of Sir George Gilbert Scott, designed the Church of Our Lady and St Alphege in Oldfield Park (1927–29). It was one of Scott's favourite works, and there was an interesting experiment using pieces of linoleum on the floor in the manner of marble.

Bath's only Modernist building is Woodside House on North Road. Originally called Kilowatt House, because of its elaborate and unique lighting system, it was designed by Mollie Taylor (later Gerrard) in 1937, for Anthony Greenhill, chief engineer with Wills Engineering Ltd. Taylor would later explain that when she designed Kilowatt House, she was just starting out in her father's architectural practice (Alfred J. Taylor & Partners) and he did not want the company name associated with her design because 'he didn't think a modern house in a beautiful setting was right for Georgian Bath'. The house was given planning permission on the grounds that it would be completely obscured, which it still is today for anyone keen to locate it. Taylor was cross, she was rightly proud of her first major commission and wanted to show it off.

Built of reinforced concrete, the main block is two storeys with a flat roof masked by a well-proportioned projecting slab. A single-storey wing on the left balances the single-storey garage. The ballroom is set back from the projecting wing and is of one and a half storeys. The roofs on the wings are flat and were designed so they could be flooded in the summer to cool the house. A viewing platform with curved ends surmounted the main roof. The semi-circular stairwell projects out on the garden front and is lit by a 15ft (4.5m) high curved window. As with all the windows at Kilowatt, it is metal framed and barred and produced by Crittall. The entry was through double wooden doors, deeply recessed, with art deco ornamentation.

Many of the rooms doubled up as recording studios: there was even an echo chamber on the roof and all the rooms were soundproofed. The main studio was a cavernous 45ft (13.7m) long by 23ft (7m) wide and 16ft (4.8m) high.

Greenhill had grown up in Bath and had always been fascinated with electricity, filling the rooms of his parents' house at No. 12 Royal Crescent with equipment and carrying out electrical experiments there. One such experiment with colour lighting set to music went wrong and nearly burnt the house down! Kilowatt House was to be Greenhill's laboratory for electronic art or 'coloured music'. Working with a friend, Greenhill installed 22,000 yards of cable. It took them six weeks, but then again they were still working full time at Wills'.

Kilowatt House had its own electricity supply direct from the works via the building's own substation. There were coloured lights reacting to music which, amongst other things, lit up an indoor fountain. Twelve amplifiers, forty microphones, forty loud speakers and 700 colour lighting points were all controlled from one huge console desk. Outside the drawing room, on open display, was an entire wall taken up with fuse boxes, switches and dials.

As the house went up there were many rumours about what was actually being built. Greenhill indulged the speculators and soon there was a buzz that is was going to be a zoo, a swimming pool and then a lunatic asylum. Greenhill wrote, 'possibly the latter was fairly near the truth'.

The house was renamed Woodside after Greenhill's death in 1958, due to its woodland setting in a former quarry which Greenhill had spent three years levelling and clearing of tons of stone before the build could commence.

※ ※ ※ ※ ※

St Bartholomew's Church on King Edward Road, Oldfield Park, was designed by A. Taylor and the foundation stone was laid in November 1936. It has the misfortune to be known as the unluckiest church in Bath. It had taken thirty-four years to raise the money for the scheme, the balance of which was financed with a bank loan. Fundraising efforts ensured that the mortgage was eventually paid off on 15 March 1942 – St Bartholomew's was finally debt free. Disastrously, the church suffered a direct hit from a high explosive during the Bath Blitz. The damage to the church was catastrophic, and very little remained structurally sound. The Luftwaffe did intentionally target churches to undermine civilian morale and, perhaps in defiance, services continued to be held within the ruins of the church. St Bartholomew's was rebuilt with the help of a grant from the War Damage Committee and reopened on 17 March 1951; the first of Bath's bombed churches to do so.

※ ※ ※ ※ ※

On 20 November 1929 at about 6.35 p.m., fumes in the Combe Down Railway Tunnel (built in 1874) overcame the driver and fireman of a Somerset & Dorset

St Bartholomew's Church, Oldfield Park, April 1942. (Bath Central Library/Bath in Time)

goods train. The tunnel was the longest railway tunnel in Great Britain without intermediate ventilation. The train, laden with thirty-two wagons of coal, another of general goods and one with an empty oil tank, ran down at increasing speed towards the entrance to the Bath Yard. The train collided with and completely wrecked the end of the Railway Clearing House building. It was estimated that the total weight was nearly 500 tons.

The train derailed, leaving three dead and two injured, including the driver, J.H. Jennings, and Inspector Norman and J. Loder, who were in the yard, Fireman Pearce and the guard, Wagner, were seriously injured. Tragic as this is, if this had been a passenger train then the loss of life would surely have been overwhelming.

The Combe Down Tunnel was closed in 1966, along with the rest of the Somerset & Dorset line. In 2013 it reopened as part of the Two Tunnels Greenway walking and cycle path. This project was partly funded by the King Bladud's Pigs Public Art Project, which saw 106 individually painted and styled life-sized pigs located across the city during 2008. The pigs were auctioned off, raising an impressive £200,000.

✳ ✳ ✳ ✳ ✳

In 1934 the Bath Preservation Trust (BPT) was founded. As a charitable trust they could undertake fundraising and buy property, unlike their parent body, the Old Bath Preservation Society. Today, the BPT remains an independent charitable organisation which campaigns to preserve the architecture of Bath, and to ensure that new developments enhance the existing city, not mar it. The Trust is not funded by national or local government, and has no special powers to stop developments in Bath. Its strength, however, is through its members.

From the start, the BPT were prepared to stand up to the Council. In the 1930s the city was under increasing pressure to modernise. The ancient layout of the town was not suitable for cars and shoppers and the Corporation (council) were ready to propose radical change, including the extension of Milsom Street northwards to the Assembly Rooms, the demolition of the block in Old Bond Street, the widening of Broad Street, and the widening of many other streets to make way for a new east–west road.

The Trust launched an appeal called the 'Preserve Bath Movement', and Sir Alexander Lawrence, a trustee, wrote a letter to *The Times* calling attention to the way the proposals had been presented to the City Council. He claimed that the councillors passed the plans without any real idea what it was about, many having never seen the actual bill. Instead they were given a summary by word of mouth and a list of street works to be carried out. He encouraged a wide debate in the local and national press. Alderman J. Wills, who was responsible for piloting the bill through Parliament, resigned from the chairmanship of the City Improvements Committee and the Council was thrown into confusion. At this point relations between the Council and the Trust were very sour.

It was after this great success that the Trust gained greater influence. They put forward their own agenda for enhancing Bath and they also helped to restore some of the most iconic parts of the city, including the Palladian Bridge at Prior Park, the Greville monument at Lansdown, and the stone acorns in the Circus. The Trust also began one of its lengthiest campaigns: to protect the setting of Bath – the green belt which surrounds the city and provides a romantic foil to the stone buildings.

❊ ❊ ❊ ❊ ❊

Again, butting the norm, Stothert & Pitt Co. continued to expand during the interwar period. By the Second World War their heavy lifting and pumping equipment was in great demand. During the war the firm provided the gun-mounting and turret-traversing mechanism for every Challenger tank, seaplane-lifting cranes and, after the Admiralty moved to Bath in 1942, they worked in conjunction to develop a top secret mini-submarine called the 'Human

Torpedo'. The other main industry of stone quarrying floundered as the quarries were requisitioned for wartime storage.

The escalating crisis in Europe meant that by July 1939 the local authority had spent over £7,000 on eleven public shelters in Bath. Anderson shelters could accommodate up to six people and were made from corrugated iron. They were 6ft (1.8m) high, with 4ft (1.2 m) needing to be buried in the ground. The excavated soil would then be used to cover the roof to provided extra protection. These earth banks were often sown with flower, grass or vegetable seeds to help disguise them from aircraft, but also to make them a more attractive and useful feature of the street or garden they occupied. They were extremely effective at absorbing the shock of an explosion.

The majority of houses without alternative cover were issued with Morrison shelters, made from steel with wire mesh sides. Despite feeling extremely claustrophobic, families could take refuge and survive even with their whole house collapsing on top of them. They were, however, extremely large and had to double up as dining room tables when not in use.

On 3 September 1939 Britain was forced to declare war on Germany. There were no anti-aircraft guns or barrage balloons in Bath, and only one or two searchlights at Lansdown. At the start of the war both Germany and Britain restricted themselves to military targets where there was no threat to the civilian population. This period became known as the 'Phoney War'. Bath was, therefore, not perceived to be at risk.

In fact, it became a designated 'receiving area' for evacuees. In the first four days of September 1939 over 4,000 people of all ages arrived by special trains, the majority from London's East End. Some moved on to surrounding villages, but over half remained in Bath. The 'vackees', as they were known, combined with the influx of Admiralty workers evacuated from Whitehall put a huge strain on the city's accommodation. In October 1940 councillors warned that Bath was almost at 'saturation point'. The visitors were billeted with willing families who were paid 1 guinea a week for their board and lodging, leading to the nickname of 'guinea pigs'.

The sound of enemy aircraft overhead was commonplace, Bathonians had become used to the drone of the planes as they headed for Bristol. As a consequence, between May 1940 and August 1941, Bath endured 875 red alerts but very few of those led to bombs actually falling on the city. The first high explosive to land near Bath was on 24 August 1940, followed by a short spate of bombs that September and, although two people were injured, no one died.

The first casualties were from a lone German bomber trying to evade a British fighter plane. He dropped his cargo of weaponry in order to pick up speed. The incendiaries fell across Englishcombe Lane, but were quickly extinguished. The high explosives, however, destroyed two houses on Twerton High Street, killing three members of the Randell family and two passers-by. Shrapnel claimed another victim near West Twerton School.

Bath's first wide-scale devastation from enemy action occurred on 11 April 1941 when five bombs fell on the Dolemeads area of Widcombe, killing eleven, seriously wounding nine and injuring a further forty-three. Photographs of the devastation to the brick-built houses of Broadway, Princes Buildings, Archway and Excelsior Streets were censored at the time.

It was twelve months later that Bath suffered a series of terrifying raids inflicted on the mostly undefended city – known as the Bath Blitz. In March 1942 Britain's Bomber Command, as part of a new policy of 'Area Bombing', achieved its first successful attack on a German city. Their prey was the mostly undefended north German port of Lübeck. Britain had been unable to match the Luftwaffe's strength, but until 1942 both sides had attacked only legitimate military targets. Lübeck did manufacture armaments and the port was used for supplying the German armies in Northern Russia, but these industrial areas were far from the tightly packed medieval city centre where the RAF offensive resulted in extensive damage. Although Lübeck was a 'soft' target, its destruction boosted Allied morale and seriously hurt the German High Command.

As a direct consequence, over the weekend of 25–27 April 1942 Bath suffered three horrifying reprisal raids. Eighty Luftwaffe planes took off from Nazi-occupied northern France. As the sirens wailed, few people took cover; even when the first pathfinder flares fell, the people of Bath still believed the attack was destined for Bristol. During the previous four months Bristol had been hit almost every night. It is therefore understandable that Bathonians did not expect the bombs to fall on them.

The first raid struck just before 11 p.m. on the Saturday night and lasted until 1 a.m. The enemy aircraft then returned to France, refuelled, rearmed and returned at 4.35 a.m. Bath was still ablaze from the first raid, making it easier for the German bombers to pick out their targets. The third raid, which only lasted two hours but caused extensive damage, arrived in the early hours of Monday morning. The bombers flew low to drop their high explosives and incendiaries and then returned to rain the streets with machine-gun fire.

With civilian morale now a legitimate target for both sides, the poor accuracy of the night-time bombing raids was paradoxically justified. Citizens would become despondent if their workplaces were damaged, roads blocked, utilities cut off and homes in ruins – the fact that many would also die was glossed over by both sides.

As a primarily working-class, high-density area, Wellsway and Oldfield Park saw the greatest destruction and loss of life. Of all the so-called 'Baedeker raids',

Bath's death toll was the greatest. Bear Flat was hit during two of the assaults and had to be almost completely rebuilt. Although the modern buildings do follow the same curve in the road there are a number of notable differences including, for instance, the Bear Inn, which was rebuilt further down the road. The pharmacy building was restored and is still a pharmacy today, even though its outside walls are covered with shrapnel scars.

Harry Patch, of Combe Down and the last surviving 'tommy' from the First World War, died in 2009 at the age of 111. Patch spent the Second World War as a member of the Auxiliary Fire Service. Whilst working on the Wellsway during the Blitz, Patch and his crew were machine-gunned as they tried to douse the flames created by the illumination flares. Patch wrote that the raids on Bath were so horrific that they reminded him of his time fighting in Ypres in 1917.

The German bombers did not threaten the nearby Admiralty barracks at Foxhill, the closest they got was Ralph Allen's Prior Park. If they had targeted Foxhill they would have almost certainly undermined the Forester's Arms opposite. It was here that the Control Centre for the Civil Defence Services had been relocated after the telephone system had been disrupted at Apsley House in Lower Weston. The fact that they moved the headquarters to within metres of an Admiralty stronghold shows that the authorities realised at the time that Bath was not being targeted for its military status.

In 1941, guidelines had been agreed on how to deal with enemy damage to historic Bath buildings. Architect Mowbray Aston Green (1865–1945) was appointed by the Ministry of Works as Bath's panel architect. He identified and photographed Bath's scheduled buildings, ensuring there was an up-to-date record of each building should they ever require restoration. In the case of an enemy attack, City Engineer John Owen would send out inspectors who would report to Green any damage to buildings on the Schedule. Repairs could only commence after an inspection by an approved architect and they had to be undertaken by an approved building contractor. By February 1943 Green and his assistant had examined and reported on 303 historic buildings and twenty-six churches affected by the bombing of Bath.

The Royal Crescent was almost certainly a target of the Baedeker raids; it was then, as it is today, a world-renowned representation of Bath's architectural heritage. It is therefore gratifying that John Wood Junior's spectacular feat of eighteenth-century geometric engineering suffered relatively minor damage. During the first raid the pilots flew at 10,000ft and during the second at 30,000ft – it was therefore difficult to be entirely accurate. As a consequence, the Julian Road area, behind the Royal Crescent, suffered badly.

No. 2 Royal Crescent was burnt out by an incendiary, and No. 17 was damaged by a bomb that fell in the road outside. Green and Owen both reported that little damage had been done to the façade of either. First aid repairs were swift because of the symbolic status of the Crescent; nevertheless Green was frustrated by any delay, complaining that it was a 'bad advertisement for the City'. Despite being in his late seventies, Green worked ardently to protect the future of Bath's historic buildings. As it was, the internal structure of No. 17 was not rebuilt until the 1950s.

As part of the 'Dig for Victory' campaign, 26 acres of land in Bath were given over for allotments in an attempt to encourage people to grow their own vegetables. In 1942, Crescent Field (beyond the ha-ha) was also utilised; Royal Crescent lawn, however, was not used.

The Roman Baths escaped damage, but were still employed as a consequence of the air raids. Even those householders whose homes had withstood the onslaught found themselves without water, electricity and gas. A free emergency laundry service was set up at the Roman Baths. Those in need could take a maximum of eight items (cot blankets, bedding, underwear and shirts only) to the Hot Mineral Baths laundry in York Street between 9 a.m. and 6 p.m. Within twenty-four hours the items would be returned to your address washed, dried and ironed. Contemporary photographs show shirts and sheets strung up to dry between the statues of Roman dignitaries Julius Caesar and Claudius, and a lady using the flat top of the stone balustrading surrounding the Great Bath to iron a shirt!

The adjacent Pump Room also played its part during the war by providing office space for a number of key emergency staff. It also became a 'British Restaurant'. These were establishments where people could pay for a meal, usually consisting of non-rationed and luxury foodstuffs. Bath had three purpose-built British Restaurants, including Parkside, not far from the war memorial at the entrance to Crescent Gardens, which still operates as an eatery today.

In all, 417 people were killed and another 1,000 injured. Over 19,000 buildings were affected, of which 1,100 were seriously damaged or destroyed, 218 of which were of architectural or historic interest. These included the Assembly Rooms, the Royal Crescent, Queen Square, the Mineral Water Hospital, Lansdown Crescent, the Circus, Prior Park and Abbey Church House. The churches that were hit included St James's, Holy Trinity, New King Street Methodist Chapel, St Andrew's, St Mary's, St Bartholomew's and St John's.

Along with the attacks on Exeter, York, Canterbury and Norwich, the raids on Bath have become known as the Baedeker Blitz. The term originated with Baron Gustav Braun von Stumm, of the German foreign press division. He broadcast that the Luftwaffe had been instructed to attack every building rated highly in the well-known travel guides published by the firm of Karl Baedeker. This announcement spread quickly and brought terror to Britain. The cities of the Baedeker raids were never legitimate military targets, but the raids created a momentum of fear because now nowhere was safe from enemy air attack.

Within a week of the bombing, on 2 May, King George and Queen Elizabeth visited Bath. They were escorted by the mayor, Alderman Aubrey Bateman, up to Beechen Cliff, a famous viewing point, where they 'gazed with sorrow' on the devastation spread out below them. They toured affected areas in Oldfield Park and saw the gutted remains of the Assembly Rooms. In the *Chronicle* that day Bateman, who wrote that his heart ached for the people of Bath, encouraged everyone to carry on – 'battered but unbowed'.

By 1944 arrangements were in place to facilitate the rebuilding of people's homes. Approvals had to be obtained from two government divisions and a Bath Council department. Authorisation was given once it was established that there were resources available with which to rebuild. Dwellings would be replaced on the same footprint, but materials had to be economised on. For instance, there would be no decorative stonework unless it had been recovered from the rubble. Skirting boards would be half-height at 3in, and garden walls, gates, fences, would be omitted until much later when materials became more plentiful. A number of sites still retain their salvaged gateposts. Council contractors undertook the works, but after the war they were only permitted to repair; rebuilds then became the responsibility of the government, who had to approve an independent contractor's tender. By the end of September 1945, Bath had received over £1.5 million from the government to pay for repairs.

The people of Bath were sitting targets. Survivors believed that Bath was finished and could never recover. A German journalist reported that the Luftwaffe had truly shown their strength; that the terrible raids of destruction and 'fire of annihilation' would go down in history. In reality Bathonians would not allow their spirits to be broken. Through a mixture of stubborn denial, public morale and government censorship the Blitz on Bath was widely forgotten. And until 2003 there was no city-centre memorial to the 417 civilians who had lost their lives.

Today, visitors and residents alike are shocked to learn that Bath was bombed. Although now restored, on close inspection evidence of the devastation can be found – shrapnel scars and scorch marks on heritage buildings and, equally, the areas of 'packing case' architecture of the 1960s and 1970s that eventually filled the areas left derelict as a consequence of post-war building blight.

Twelve

PLANS FOR BATH

By the 1940s the years of fashionable decline and neglect were exacerbated by war damage. This led the Bath and District Joint Planning Committee, at their meeting on 21 June 1943, to recommend that a report, through consultation, be prepared by Sir Patrick Abercrombie (Consultant), John Owens (City Engineer) and H. Anthony Mealand (planning officer to the joint committee). *A Plan for Bath*, published in 1945, formed a framework for Bath's future development 'in accordance with modern requirements whilst at the same time preserving the beauty, architecture and history for which Bath is so famous'. The report has since become known as the *Abercrombie Plan*.

Sir Leslie Patrick Abercrombie (1879–1957) was professor of civic design at the University of Liverpool and later professor of town planning at University College London. He was a planning pioneer, advocating that the new housing estates being built for the heroes of the First World War be properly planned with transport links, shops and schools through a system of zones, free-flowing traffic and regional plans. He is probably most famous for his re-planning of London after the Second World War, from which came the New Towns Movement and the building of Harlow and Crawley. He was also employed by Liverpool (1914), Dublin (1923), Plymouth (1943) and Edinburgh (1949), amongst others.

His schemes gave birth to the concept of the green belt and he was closely involved with the founding of the Council for the Preservation of Rural England (1926). In his later years the British government charged Abercrombie with redesigning Hong Kong, and another Bath visitor, Haile Selassie, commissioned him in 1956 to draw up plans for Addis Ababa.

Although never fully executed, *A Plan for Bath* was a momentous task, considering each area of the city and its environs and aiming to understand every aspect of Bath life. It contains maps and photographs and a number of exquisite aerial illustrations of the proposed new buildings and roads, drawn by architects A.C. Fare and J.D.M. Harvey. Abercrombie speculated that as the citizens of Bath recovered from the raids of 1942, their minds would turn to planning and they resolved to restore their city by clearing away the slums, improving the communications and modernising the city's architectural heritage to make the 'City worthy of its traditions'.

One of the main legacies of the *Abercrombie Plan* is the enduring hierarchy of Bath's architectural heritage. Abercrombie identified and zoned off the buildings (almost entirely from the mid-Georgian period) that were considered worth preserving, often at the expense of Bath's 'less important' buildings. For instance, the central area of Bath was divided into ten precincts. Precinct No. 1, surrounded by an inner ring road and roughly occupying the area within the city walls, was referred to as the Roman Precinct. Within it, several roads were redesignated as pedestrian-only to allow for greater functionality as an area for shopping and commerce. To achieve this, however, the plan called for the demolition of a wealth of historic buildings including the Blue Coat School, the Mineral Water Hospital (damaged during the Bath Blitz), a number of the shops in Orange Grove and Terrace Walk, North Parade Buildings, the body of St James's Church (also damaged during the Bath Blitz) and Weymouth House. Business premises were also to be removed from Stall Street to allow for an extension of the baths. The Friends Meeting House (1817–19) on York Street was to be sacrificed in order to open the view to John Wood's ostentatious façade (*c.* 1727) of Ralph Allen's townhouse.

Abercrombie despaired at the neglect of Bath's riverfront and proposed a brand new sweeping road to connect Cleveland and Pulteney bridges. Admittedly, some of Bath's most historic buildings would also have been swept aside, but when one considers what was eventually built in the form of the Hilton Hotel and the Podium, both of which turn their backs stubbornly on the River Avon, Abercrombie's idea seems visionary.

Abercrombie was a pioneer when it came to offering solutions for controlling traffic. In Bath he set out to separate and redirect Bath's through traffic. 'In an ideal world', he declared, 'there should be no genuine through traffic … in no sense should Bath be considered as a mere incident upon a national route from London to Bristol.' Unfortunately, today it is certainly on the route from the south coast to the M4 for the haulage trucks that pound Bathwick Street, Cleveland Bridge and London Road.

Abercrombie's Arterial Road No. 5, which would have come off the A36 at Dry Arch, crossed the canal and railway before joining the London Road at Lambridge. This might have solved the problem, and although it is still occasionally mooted, is highly controversial. Arterial Road No. 5 was also meant to improve communication links in this area of Bath and therefore support another of Abercrombie's proposals, which was to turn 40–50 acres of the Bathampton Meadows into a 'zone' for heavy industry.

Sir Patrick Abercrombie: A New Plan for Bath, Northgate Street, 1945. (Bath Central Library/Bath in Time)

Despite Abercrombie's hope, he was realistic that there would always be a certain amount of through traffic, but primarily on the east–west axis. The plan saw the development of a number of roads, such as the new Arterial Road No. 1, running east and west through Bath with a width of between 68ft (20.8m) and 80ft (24.3m). One of the most striking illustrations shows this road and its proposed junction between Julian Road and Guinea Lane. The land is cut dramatically away and a bridge formed to take traffic under Lansdown.

Where this same road passes the junctions with Marlborough Buildings and Church Street, a large open space would be created to house the new Civic Centre. It was found that the existing accommodation at the Guildhall was inadequate for the scope and responsibilities of a post-war local authority. A solution was proposed in which the sixteen central houses of the Royal Crescent would be converted to form a centralised office for (almost) all the departments of the Corporation. This development was to see the removal of both the 'unbalanced and unsightly appendages' to the Royal Crescent and the dilapidated Mews behind. Facing the widened Julian Road would be a brand new council chamber set within spacious gardens. 'The development of this great Crescent as a Centre of Local Government would create one of the finest civic centres in the country. It would be a bold scheme calling for wisdom and great courage.'

The *Abercrombie Plan* proposed alterations and solutions for every single part of Bath, from new estates with community and shopping centres to a grand concert hall near the Abbey, each reliant on the other for the plan to fully succeed. The premise to cover every aspect without bias and thereby create a future plan of absolute balance seems, at best, naive. Abercrombie criticised previous plans for having put too much emphasis on the monumental and architectural over his stated commitments to convenience, healthy living and recreational open spaces. Although Abercrombie's influence can be detected in some later 'solutions' imposed on Bath, had *A New Plan for Bath* been executed in its entirety, Bath's 'sack' would have been even more devastating.

The sad fact is that after the 1940s the trademark Georgian buildings of Bath were hopelessly redundant. Society's structure had changed; too many young men had been lost during two world wars (and countless other conflicts). Families simply did not have the staff, or the lifestyles, to maintain a townhouse of five storeys.

In 1944 the Bath Preservation Trust commissioned a report by SPAB (Society for the Protection of Ancient Buildings) to help find a use for the old buildings. The report looked at houses in the Royal Crescent, Northampton Street and New King Street, but noted rather despondently, 'Since families are greatly reduced and service almost unobtainable, these buildings as they stand are admittedly out of date and redundant … They have served their purpose and for the most part are no longer wanted in their present form.' Rather than becoming 'ghosts of a past age', the report asserted that they could, and should, be carefully and sympathetically converted into flats.

Directly after the war, in 1946, there was a patriotic desire to rebuild homes for those bombed out during Bath's Blitz. The immediate housing needs of the community were answered by the erection of prefabricated units that had 'come to rest for all to see on Odd Down'. Even the Bath Preservation Trust could see the value of these homes encroaching on the green belt. The Annual Report for 1946 states, 'Whatever the impression en masse of these snug little homes, there is no doubt that they have brought happiness to scores of families.'

The Moorlands Housing Estate (1950), by City Engineer John Owen, with P. Kennerell Pope, was the first completely new city council development after the war. Architect and academic Michael Forsyth praises the mix of semi-detached and terraced houses, using Bath stone – equally showing respect for the Georgian tradition 'while being unashamedly modern'.

Council housing was also provided in Upper Weston in 1948 and at Snowhill in 1954–61. The Snowhill development, by Terence Snailum of Snailum, Huggins & Le Fevre, included Berkley House (1958), Bath's first tower block. Snowhill was built on a steeply sloping site after 'slum clearance'. Long parallel blocks of flats are set along the contours with one stepping uphill 'for contrast' and a point block for 'focus'. The buildings are faced with ashlar and they have green copper roofs visible across Bath. It is a Scandinavian interpretation of Bath's Classicism. The development won a Civic Award in 1961.

Kingsmead Square suffered greatly during the Blitz, and after the war – primarily due to its proximity to the poorer areas of Avon, Milk and Corn Streets – was gripped by building blight as various schemes to improve Bath's transport and infrastructure were considered. Today Kingsmead Square seems to be the last bastion of historic Bath before you are affronted by the mass of post-war redevelopment.

The flight path of the Luftwaffe's Junkers Ju 88 and Dornier Do 217 bombers was orientated north to south and then east to west, and these two axes crossed at Kingsmead causing extensive damage. Kingsmead Street, which originally joined New King Street, was the main and very busy route to Bristol. It was targeted primarily to disrupt communication and transport links. There were twenty-two victims in the Kingsmead area alone, and as you read the names you appreciate that whole families were wiped out.

The destruction immediately closed Kingsmead Street, and it quickly took on a new role as the salvage yard for all reusable stone and building supplies. By the time all the materials had been used and the street was clear again, Bathonians had found alternative routes. It was quietly accepted, therefore, when Kingsmead Street and the thoroughfare to the west was truncated by Rosewell Court (1961) and its adjoining car park. There is a dramatic difference in levels here, illustrating the depth of the cellars and basements of the obliterated eighteenth-century buildings.

The large hotels that had been requisitioned during the war continued as military offices, but as the Admiralty started to leave Bath so large 'white elephants' started appearing on every street corner. The Grand Pump Room Hotel, which had found itself as the battlefield of the Old Bath Preservation Society in 1909, was taken over and revived by De Vere Hotels Ltd and, whilst enjoying another heyday, was requisitioned by the Admiralty in 1939. The hotel remained the offices of the Electrical Engineering Department until September 1946. In 1944, De Vere's had sold the lease to Great Western Railway for £36,000. Once the hotel was released by the Ministry of Works, GWR planned to spend £100,000 over five years to update and improve the hotel. This renovation, like so many others, was held up by a shortage of labour and building materials after the war. But soon there was added uncertainty caused by the Transport Act (1947), which saw the railways nationalised in 1948.

It was hoped that the hotel would reopen at the end of 1950, in time for the Festival of Britain in 1951 – Bath was one of eight provincial festival cities. Yet the hotel continued to lie derelict, and so in 1953 the council served a writ against the British Transport Commission (BTC) for failing to carry out its contractual obligations. As a result, in 1958 the BTC were ordered to pay £100,000 compensation. As the building lay empty and all hope of it being revived as a hotel faded, the public made suggestions for possible uses such as council offices with flats above and, on the ground floor, the city art gallery and library. In 1957 local businessmen had ambitions to convert the hotel into a casino, but the necessary investment could not be raised. Thus, in 1959 the Grand Pump Room Hotel was demolished to make way for Arlington House, a development of thirty-three luxury flats and nine shops by Ravenseft Properties.

The Admiralty had also requisitioned the Empire Hotel in 1939, and had removed a number of architectural details such as the finials and a number of balconies. The Ministry of Defence eventually moved out in 1988 and the building fell rapidly into decline. The Empire was earmarked for demolition, but after local protests it was saved and converted by PRP Architects in 1995–96 into forty-five retirement flats, with a roof garden, library and card room.

Even today there is a noticeable undulation in the central grass area at the Circus from a huge bomb crater. Nos. 17 and 20 were extensively damaged and the elderly owners did not have the resources, or lifespan, to restore their properties. Instead, both hoped to settle with the War Damage Commission and literally walk away with a payment equivalent to the 1939 value of their homes. The Housing Act of 1949 provided grants so that houses could be converted into self-contained flats. By the mid-1950s a number of houses in the Circus were empty and rapidly falling into a worrying state of disrepair. Bath City Council purchased six houses and converted them to create twenty-five self-contained flats.

In 1953 the Historic Buildings and Ancient Monuments Act made government funds available for the preservation of significant buildings. This led, in 1955, to the establishment of the Bath Terraces Scheme under which grants became available for conservation. The first project was to restore the badly eroded façade of the Circus. A large number of the precarious acorns had to be replaced, whilst the Council specified that the variety of historic openings broken through the parapet become unified ovals. Only seven of the façades were considered to be in a reasonable condition, mainly because they had been previously restored.

Whilst the Council converted the interiors, work started on the façades, commencing with Nos. 21 and 22. The soot and grime of two centuries was cleaned off by the use of water delivered through a fine jet spray. By 1966 six of the eight houses owned by the Council had been cleaned and the stonework restored.

Seventeen privately owned houses had also been restored. This was achieved through a government grant scheme that provided 50 per cent of the cost, whilst a further 25 per cent was received from the city rates. There were eight privately owned houses that still needed to be restored, but the cost was prohibitive to the owners – the average cost to clean and restore one façade at the Circus was £4,000 (the equivalent of around £67,000 in today's money). Despite this being far beyond the finances of the owners, it was actually a conservative estimate;

the lack of skilled labour and the extent of the erosion meant that the final outlay usually far exceeded £4,000. Urban myths propound (although I know them to be true) that owners were willing to give up a house on the Circus, complete with furniture, for £1 (less than £20).

In 1950, the Bath Extension Act added a further 1,130 acres to the city of Bath, taking in parts of the parishes of Charlcombe, Claverton, Englishcombe, Monkton Combe and Weston. The reactions were mixed: those in Bath felt that the parishes would be a financial burden because a significant amount of investment would be required to bring their infrastructure, education, drainage, roads, etc., up to Bath's standards, and equally the parishioners were concerned that their rates and taxes would rise.

The name of Colin Buchanan (1907–2001) is still vilified in Bath. He faced one of his greatest professional defeats in Bath, and so outraged were the conservationists at his company's 1965 suggestion to put a tunnel under the historic city of Bath that few would have thought his career could have survived such a public lashing, let alone see him knighted in 1972. However, as one of those conservationists admitted in more recent years – perhaps, with hindsight, Buchanan had the answer after all.

Colin Buchanan & Partners was founded in 1964 on the back of the success of the seminal *Traffic in Towns* report, a document still 'regarded as the starting point of modern transportation planning'. Their task for Bath was to produce an interim-style report which would both assess the relevance of previous findings, and offer the most desirable solution – irrelevant of cost. This would clear the way for the Council to begin a more in-depth consultation. *Bath: A Planning and Transport Study* was a progression of *Traffic in Towns* and *Traffic in Bath*, in which the main principles of modern urban planning were outlined.

Buchanan stated that too many roads in the past had been planned around hypothesis and guesswork – *their* findings were based on statistics taken in the field, and their plan was to improve areas where they believed movement demands were certain to rise. Their surveys, carried out in July and August 1964, showed that the east–west routes of the Upper Bristol Road (A4), including Queen Square, and Lower Bristol Road (to A36) were the most used and congested. Both routes carried 10,000 vehicles per day, and the London Road carried about 30,000 vehicles per day. The A46 from the north and A367 from the south, were also heavy. They also found that 67 per cent of the HGV lorries on Bath's roads were using it as a cut through and had no business in the city. The main traffic black spots in 1964 were identified as being Lambridge and Cleveland Bridge – all of which still sounds horribly familiar!

The introduction to *Bath: A Planning and Transport Study* warns of no quick fix, 'unhappily there is no prospect whatsoever of such expectations being gratified. This is because the problems are intensely difficult even to define, let alone solve.' Increases in traffic volumes were affecting the whole country, and towns with historic street systems that were unsuitable for motor vehicles faced a major dilemma. Bath, however, with its unique topography and architectural heritage, faced far greater problems than most. Buchanan particularly disliked 'the intrusion into the [heritage] scene of continuous rows of parked vehicles on both sides of the street'. It went 'without saying,' wrote Buchanan, 'that a main objective of planning should be to preserve the character' of the central part of the city whilst also respecting 'to the uttermost the Georgian heritage' and 'the landscape heritage of Bath'.

The year 2000 was seen as the point that the 'saturation' of private car ownership would be reached. The study showed that the road requirements and car parking spaces needed to accommodate this theoretical scale of car ownership was impossible to achieve. In answer to this dilemma, the plan looked at alternative solutions, such as the improvement of the public transport network:

> There is a certain measure of choice regarding the amount of motor traffic which need be accepted in urban areas, but all the indications are that the motor vehicle is an extremely useful method of transport which is here to stay for as far ahead as one can reasonably look.

Buchanan advocated the egalitarianism of both drivers and pedestrians. Vehicles had the right to 'move easily from one part of a town to another, to penetrate destinations, and to stop there on arrival', whilst residents and pedestrians should be free from danger, noise, fumes, vibrations, visual intrusions and to be 'reasonably protected from cross-penetration by extraneous traffic'. These conflicting demands could be solved by a network, 'the purpose of [which was] to provide both for efficient movement and to permit the establishment of "environmental areas"'. A number of streets were to be made permanently traffic free, whilst others, such as Milsom Street and the High Street, would be closed to traffic during shopping hours. In order to service the shops, depots would be set up on the edge of town and goods distributed from there. The inner ring road, meaning the series of roads past Bath Spa and Green Park railway stations leading to the Upper Bristol Road, would be serviced by an extensive series of car parks.

To provide for the free movement of vehicles across Bath three main routes were considered, but all were deeply hampered by Bath's topography and heritage. The only solution was to find a route that actually passed through the heritage area. 'We were led, quite inexorably, to the conclusion that there was one answer and one alone – to construct a tunnel underneath the central area.' A twin-tube tunnel, 540 yards long and dropping down under the Paragon, would carry the heavy east–west traffic. The tunnel would reappear just beyond Gay Street, from where the route was to follow the soon to be abandoned railway line out of Green Park Station. At £5 million, the cost of the scheme was unprecedented, and as a result the build was to be staggered over a twenty-year period – the first tunnel to be completed by 1975, the second by 1985.

A central cross route was also planned to service local traffic from Walcot. This road is described in the report as 'a delicate act of urban surgery', although it would have wiped out at least thirty-five Georgian buildings. 'To maintain the continuity of pedestrian movement in the old heart of the City, and to avoid physical severance of the destruction of Bath's architectural heritage', a cutting, sunk 20ft below New Bond Street, would have carried the traffic.

Buchanan's plan was supported by the Ministry of Housing & Local Government; many of the councillors, the Bath Preservation Trust and the *Bath Chronicle* felt it was the only acceptable solution. Nevertheless, public opinion was divided and in May 1966 after reaching deadlock, Bath City Council looked to government ministers for counsel. Mr Crossman, the Minister of Housing & Local Government, advocated a further consultancy report to advise on the practicality of Buchanan's proposals.

However, the main objections to the plan were actually generated by the far more destructive modifications proposed by the Council. They had taken elements from the Buchanan report and created their own scheme, including motorway-style roads and junctions ripping a path through Bath's heritage. This indecision created slums, as building blight saw all earmarked development areas deserted and neglected. The plan was eventually abandoned in 1979 due primarily to escalating costs. However, attitudes to conservation and preservation had improved greatly since the mid-1960s, and those protestors who had demanded 'Buchanan out of Bath!' claimed a victory.

There is still one period in Bath's recent history that still shocks and embarrasses us all – the infamous 'Sack of Bath' of the 1960s and early 1970s which saw thousands of Georgian buildings destroyed in the name of progress. Testament perhaps, is the fact that *The Sack of Bath – And After*, the Bath Preservation Trust's 1989 reprint of Adam Fergusson's seminal work of 1973, with an update by Tim Mowl, is still in print today and in 2011 interest was such that Fergusson reissued the 1973 edition with a new preface.

Before the Second World War, Bath was held up as an example of sympathetic preservation. Acts introduced in Bath in 1925 and 1937 helped prevent incongruous buildings being put up, but also protected the older ones from unnecessary alteration. These acts were subsequently adopted by other local authorities. Bath was a beautiful example of a Georgian 'new town', planned and organised with the artisan housing closely situated, to serve the grander set pieces. Both grand and modest were conceived and built together in freshly quarried, honey-coloured Bath stone. 'All Bath grew old together. It was unique.' After the devastation of the Blitz, however, there was a change in attitude. What followed was a 'lust to develop' and modernise, with new shopping centres and flats with 'mod-cons' to help solve the housing crisis.

The 'Sack' saw seventeenth-century, Grade III listed buildings in Holloway demolished. They were replaced with what has been described as 'rows of hencoops'. The clearance of the Dolemeads was underway before the First World War, and Avon Street and Peter Street were being assessed before the Second World War, but Bath of the working classes – the infrastructure, the artisans, the balance, the picture of complete society and, possibly of more current concern, the first rung on the modern housing ladder – were being indiscriminately swept away.

Few original working-class housing districts exist anywhere in this country, so why the great outrage? Because Bath had effectively been slumbering since the end of the eighteenth century and the investment to rejuvenate on a major and natural scale had not been here, Bath had become a time capsule. As a piece of history, it had much more to offer before 1950 than it does now.

The national attitude at this time is probably best illustrated by the 1966 proposal to build an uncompromisingly modern new headquarters for the Bath and Portland Stone Group just a few feet from Bath Abbey's south transept. The four-storey building of Bath stone, with amber-tinted glass and bronze window surrounds was designed by award-winning Robert Matthew, Johnson-Marshall & Partners (now RMJM), who were concurrently working on the University of Bath's main campus buildings. The design was described as 'distinguished' by its supporters, who believed the building would not only blend with the Abbey, but would actually enhance its beauty.

In December 1966, the Bath Planning Committee approved the scheme and recommended that the Council grant permission. The Council's expert advisors, Sir Hugh Casson and Professor Colin Buchanan, both agreed that the application be approved. The Bath Preservation Trust reported that 60 per cent of its members saw the design as being worthy of such a significant site (although the remaining 40 per cent fervently objected).

Bryan Little, *The Bath & Wilts Evening Chronicle* architectural correspondent, whilst questioning the legitimacy of placing such a modern building so close to Bath's medieval centrepiece, did consider that if the design was rejected, he would regret the loss of 'what could intrinsically and without account of its surroundings, be the best modern office building in Bath'. Councillor W.E. Evans, however, condemned the building, saying it 'would stand out as an extraneous wart on a pretty girl's face'. By just one vote, the Council sent the matter back to the planning committee for further consideration at its meeting on 7 February 1967. The Bath and Portland

Stone Group naturally appealed, which led to a three-day inquiry presided over by Anthony Greenwood (1911–82), Minister of Housing & Local Government.

During the inquiry, the Bath and Portland Stone Group were represented by Ernest F. Tew, who pointed out, 'the Abbey had been surrounded by buildings for hundreds of years. Over the centuries these had changed in style and character and it was an evolution that should continue'. The Bath Preservation Trust were not invited to give evidence at the inquiry, but they did let Greenwood know that there had been a wide division in the opinion of its members concerning the appropriateness of the design for such an important position in the heart of the city.

The Trust's *Annual Report* for 1966–67 described the division as:

> … an unhappy episode in the history of the Trust, but it has established the fact that the Trustees are not dyed-in-the-wool preservationists, but are sincerely seeking to achieve what they believe to be in the city's best interests, which lie as much in the future as in the past.

Bryan Little praised the design of the building, believing it to be 'better than any commercial building [proposed] for the central area … since the war', but he did believe it was unsuitable for a site so close to the Abbey, whilst Yehudi Menuhin described the scheme as 'outrageous'. The inquiry found against the Bath and Portland Stone Group, with Greenwood summing up that whilst he agreed 'forceful contrast in architectural compositions and townscapes was not necessarily wrong, [he felt that as] the present building on the site fitted in with its surroundings, any new building should have the same quality of restraint, leaving the Abbey to dominate the scene'.

Many declared that the defeat of the application was the direct result of a monumental two-year campaign by one woman – Philippa Savery. Described by *The Times* as a 'passionate protector', she resigned her membership of the BPT in order to fight the plan. At the time, the 65-year-old antiques dealer ran a successful business from her bow-fronted shop in Abbey Green, but she was so consumed by her crusade that she closed her business in 1967, instead using the shop as her campaign office. She replaced the collectibles in her window with slogans and a model of the Abbey with a cube of matchboxes next to it to represent the new scheme. She collected over 4,000 signatures from passers-by, many of whom were international visitors to the city.

Philippa wanted the historic building saved, and although that part of her campaign did not win universal sympathy, most agreed the building had little architectural interest. Bath Stone Firms Ltd, quarry masters and stone merchants, had occupied No. 7 Kingston Buildings since the 1880s, taking over the premises from Isaac Pitman and his Phonetic Institution. By 1901, John Pearce, Portland

Stone Co. (Ltd) occupied No. 6 Kingston Buildings and eventually the two companies formally amalgamated to create the Bath and Portland Stone Group. Kingston Buildings, including the run of properties behind the Bath and Portland Stone Group's headquarters, had been condemned for residential purposes and were threatened with demolition. According to friends, Savery's forthright opposition was quite out of character, although perhaps not surprising when one considers that she claimed centuries of Bath lineage and lived, quite literally, in the shadow of the Abbey. Savery attended the inquiry, anxiously listening to every point.

Having outgrown their Bath office building, the Bath and Portland Stone Group was forced to leave the city centre. No. 7 Kingston Buildings (now the home of Bath Tourism Plus) remained empty until 1971 when the City of Bath Architectural and Planning Department, which was waiting for its new purpose-built office block on Trim Street, took up residence. The Abbey Authorities purchased the run of properties to use as their offices.

The Bath Preservation Trust declared that the restoration of Kingston Buildings 'relieves a great anxiety concerning their future. No happier solution could have been found.' And Savery, of course, was 'overjoyed' at the inquiry's refusal. We will never know how the block may have stood the test of time, but I suspect it would not have been popular today.

Building preservation orders were introduced nationally in 1932, but the first survey did not commence until 1 January 1950. In actuality, 'listing' did little to protect Grade III listed buildings from being altered or even demolished. The conditions merely called for the local authority to be informed of changes. In addition, Bath had hundreds of unlisted buildings which, elsewhere in the country, would have been considered for statutory protection. At the height of the 'Sack', Grade II listed buildings were not safe either. Georgian Bath was ripped up and junked and replaced with 'packing case architecture'.

The only way to stop the destruction was to shame the authorities. The editor of *The Times*, William Rees-Mogg, lived near Bath and encouraged his feature writer, Adam Fergusson, to cover the city's plight. In two articles – on 23 and 29 September 1970 – Fergusson estimated that more than 18,000 listed buildings had been destroyed in Bath since the Second World War. Adding insult to injury was the unsympathetic replacement architecture; Fergusson described St Patrick's Court on Bathwick Hill, for example, as 'lurch[ing] inelegantly down the slope, like a juggernaut with a flat tyre'. His exposure of Bath's systematic destruction stirred such national outrage that the pages of *The Times* were filled with horrified assertions against the scandal. 'Smashing the totality of this city is even worse than cutting up a Rembrandt. The destruction must stop and the restoration and protection of Bath be undertaken as an urgent national task,' cried *The Architectural Review* in 1973.

Lord Snowdon: View from Beechen Cliff, blighted by the Technical College, 1972. (Private Collection/ Bath in Time)

As a consequence of Fergusson's articles, Sir Christopher Chancellor, president of the Bath Preservation Trust, approached him to write a book. Initially Chancellor wanted to call it 'Bath in Danger', but the title chosen, inspired by the Sack of Carthage, had a far more dramatic effect. Lord Snowdon came to Bath for three days in March 1972 to take photographic evidence and Lord Goodman, a lawyer who was known as the most powerful non-elected man in the country, was purposefully asked to write the foreword, to serve as a warning to anyone who thought they might make libel charges against Fergusson.

After reading Fergusson's draft James Lees-Milne, the celebrated architectural conservationist and writer, was duly impressed but he felt concerned that the book did not leave readers with a plan of action. Lees-Milne suggested an alternative ending:

> I think the last note of this splendid fanfare ought to be a positive one. Let us beg the Government to take over. Let us march to Downing Street. Let us strip ourselves naked and slash ourselves with knives on 1 April 1973 in the Town Clerk's Office.

John Betjeman had already written to congratulate Fergusson on his articles in *The Times*, but now his friend Lees-Milne asked him to get more involved. To serve as *The Sack of Bath*'s introduction, Betjeman produced *The Newest Bath Guide*, a parody of Christopher Anstey's Georgian verses. Betjeman was happy for the 'rhyme' to be altered or cut. Fergusson changed the first six lines into the third person and cut lines 19 to 26. The full and original version was reproduced for the first time at the Building of Bath Museum during the 2006 *Poetry in Stone* exhibition, part of the anniversary celebrations of John Betjeman's birth. The most quoted verse, however, remains:

> Now houses are units, and people are digits
> And Bath has been planned into quarters for midgets.
> Official designs are aggressively neuter,
> The Puritan work of an eyeless computer.
> Goodbye to old Bath. We who loved you are sorry
> They've carted you off by developer's lorry.

The Sack of Bath was instrumental in bringing the destruction of Bath to a halt. The greatest achievement was the introduction of the Conservation Area Act of 1974, which helped save other English towns from needless destruction. The national outrage reached the ears of the government, who felt compelled to intervene. The Secretary of State for the Environment became directly involved in the planning process in Bath. He discounted the idea of holding a public inquiry into the proposed traffic schemes, and instead encouraged the City Council to work with, rather than against, the BPT.

In July 1974 the Trust was invited to join a joint steering group with the Department of the Environment, Avon County Council and Bath City Council. This steering group began to commission experiments in traffic management, draw down funding from national government for more specialist conservation staff in the planning offices and, what's more, looked into developing a policy of 'Minimum Physical Change' to the historic buildings. In addition to this, the conservation areas across Bath were extended. This meant that no historic building in these areas could be demolished without permission.

By 1978, Fergusson believed the scandal had stopped and 'so long as one is prepared to wear blinkers from time to time it is still a complete city'. The tide of destruction was turned, so much so that the same Bath City Council produced a document called *Saving Bath*, again written by Colin Buchanan.

※ ※ ※ ※ ※

We know so much about Bath's 'lost' buildings because of the Bath Buildings Record. This archive consists of about 5,000 items, including exquisite drawings by Peter Coard, meticulously catalogued surveys by Ruth Coard, architectural fragments and photographs by Lesley Green-Armytage.

Peter and Ruth Coard moved to Bath in 1957. Peter became head of art at Bath Technical School and Ruth worked as a library assistant at the Bath Reference Library. Initially Peter had little interest in old buildings; it was Ruth who suggested that he contribute some drawings. He got so enthused by it that Peter was still recording buildings in his own unique style, using black biro on card, long after everyone else had moved on.

Peter and Ruth had grown increasingly concerned with the seemingly indiscriminate policy of demolition that was blighting Bath during the 1960s and '70s. They recognised the need for progress, but were concerned with the mass clearance of Bath's historic Georgian artisan housing and the unsympathetic developments that were taking their place. With other like-minded people, they set out to record these historic buildings before the bulldozers caused them to vanish forever.

As founder members of the Bath Buildings Record Group, their motivation was as recorders rather than protestors; their work, however, soon added to the cries of outrage as vast areas of Bath came under the threat of the developers. The group was active from about 1963 to 1976, meeting initially once a month at

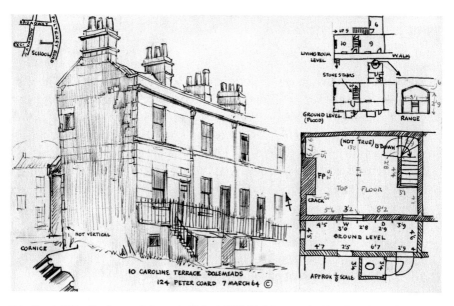

Peter Coard, 10 Caroline Terrace, Dolemeads, 7 March 1964. (Bath Preservation Trust/Bath in Time)

7 p.m. on a Thursday at Bath Reference Library, then housed at Queen Square, where Ruth worked.

At its height in 1966 there were sixty-three voluntary recorders, but a core of six to eight members undertook the majority of the work. They contributed photographs, illustrations, sketches and surveys. An early information sheet produced by the group stated that they were interested in all buildings, whatever their age or function and whether they were considered to be of architectural merit or not. This basic objective to record, without bias, did not alter. The members of the group undertook this phenomenal record in their spare time – at weekends or after work. Elizabeth, the Coards' daughter, remembers 'playing' on the demolition sites whilst the adults worked against the clock, Peter often having to sketch by torchlight. Peter also removed architectural elements from buildings due for demolition. He stored them at home in an 80ft (25m) lean-to shed for over twenty-five years until they were moved to what is now the Museum of Bath Architecture.

The group had a sense of urgency as many buildings had already been lost and, as Ruth wrote in her introduction to *Vanishing Bath*, 'demolition waits for no-one'. As Adam Fergusson summarised:

> The destroyers work from nine to five every day, sitting in comfortable offices ... and they get paid for what they do. The preservers have to make their own time, acquiring what facts and figures and plans they can get hold of, often finding that action is too late, too difficult or too expensive; and they have to raise the money for it themselves, organise petitions, and pay for legal and architectural expenses out of their own pockets.

Vanishing Bath was published in three volumes (Kingsmead Press, 1970, 1971 & 1972) and then as a combined volume in 1973. The books feature a short historical introduction by Ruth, followed by uninterrupted pages of Peter's drawings. Peter's considerable skill as an artist, illustrator and draughtsman enabled him to capture the unique and beautiful features of these condemned architectural treasures. Ruth wrote:

> Every building, every detail, every article of street furniture illustrated in [*Vanishing Bath*] has been demolished, removed or threatened with demolition ... this [publication] is intended primarily as a record rather than a protest.

Without the examples of the homes of the regular working inhabitants of the city, wrote Ruth, the grander houses are meaningless, 'a record [of all] is necessary for a balanced view of eighteenth and nineteenth-century Bath'.

As a consequence of Dr Richard Beeching's (1913–85) report, *The Reshaping of the British Railways*, Green Park Station closed in 1966. Almost immediately, it was earmarked for demolition to make way for a new dual carriage as part of the Buchanan Transport Plan for Bath. The station had been slowly run down before closure and had probably not been maintained for the previous twenty years. Left empty, it quickly became dilapidated. Nevertheless, in 1971 the buildings were upgraded from Grade III to Grade II, but their 'disgraceful condition' was noted. All the glass was broken, billboards with posters and graffiti covered the stonework, buddleia grew from crevices, rubbish was dumped outside, and it had become a notorious hideout for hippies!

Throughout the 1970s it was known as Bath's 'white elephant'. Run down and ramshackled, finding an agreeable use for the site was fraught with conflict and politics. In 1973 the roof had started to shower debris onto the former platform and the need to find a new use, with renovation expenditure, was urgent. The fear that the station would become another victim of the 'Sack' led to it being recorded by the Bath Buildings Record as well as by Lord Snowdon, who photographed it for possible inclusion in Adam Fergusson's *The Sack of Bath* book. After protracted negotiations and much secrecy, Bath City Council eventually purchased the premises from British Rail in 1974 for £58,000.

The Council called for proposals for the reuse of the premises, and numerous schemes were put forward for the 4 acre site, including a design by William Bertram for Bath's own festival hall. The lack of a suitable venue meant that a number of the music festival's events were actually held in Bristol. Bertram's split-level structure – sandwiched between the platforms and under its own ceiling, independent of the original cast-iron roof – could have provided an auditorium for 1,000, a stage for an orchestra of 150 and a choir of 300, a lecture hall, an all-glass exhibition hall and restaurants. Sadly, Luke Rittner and Anthony Tootal, administrators of the Bath Festival, had to announce that they had failed to find the finance needed for the private project to go ahead; not surprising when they had only been given five weeks to raise the money.

There was also a hope that Green Park might be used as a railway station again. Sarcastically, Edward Foring wrote in his *Sul's Day by Day* column on 24 October 1974, 'the idea of using Green Park railway station as a railway station is too original to be considered by Bath Corporation'. Enthusiasts from the Bristol Suburban Railway Society campaigned to restore the line from Bath to Mangotsfield. A supercilious, but realistic, letter from Steve Ehrlicher pointed out that to reinstate this section of railway would require the purchase and relaying of track on a stretch of line which included fifty-three bridges, a viaduct, a tunnel and three level crossings. Combined with labour and rolling stock, Ehrlicher predicted that the venture would cost at least £7 million (£65 million today).

Other proposals submitted to the council included a home for the city's new law courts, casino, coach park and a leisure centre. There were also schemes for housing, but these mostly required the demolition of the station buildings. Tesco made a proposal in 1976 to build a store and car park, but their designs called for considerable internal alteration, which would not be tolerated. The Council eventually rejected their application and Tesco lodged an appeal. Whilst the Council procrastinated, so the station buildings deteriorated further. Locals were concerned that soon Green Park Station would go the way of other sites in Bath, where constant indecision had led to demolition being the only viable solution.

The Council favoured hotel projects, but no company went as far as completing the planning process and by 1977, despite advertising the land as a prime site for a hotel, there were no bidders, and so an offer by a supermarket seemed the only option.

In June 1977, J. Sainsbury Ltd submitted a scheme in partnership with Stonechester of Bristol, with C.H. Peare & Sons, contractors. Their proposal saw the train shed restored, the booking hall become a museum and a new supermarket. Sir John Betjeman volunteered as their advisor and the scheme was supported by the Bath Preservation Trust. The restoration work was undertaken by Stide Treglown Partnership in 1982–84, at the expense of Sainsbury's. Happily the station buildings now house a thriving, bustling complex of independent shops, market stalls, restaurants and meeting rooms.

✳ ✳ ✳ ✳ ✳

Probably the most important work undertaken for Bath was the Flood Alleviation Scheme of the 1960s–70s. Just to the south of Pulteney Bridge is the horseshoe weir, perhaps unremarkable to the many admirers of Bath, but this exceptional piece of modern engineering has saved Bath from the regular and devastating floods the city has often had to endure. In December 1960 alone the damage caused amounted to £1.14 million; something had to be done. Work commenced in 1963 and included new retaining walls, the introduction of steel sheeting to line the river walls, the construction of Churchill Bridge and footbridge, the redirection of mains gas and electricity, and finally – below Pulteney Bridge, a new three-step weir and radial gate which automatically adapts to the water flow. Downstream, at Twerton, the scheme includes gates that span the width of the Avon, impounding a constant water level under low-flow conditions, but raising during floods. The Flood Prevention Scheme has been a resounding success.

Recognised with a Civic Trust Award in 1973, it has kept Bath safe from flooding for forty years.

❋ ❋ ❋ ❋ ❋

As we have seen, the opening of the Great Western Railway had seriously undermined the canal. In 1852, the Kennet and Avon Canal was sold to the GWR, but was rapidly run down and neglected. By the 1950s a survey showed that the canal was carrying insufficient trade to justify it being retained as a commercial waterway. Over the years many leaks had developed and the canal was closed, in some areas becoming completely dry. The last voyage along the Kennet and Avon was made in 1952.

In 1962, control of the canal passed to the British Waterways Board who, with the newly formed Kennet and Avon Canal Trust and a legion of volunteers, set about restoring the canal. The work took almost thirty years and to mark their success, on 8 August 1990, Queen Elizabeth II navigated through one of the locks at Caen Hill and announced the canal's official reopening. Today, the canal is a very popular and attractive place to spend your leisure time – a world away from its industrial origins.

❋ ❋ ❋ ❋ ❋

Frederick Gibberd's Bath Technical College on James Street West (1957–63) was deplored by Betjeman for its 'pointy behind'. Unlike the majority of the other large and jarring post-war buildings in this area, it seems unlikely the college will be redeveloped anytime soon, mainly because it is an extremely good college with exceptional catering and hair and beauty departments.

Away from the city centre, on a 150-acre site in Claverton Down the University of Bath was established. The architects Robert Matthew, Johnson-Marshall & Partners (RMJM) published its development plan in 1965 and phase one of that scheme was completed in 1966–67 and the rest by 1980. The main principle was to separate traffic from the pedestrian areas. The main spine of the university, with the library, lecture theatres, cafes, etc., sits on a deck above the central service road. Alison & Peter Smithson added further buildings in the 1980s, before a further master plan was undertaken by Feilden Clegg Bradley in 2001. There is a wealth of modern buildings on this site, which is constantly being added to and upgraded.

Again, Betjeman did not like the architectural styles here, thanking the university for building its 'factories' away from the historic centre of Bath. No. 8 West, the School of Management (1992–94), was designed by Nugent Vallis

Brierley architects and Nos. 7 & 9 West, the Pharmacy and Pharmacology Department building (1994–97) and the Chemical Engineering Department building (1999–2001), are both by de Brandt, Joyce & Partners. Planned as two buildings, and housing two separate departments, it reads as one. The building follows the slope with three and four storeys. The gleaming, heroic flue towers and stair towers clad with glass blocks single this building out even amongst all the other modern buildings on site.

Nearby, on Claverton Down Road, also away from the heritage centre, is the headquarters of Wessex Water, designed by Bennetts Associates in 1998–2000. The design philosophy was around the company's commitment to environmental sustainability. The scheme is a sensitive, low-key response to the rural, steeply sloping site that looks out over Monkton Combe and Limpley Stoke. It is, however, considered by many to be far too modern for a site any closer to the centre of Bath.

※ ※ ※ ※ ※

Bath certainly lost its way during the second half of the twentieth century, but the importance of Bath's heritage to its continued popularity and economic growth was thankfully recognised by some far-sighted preservations. The more recent examples of high-quality, modern architecture show what can be achieved with some thought and sound principles.

Thirteen

WORLD HERITAGE CITY

Bath is rightly proud of its UNESCO World Heritage Site status, yet despite its historic image, Bath is constantly regenerating and it is surprising how abundant the modern architecture and new building is. The recent £360m SouthGate shopping area (2006–10), designed by Chapman Taylor for Morley Fund Management and Multi-Development, replaced Owen Luder's unpopular 1971 version. The 9 acres of new shops and residential apartments, whilst not great architecture, does appear to be 'fit for purpose'; the area is alive with hundreds of shoppers on a daily basis.

As part of the wider SouthGate scheme, a new transport interchange designed by Wilkinson Eyre was introduced to enable more streamlined travel between train and bus. One of the aspects that makes Bath so successful and loved is its ability to embrace its heritage, but equally not becoming a slave to it. Bath is a modern, thriving city providing homes, jobs, education, entertainment and visitor attractions – whilst continuing to tell its very impressive story. The once redundant space between the railway and the bus station has been transformed into a hive of restaurants and bars, all making their individual and idiosyncratic use of Brunel's railway arches.

Despite a five-year delay, £30 million over budget, materials that could not stand up to the environment, costly legal proceedings (ending in an out-of-court settlement) and insistent cynics, Bath's new Thermae Spa has got to be the greatest thing to happen to this city in decades. Nicholas Grimshaw and Partners' new facility opened on 7 August 2006, and in its first year welcomed over 130,000 visitors. Consequently, staff numbers had to be increased by 100 per cent and the knock-on benefit for accommodation providers, restaurants and shops in Bath has been marked.

Bath's last bastion of industry, Stothert & Pitt, which had ridden major economic depressions for over 200 years, was forced to contract its business in the 1970s and this led to its final closure in 1989. The works were left derelict for twenty-five years before the brownfield site was cleared and developed for housing by Crest Nicholson in 2011 (the first residents moved in at the end of

Oriana Viall: Brunel Square at night, 2015. (Author's Collection)

that year). Bath Western Riverside will eventually offer over 2,000 new homes, two new parks, cafes and restaurants. The project is phased and is not expected to be completed until 2030. Its entrance is suitably marked with a Stothert & Pitt crane from 1908.

Horstmann Controls Ltd founded a factory for the manufacturing of car gearboxes on the Newbridge Road in 1903. The company was sold to the Roxboro Group in 1998, who then sold the 5-acre site for development. The complex of seventy-five units was developed by Crest Nicholson and designed by Le Lay Architects in 2003.

Bath's museums have also undergone revamps. Elsewhere in the country heritage attractions are being forced to reconsider their offer by reducing their activities, opening hours and, sadly, in some places being forced to close. The Holburne Museum has been recently transformed with an extension of ceramic and glass, designed by Eric Parry (b. 1952). The proposals for the museum split public opinion, but the results of the project are – without doubt – exceptional. The museum welcomed over 160,000 visitors in the first year after reopening.

The Holburne Museum's success is reflecting positively on Sydney Gardens, too. As more people discover and enjoy this picturesque urban open space so current restoration plans are gaining momentum. The gardens are listed and the

Admiralty Camera Club: Giants of Industry: Stothert & Pitt Crane makers, 1970s. (Bath Central Library/ Bath in Time)

Council have undertaken a number of important renovation projects since 1995. It will be interesting to see these develop.

The Roman Baths Museum, designated as 'an outstanding collection' of national and international significance, has managed to introduce updated facilities, interpretation and improved access in phases, keeping the museum open to the 1 million visitors it welcomes every year. Currently the Council is working on the Archway Project, which will provide a Roman Baths Learning Centre and World Heritage Interpretation Centre in the old Victorian laundry on York and Swallow Streets.

No. 1 Royal Crescent opened its doors again in June 2013 after completing a £5 million project that saw the principal house reunited with its domestic service wing once more. Again, with the visitors in mind, the project team managed to structure the works so the museum was closed for less than a year. The actual project, from Chairman Edward Bayntun-Coward's initial concept to opening, was seven years.

※ ※ ※ ※ ※

The global economic downturn of 2006–08, which led to the Great Recession, is considered by the International Monetary Fund to be the worst global recession since the Second World War; there is also some debate over whether it has run its course or not. Bath was obviously affected, but again far less so than other towns and cities across the Western world. Tourist demand is such that new hotels seem to be opening with increasing regularity, from the high-end luxury Gainsborough Hotel to the provision of a new budget – or mid-range – Z Hotel at Sawclose (due to open in 2016). The Gainsborough, which opened in July 2015 offering ninety-nine rooms, is the only hotel to currently have direct access to the thermal waters – the Grand Pump Room Hotel was the last to be able to lay such a claim. Whilst the redevelopment of Sawclose will also see a new casino and two new restaurants.

※ ※ ※ ※ ※

Bath has always embraced its high-status patrons. Their approval and benefaction has consistently brought hundreds of 'followers of fashion' in their wake. Previously it was the visits by royalty and the aristocracy that the city courted, but today modern culture favours celebrity musicians, actors and authors far more. Thankfully, Bath can still be seen as a place to visit because so many well-known personalities have associations with the city – from Peter Gabriel, Clare Teal and Jamie Cullum to Alison Goldfrapp, Midge Ure and

Gabrielle Aplin. Sadly, Bath's other claim to modern musical fame is as the death place of American rock 'n' roll icon, Eddie Cochran. On Saturday, 16 April 1960 at about 11.50 p.m. Cochran was thrown from a car during a road traffic accident in Chippenham. He was taken to St Martin's Hospital in Odd Down, where he died at 4.10 p.m. the following day of severe head injuries. He is buried at Forest Lawn Memorial Park in Cypress, California.

Throughout Bath's history significant figures from the world of art, literature and politics have found refuge and inspiration here. Emperor Haile Selassie spent his years of exile in Bath between 1936 and 1941. Kenneth Horne, famous for his radio programmes *Ack-Ack, Beer-Beer* (service jargon for anti-aircraft balloon barrage) and *Round the Horne*, was stationed at Claverton Manor between 1941 and 1944, with No. 32 (Balloon Barrage) Group. He was billeted at Bathwick Grange. The Beatles stayed at the Francis Hotel on Queen Square when they played the Pavilion in June 1963 – Jimmy Hendrix played the same venue four years later.

Princess Margaret used to stay with her friends, Jeremy and Camilla Fry, at Widcombe Manor in the 1960s. American textile artist Kaffe Fassett (b. 1937) also had a studio there. Pop artist Peter Blake (b. 1932) lived at nearby Wellow in the 1970s. Inventor James Dyson (b. 1948) has a long association with the city, as does shoe designer Manolo Blahnik (b. 1942). Film director Ken Loach, actors Nicolas Cage, Johnny Depp, Anthony Head, Jane Seymour and John Cleese have all – at one time or another – owned homes in the Bath area.

Two of our most famous home-grown personalities are Dame Jacqueline Wilson (b. 1945), the ground-breaking children's literature writer, and celebrity chef Mary Berry (b. 1935). Mary is a Bathonian, and her father was mayor in 1952. She trained at the Bath College of Domestic Science, but really honed her skills when she worked for the electricity board visiting customers in and around Bath to demonstrate how to use their electric ovens by baking a Victoria sponge cake.

From the world of sport, Bath can claim links with such luminaries as former Rugby Union player (Bath, England and the British and Irish Lions) Jeremy Guscott (b. 1965 and educated at Ralph Allen School), and Jason Gardener (b. 1975). Amy Williams (b. 1982), although born in Cambridge, was brought up in Bath and went to Hayesfield School – her welcome in Bath after she won gold at the 2010 Winter Olympics left no doubt as to which city was her home. The city's position in the sporting world is supported by facilities at the University of Bath. Whether Bath Rugby will secure the necessary expansion to its home on the 'Rec' is still to be determined, but it would be devastating to the hoteliers, restaurateurs and retailers should Bath Rugby be forced to leave Bath.

Bath's position as a cultural centre is supported by the many festivals it now hosts: from the music festival, literature and children's literature festivals, food festivals, Bath in Fashion and the fringe festival to the hugely successful Christmas Market. Combined with the many acclaimed museums in the city, in 2013 alone tourism attracted 967,000 staying visits from UK and overseas visitors, plus an impressive 4.8 million day visits. An estimated £405 million was generated for the local economy, and 10 per cent of jobs in the region are tourism related, which is equivalent to 9,300 jobs. Bath's great asset is Bath.

※ ※ ※ ※ ※

Until the 1960s flooding was probably the town's greatest cross to bear. Looking at an historic map, a number of the place names perhaps suggest why: Bathwick and Kensington Meadows denote their agricultural use, but meadows also could be (and often needed to be) flooded. Dolemeads and Kingsmead also suggest meadows (or 'mead', meaning the colour of the water), and the Ham is an area in the loop of a river often cut off. Those aspects that made Bath an easier place to cross the river equally make it susceptible to flooding – which is fine when the abutting land is left as flood plain.

And the Romans knew this, concentrating the settlement of Bath on a terrace rising about 50ft (15m) above the (normal) level of the river. 'For the greater part of three centuries,' points out Angus Buchanan, 'Roman engineering and drainage coped adequately with any tendencies to succumb to flooding.' The first major development off this plateau was Southgate Street, which was mainly built up during the sixteenth century. Increasing riverside industry and the regular, devastating floods saw Bath turn its back on the river.

Even with improved safety and awareness, the number of tragic drownings has increased in recent years, adding to our revulsion of what could – and should – be a major benefit. The bad publicity may well have forced the council's hand, but they are now committed to an infrastructure project to update Bath's flood defences, and also to build a more positive relationship between the city centre and the River Avon.

There are a number of developments on the cards at the moment, which – if they all go ahead – will change our relationship with the river. The first phase of the flood defence works for the Bath Quays Waterside Project started in January 2016. This will see essential flood mitigation and defence works between Churchill and Midland Bridges, the rerouting of Green Park Road through the Riverside Coach Park and the relocation of the long stay coach parking to Weston Island. This is also being actively seen as an opportunity to reverse Bath's history of turning its back on the river. The project plans to enhance the riverside, provide better access and make it more enjoyable and beautiful.

It is all part of a major master plan – the Bath City Riverside Enterprise Area – which will also see the redevelopment of the Avon Street car park and former Newark Works areas to create a business park to be called Bath Quays. With a new pedestrian bridge by Marc Mimram, the winning design having been chosen late last year, Bath City Riverside Enterprise Area has the capacity to deliver 9,000 jobs and 3,400 homes in Bath by 2030. We have already seen the progress of the redevelopment of 17.5 acres of key brownfield site on Bath's western riverside by Crest Nicholson. One of the main marketing aspects is its proximity to the river. Perhaps we are at last going to make the most of our waterways.

In recent years, a number of the monolithic 'packing case' buildings of the 1960s and '70s have also been demolished, although it is extremely doubtful that one of Bath's most hated buildings, the Hilton Hotel by Snailum, Le Fevre & Quick (1972), will be replaced in our lifetimes. It is one of the Hilton's Groups most profitable properties, and at least the views out are magnificent!

❋ ❋ ❋ ❋ ❋

The extraordinary story of Bath extends over six millennia; a constant theme is the lure of its hot springs. An international icon of elegant architecture, boutique shopping, fashionable restaurants, inspiring cultural events and renowned personalities, its popularity and prosperity has certainly wavered over the centuries. But in the early years of the twenty-first century Bath is triumphant again. It is exciting to think what stories Bath will tell in the future.

SELECT BIBLIOGRAPHY

Cunliffe, Barry, *Roman Bath Discovered* (London: Routledge & Kegan Paul, 1971).

Defoe, Daniel, *Tour of the Whole Island of Great Britain (1724–26)* (Middlesex: Penguin, 1971).

Fergusson, Adam, and Tim Mowl, *The Sack of Bath – and After* (Bath: Bath Preservation Trust, 1989).

Fiennes, Celia, *Through England on a Side Saddle (c. 1700)*, 1888 (Cambridge University Press, 2010).

Forsyth, Michael, *Bath – Pevsner Architectural Guide* (London: Yale University Press, 2003).

Green, Mowbray A., *The Eighteenth Century Architecture of Bath* (Bath: George Gregory, 1904).

Ison, Walter, *The Georgian Buildings of Bath from 1700–1830* (London: Faber and Faber, 1948).

Leland, John, and Thomas Hearne, *The Itinerary of John Leland the Antiquary*, Vol. 2 (Oxford, 1711).

Mowl, T. and Earnshaw, B., *John Wood: Architect of Obsession* (Bath: Millstream Books, 1988)

Neale, R.S., *Bath: A Social History, 1680–1850 or A Valley of Pleasure, Yet a Sink of Iniquity* (London: Routledge & Kegan paul, 1981)

Smollett, Tobias, *The Expedition of Humphry Clinker*, 1771 (London: Penguin Classics, 1985).

Spence, Cathryn, *Bath in the Blitz: Then & Now* (Stroud: The History Press, 2012).

Spence, Cathryn, *Water, History and Style: Bath World Heritage City* (Stroud: The History Press, 2012).

Swift, Andrew, *All Roads Lead to France: Bath and the Great War* (Bath: Akeman Press, 2005).

Various, *Bath History*, Volumes I–XII, 1986–2011.

Wood, John, *An Essay Towards a Description of Bath* (London: 2nd edition, Bathoe & Lownds, 1765).

Wroughton, John, *Stuart Bath: Life in the Forgotten City, 1603–1714* (Bath: The Lansdown Press, 2004).

Wroughton, John, *Tudor Bath: Life and Strife in the Little City, 1485–1603* (Bath: The Lansdown Press, 2006).